LAWYERS' LANGUAGE

The law presumes that everyone knows the law, yet the obscurity of lawyers' language puts it out of reach of those who are presumed to know it.

The aim of this book is to establish that, on the contrary, the development and maintenance of the law's special language can be justified. The notion of representation is applied to the relationship between legal language and ordinary language. In a judge's use of a language designed to build a coherent and internally consistent body of applied law, which will stand in a relationship of representation to ordinary language, the judge can properly be said to be the people's representative.

Cases are used throughout the book to underpin the author's argument. *Lawyers' Language* justifies the transformation of ordinary language into a special discourse for the purposes of the legal system.

Alfred Phillips is a jurist, experienced in most important areas of law as a practitioner, university lecturer, journal editor and writer. He was the editor of *The Journal of the Law Society of Scotland* for 25 years, having founded *The Conveyancing Review*, which merged with *The Journal of the Law Society of Scotland*. He also founded and lectured on the course in Professional Skills and Professional Ethics for postgraduate students in the Faculty of Law, Glasgow University.

LAWYERS' LANGUAGE

How and why legal language is different

Alfred Phillips

LONDON AND NEW YORK

First published 2003
by Routledge
2 Park Square, Milton Park, Abingdon, Oxfordshire OX14 4RN

Simultaneously published in the USA and Canada
by Routledge
711 Third Avenue, New York, NY 10017

First issued in paperback 2015

Routledge is an imprint of the Taylor and Francis Group, an informa business

© 2003 Alfred Phillips

Typeset in Sabon by
HWA Text and Data Management, Tunbridge Wells

All rights reserved. No part of this book may be reprinted or reproduced or utilised in any form or by any electronic, mechanical, or other means, now known or hereafter invented, including photocopying and recording, or in any information storage or retrieval system, without permission in writing from the publishers.

The publisher makes no representation, express or implied, with regard to the accuracy of the information contained in this book and cannot accept any legal responsibility or liability for any errors or omissions that may be made.

British Library Cataloguing in Publication Data
A catalogue record for this book is available from the British Library

Library of Congress Cataloging in Publication Data
A catalog record for this book has been requested

ISBN 13: 978-1-138-86836-6 (pbk)
ISBN 13: 978-0-7007-1688-3 (hbk)

CONTENTS

	Introduction	1
1	Breaking ground	28
2	How critical language theory seeks and then struggles against its own undoing	51
3	Interpretation	89
4	Constructive interpretation	114
5	Conclusions	145
	Notes	179
	Index	186

INTRODUCTION

Sociopolitical background

This book's aim is to make a contribution to the alignment of law and democracy. Today, there is a need to study at all levels how the legal system fits into and works in a modern democratic society. A project to align law and democracy would not only explain how law adjusts to democratic change; it would also produce a critical background of theory against which the present-day anxieties about the location of power, as well as the programme of reforms now under way or discussion in Britain and in France, could be assessed. I mention some of these later in this Introduction. The book's precise objective is to provide a buttress for the democratic credentials of the law. For, most obviously, the judges who apply and articulate the law can be attacked as being unelected and unaccountable. How can they be regarded as the people's representatives? I aspire to dissolve the problem by a study of the nature of the language of the law against a linguistic background, showing in conclusion the link between legal language and ordinary language. In this, I lean heavily on the ideas of Habermas displayed in his masterly work *Between Facts and Norms*. While the argument is focused on British law (including particularities of Scots law), a great deal of comparative material is introduced from US law and some from France, taken as a representative Continental system.

The procedures of representative democracy, and a legal system which incarnates the rule of law and acts as a pillar of democracy, are both now taken for granted in the West. But, as regards the procedures of representative democracy, strains have progressively emerged. The crusading fervour which, in their time, powered the old Left and Thatcherism, has evaporated. The absence of any sharp ideological division between the mainstream parties, which makes the prospect of their alternance in government seem unexciting or even meaningless, conduces to apathy. There is a general impression that politics has become marginalised or personalised. Instead of the politician's ideas, it is his integrity, allegiance, celebrity status and the titillation value of his private life that engage the public. Low turnout in key elections reflects this anomie. Recent events in Austria and more recently elsewhere in Europe show that, against that background, opportunistic, extremist (right-wing) parties led by mediatised personalities, using a cloaked xenophobic, nationalist, populist discourse, can find a way to power. When the political system weakens in this way, the other institutions of democracy, *particularly the legal system*, must take the strain.

The source of the malaise lies in the communication gap between representatives and the represented. It is the shortfall between parliamentary sovereignty and popular sovereignty that is the measure of the democratic deficit. This insight seems confirmed by a public opinion poll carried out in October 1999 in France,[1] where a similar disaffection with politics has been noted. While the *institutions* of democracy are not themselves questioned, there exists at the same time a massive rejection of politics: thus 57 per cent of the sample of 1,000 expressed mistrust, 27 per cent boredom and 20 per cent disgust;[2] on the positive side, 26 per cent experienced hope, 20 per cent interest and 7 per cent respect. The preponderance of negative attitudes reflects 'a crisis of representation and leadership'. A large majority consider that the politicians 'worry themselves very little or practically not at all with what the French people think'.

The complex relationship in the form of representation which connects parliamentarians and citizens is not working well. It seems as if the cynical assessment of democracy is right, that the people are given power once every five years only to give it away again immediately to its representatives. In the run-up to the general election in Britain in 2001, both Labour and Conservatives told the electorate that they had undertaken to 'listen to the people'. In the Government's case this was said once the memories of the terms of its previous mandate had faded and in the case of the Opposition when the faults and errors of its previous long period in office had mostly receded into historical oblivion. In particular, the result of the Conservatives' exercise is worrying. For the discourse that was produced just approximated to a paler version of the rhetoric used (with a degree of electoral success) by the Continental parties of the far-Right. It claimed attention with a shock-horror style of language.

INTRODUCTION

In the event, it turned out that the Government had heard the people's voice aright, not the Conservatives who seriously misjudged their uppermost concerns.

Nonetheless the rage against Europeanism, criminals, asylum-seekers and minorities conveyed or connoted by speech of this sort both marks and makes for uneasiness in society. It is significant, too, that the idea of political correctness, which should rule such a discourse out of order, is also made an object of scorn by the same voice. Will the angry slogans of our representatives (present and would-be) drown out the liberal voice? The institution of representative democracy in itself is never challenged, but to fly contemptuously in the face of what counts as political correctness is to deny to all citizens the substantive right to equal treatment and respect. Such a right is *constitutive* of democracy. Yet equally constitutive is the procedural right to the participation in public debate and decision-making that counts as popular self-government. But what if those who are listening to the electorate are catching the right noises, that social liberalism is not in fact deeply and widely rooted in the hearts and minds of the public, that the old atavisms regarding hanging, refugees, homosexuality and 'this sceptred isle' are not far, if at all, below the surface?

In May 2000, a privately-funded referendum on homosexuality was carried out in Scotland.[3] The occasion was the publication of the Scottish Executive's bill to repeal Section 28 of the Local Government Act 1988 which banned the promotion of homosexuality in schools.[4] Of those polled 34 per cent responded, and of these, 86 per cent were against the bill and for the retention of the section. The ballot's promoter said:

> We will not stand back and allow a politically correct minority to undermine the position of marriage in society and determine morality for the majority. We did not vote for it, we're not having it

The poll itself tells us nothing, even without taking account of the inept nature of the original section and the distortion in the response which would be induced by the unofficial provenance of the ballot paper. But the discourse appropriated by the poll promoter in his statement is on the contrary highly meaningful in the way it exploits the majority/minority divide, as analysis of his statement shows. He is seen to present himself as the voice of a political majority while supporting himself at the same time on the right of any political minority to dissent on ground of conscience. He attacks elitism (i.e. minorities benefiting from an excess of power, privilege and respect). Ironically, politically correct discourse designed to displace language discriminatory of minorities is also condemned.

This episode suggests that 'listening to the people' may not be a surefire way to gain and retain political power. It shows up two problem areas. One, on the listener's side, concerns the need to *interpret* the message conveyed by the people's voice. Indeed, there are various voices and these are variously influential. Interpretation is itself a disputed concept. The other problem, on the people's side, is best packaged in the question put by Lasch: is the electorate, politically incorrigible.[5]

The permissive law on guns and the retention of the death penalty in the US show that uncertainty about the answer to that question presents politicians there with a conflict on these issues. They are aware that American prestige (at least in Europe) and American pressure in favour of human rights in other countries are undermined by the iconic status accorded to the gun and the electric chair at home. Yet, either out of conviction, or because they are unwilling to take the risk of moving ahead of what the polls tell them are the attitudes of the public, there is little enthusiasm among politicians to bring the states into line on these matters with the consensus among modern nations.

Representation

The doubtful areas that have just been identified are inherent in the relationship which we designate as *representation*. It has to be borne in mind that the relationship of representation involves an ethical dimension, which is perhaps the determinant in the last resort as regards the problem areas in this book. In the political context, this may weigh no more than in the choice between the measure which gives immediate or short-term gratification or comfort to the people and that which counts as institutional reform. Representation in a more general sense plays a part in the analysis in the last chapter. This will underline the point that to indicate problems is not to attack democracy but to mark some of the tensions inescapable in any indirect democratic system and which, therefore, underlie law as legislation.

INTRODUCTION

Media

It would be misleading to talk about the tensions in the interchange between electors and their representatives without bringing in the media. Similar tensions exist in the relations between the Members of Parliament and the media. The mass media is home to ministers who expound, are interrogated upon and defend government policies and programmes at every level from mission statement (ideological principle) down to matters of detail. Shadow ministers are given an equivalent chance to argue and criticise. Press releases flow from all sides. The object is to maintain an *informed* public opinion, for essentially involved in the idea of representation is the requirement that the represented should know and understand what the representative does and proposes to do for him and on his behalf. But, this aspect of the relationship, although necessary, can become deformed. 'Misinformation' and 'disinformation' denote the dark side to the reassuringly bland neutrality which 'information' suggests.

The media is true to its name by its role as intermediary between Parliament and public. Political communication is transformed in its passage through the media to the audience. Each section, each newspaper, each TV channel evolves its own discourse. Discourses construct what they present and are received as real, as news, as events and states of affairs. Along with the news come 'stories'. Stories are not supposed to be fictional. On the contrary, they expose another tier or layer 'behind' the news which changes its meaning or significance. So stories are represented to be more 'real' or authentic than news reports.

A serial story currently in vogue revolves around 'spin'. A term imported by the media from the States, 'spin' is used in pool to get the balls where you want them. By employing this word, the media accuses the government of presenting what purports to be information in the most favourable way through a process of selection and interpretation. According to the media, information becomes converted by spin-doctoring into propaganda. By this *interpretation* of its own of the form in which government information is provided to the public, the media not only succeeds in sullying as suspect officially-released information, but also by implication lays a claim to transparency in respect of its own role in the transmission of political news. Seemingly, its reportage is, by contrast, straight and free from spin. The media's discourse of spin is itself a skilful use of spin-doctoring. We are helped to accept the media version by the

INTRODUCTION

supreme value rightly attached to a free press in a democracy and, in association with that, the lesson from totalitarian societies that official sources are often tainted. It should not be forgotten, however, that these influences hide the countervailing fact that a 'velvet' censorship is at work in democratic societies, driven by the need to compete in the news market.

The argument is, therefore, that political news is (re)constructed in the process of its delivery to the public by the media. The purpose of the following case study is to see whether a similar process operates in the media treatment of newsworthy events in the legal domain.

CASE STUDY

California v. Simpson (*aka* the 'O.J. case') attracted the media circus, for it had all the ingredients of entertaining and suspenseful drama. It touched on many social polarities marking contemporary America: stardom and institutional power; the black–white race divide (with the additional complication that one of the victims was Jewish, so touching off the sensitivities associated with the 'ideological' hostility between blacks via the black Muslim movement and Jews); the freedom to buy virtually unlimited legal resources for the defence (the public resources available to the prosecution were pitted against a large cast of renowned criminal defence lawyers) and the theoretical fairness of the legal process; male machismo and control by women of their own sexuality; racism (which proved to be endemic in the Los Angeles Police Department) and the ethics of community policing. These polarities sharpened the adversarial relationship between prosecution and defence, and, representing as they did deep concerns in American society, ignited fierce debates all over the country. The intrusiveness and wide-ranging coverage of the media (literally thousands of hours were taken up on television) meant that, from the judge downwards, all participants in the trial would be bound to be sensitive to the unseen audience beyond the proper audience, the jury. The bombardment of TV comment, daily bulletins, psychological and social analyses, predictions, biographical and personality profiles, in enveloping and then overwhelming the televised actuality of the trial, constructed a parallel 'reality'. Whereas proceedings in court, at least at the surface level, work towards the creation of a sort of passionless monotony and neutrality, television programmes, like most other media reportage, are designed to heighten, to excite, to add colour and, perhaps most importantly, to create a narrative structure around victims and villains.

It has to be noted that the nuclear event was not the trial itself but the double murder of which O.J. was accused. The trial was itself a *representation*. In court, the authenticity of the representation of the events and states of affairs which make up the facts depends on the credibility of the evidence. This, in turn, is not measured exclusively, as the term might suggest, by a judgement of the sincerity and reliability of the witnesses, based on their demeanour, but also by the internal consistency of the facts as a whole and the correspondence between the testimony and the productions. The TV *show* on the other hand is just that, offering no more than an impression of verisimilitude. Even while it purports to be a representation of actuality, the product of the media exhibits many of the features of fiction. The lead prosecutor in the O.J. trial complained in her book that it had been turned into a 'weird and seedy game show'.[6]

How did the reception of the TV version differ from that in the court? How did the public response fed by the TV show compare with the result of the jury's deliberations on the evidence? There is some evidence on which a comparison can be based. Polls showed that assessments in the country divided along racial lines, most whites believing Simpson to be guilty and most blacks voting for acquittal. By contrast, in a memoir by one of the jurymen, he records that the jurors did not rigidly divide up along race, or indeed sex, age or class lines.[7] The temptation is to speculate about the nature of the possible link between the transformation of the actuality of the trial wrought by TV and the revelation by the polls that the question of the guilt or innocence of O.J. for the viewing public was reduced to a black and white (in both senses) issue. Did it count that the contextual material introduced by the TV programmes added a mass of analysis which could not *competently* be put before the jury?

Television's mass audience is typically dispersed in units consisting of single individuals or couples watching at home and at leisure. It is widely believed that the combination of the sensuous power of its imagery, the tension of its narrative and its projection of an authority derived from an impersonal and

INTRODUCTION

remote source (cf. Orwell's *Big Brother*) brings about a passive state in the viewer. The viewer becomes the metaphorical 'couch potato'. The same can be said to a greater or lesser degree of the effect of the print media (especially the tabloids) which ingratiates itself with its readers with elbow-nudging pictures and stories and then harangues them and polemicizes. John B. Thompson, for one, in a social psychological theory of mass communication, dissents from this negativism, arguing that televiewing does involve some form of participation. He suggests that 'the process of reception is a much more active, creative and critical process than many commentators are inclined to assume'.[8] Certainly, the televised version of the O.J. trial captivated and then shook America, producing a highly 'active and critical' public discussion. But, if the objective is taken to be the formation of a reasoned judgement, all the social and environmental advantages are seen to be with the trial jury: it formed a *deliberative* group; it could engage in two-way communication to clarify points; and, in the summing up of the judge, the relevant issues were fenced off, condensed and focused to evoke yes/no responses.

The media's inter*mediate* position between the trial and the public played in both directions. It not only relayed the trial proceedings to the public but also impacted on the trial. The representation encroached on the actuality. This produced an element of distortion. Marsha Clark felt herself turned into 'a featured player in a freak show'. She was criticised for her cross-examination technique, her trial strategy, her hairstyle and her child-care arrangements. She complained that the judge was 'too sensitive to his own press notices' and that he was ineffectual in controlling the defence because you cannot 'expect a clown to stop a circus'. Over and above these alleged effects of the media on the atmospherics of the trial, a major question is whether there was osmosis of the extraneous TV material through the barrier placed between the jury and the outside world. The original jurors who survived (many dropped out and had to be replaced) endured more than seven months in a state well-described as 'collective solitary confinement'. Yet despite the precautionary isolation, it is most unlikely that, through sources such as the permitted conjugal visits and the replacement jury members, none of the sensationalised TV outpourings came to mix in the jury's

INTRODUCTION

minds with the actual proceedings of this intrinsically most sensational of trials.

Media excesses did in fact lead to the quashing of the convictions in an English murder case.[9] In that case the Appeal Court, having agreed with the trial judge's condemnation of the press coverage of the trial as 'unremitting, extensive, sensational, inaccurate and misleading', added that the newspapers had not limited themselves to what was said in court. Mostly, 'it was not reporting at all, it was comment'. The court concluded that the press coverage of the trial had created 'a real risk of prejudice against the defendants' with the result that the convictions were 'unsafe and unsatisfactory'. Both the O.J. case and this one dramatise the conflict experienced by the media between its duty as watchdog ensuring that justice is seen to be done and its business of public stimulation. The conflict can be resolved only through an ethics of representation.

Load-bearing by the legal system

The tension between popular sovereignty and populist pressure in a representative democracy was noted earlier. The detour just ended, by way of the analysis of the influence of the media, suggested that the effect of its interposition between politician and public was to increase that tension. This is not to say that we do not get the media that we need, that we deserve, especially that we (seem to) want. Where there are excesses coming from commercial or proprietorial pressures, these can only be reined in by a system of professional journalistic ethics. Deficiencies cannot easily be made up; although a suggestion has been made that a publicly-funded newspaper might be established to be to the print media what the BBC is to broadcasting – but would anyone read it? The core principle of a system of journalistic ethics is already widely recognised and well put: the media should serve the public interest and not subserve the interest of the public. Again, this comes down to the ethics of representation. This leaves over the question of whether the media's code of ethics should be statutorily (legally) administered and sanctioned. The law is already at hand to hold the balance where individual rights like privacy, confidentiality and (respect or) reputation collide with the public interest reflected in the media's duty to investigate, comment and inform.

INTRODUCTION

It is not only at those points and in that context that the legal system holds the balance against pressures threatening the good functioning of the social systems. Most obviously, for example, a strong legal system is needed in the face of both the liberalisation of market forces, domestically and on a worldwide scale, and the opposition in the form of the non-governmental organisations and other, looser groups which claim to place themselves *outside* the law.

The nature of today's other issues points in the same direction. These mostly fall into two categories. Safety of the food supply, rationing of health resources, risk management, corporate criminal responsibility and bioethics, including euthanasia and the commercial exploitation of the sequencing of the human genome, come in the *existential* category. Another great category of contemporary issues is made up of problems of *identity*. The title of a book by Alain Touraine, *Can We Live Together: Equality and Difference*, sums it up well. In the light of this, how are the newly-emerging existential issues to be resolved; and how is the 'living together' to be managed in a self-governing society of equal yet different citizens? Although the direction will in most cases be signalled by broad political decisions, these issues will be shaped through the evolution of the law on a case-by-case basis. For example, the principle of precaution, defined for French law in the *Loi Barnier* (2 February 1995), will be tested in the European Court if the case against France for its refusal to lift the ban on British beef goes ahead. It is worth setting out the definition of the principle not only to illustrate the point just made but also to provide a foretaste of a seldom recognised feature of lawyers' language taken up in detail in chapter 5:

> the principle of precaution is the principle according to which the absence of certainty, after taking into account the scientific and technical knowledge of the time, must not retard the adoption of effective and proportionate measures aimed at the prevention of a risk of serious and irreversible damage ... at an economically acceptable cost

So the principle of precaution proposes to draw the contours of risk management for those who undertake activities presenting risks for others. Certainly, a formula has been laid down but it is the judges who will be called on to work out over time the intermediate principles governing 'proportionateness', 'seriousness of damage' and 'economically acceptable cost'. Flexible words like these are a strong feature of legal language. At the same time, it aims at precision, as is exemplified by the text just quoted, and is generally acknowledged to achieve it.

So we can anticipate a shift in decision-making from the political system to the legal process. The Human Rights Act 1998 in the UK is already starting to have its own impact on the allocation of the burden of law-making between the political and the legal system. Although the constitutional principle of parliamentary sovereignty has been left intact, the practical effect all the same is going to be that many of the issues of how we should 'live together' in a twenty-first-century democracy will be settled in the law courts rather than in Parliament.

Law on politics

Does this supposed shift impose strain on the separation of powers? Pressure may be exerted in either direction, by law on politics and by politics on law. As was said at the outset, this book's purpose is to locate the source of the 'legitimacy' of law in its connection to self-government by the citizens. This is the counter to the charge that the judges are unelected and unaccountable. It matters then whether the law intrudes into the proper province of an elected Parliament and conversely whether politics distorts the judicial process.

The former question depends on the place given to the constitution in the law-making process. As already noted, Parliament has preserved its sovereignty in the Human Rights Act. In incorporating the European Convention on Human Rights into domestic law, the power handed to the judges is purely declaratory. They can declare pieces of legislation to be incompatible with the rights protected by the Convention but they cannot overturn them. That power will be strongly persuasive in a democratic state. By contrast, the American Supreme Court has power to override or qualify federal or states' legislation. In both the UK and the US, the judicial processes can be set in motion only by individual or corporate persons so that enacted law becomes tailored to fit constitution rights on a case-by-case basis. In France, however, access to the Constitutional Council is reserved to the political authorities. Its power to declare *prospective* law unconstitutional is exercisable within one month before the law's promulgation. Exceptionally, therefore, constitutional law in France has the power to interfere in political decision-making. Indeed, lately, the Council has censured two important fiscal measures adopted by parliament. An outgoing member of the Council explains that the constitutional judge functions as a sort of 'tutor' vis-à-vis the legislator, going on to say:

> This political role adheres to the French political culture which, in name of the primacy of the general will, entrusts to the Council the task not of guaranteeing the protection of their fundamental rights to the citizens, as is the case elsewhere, but that of defending the sovereignty of the people, incarnated, above and beyond the legislator, by the constituting power.[10]

Unsurprisingly, the Council is often the object of attack by the government of the time. In France, therefore, the constitutional judges are, arguably, illegitimate players on the political scene in contrast to Britain and America where they stay out of politics.

Politics on law

Constitutional theory has it that judicial decision-making should be insulated from politics. More sharply focused, if this book succeeds in showing the direct (discursive) link between judges' decisions and popular sovereignty, then it is important that the judges' power should be immune to influence from the people's parliamentary representatives other than via the legislation which issues from them. There are two issues here: one relates to the conflicts of political parties; the other to political ideology. The first resolves itself into the question whether the political authority should have the power to appoint judges.

Proposals in England to water down the Lord Chancellor's power of appointment, and to open up the procedures for selection of judges, have so far been resisted. Supporting the resistance is the claim that the office of Lord Chancellor is hybrid, providing a foot in both camps, the legal as well as the executive, that the selection process is based on consultation with senior lawyers and that the criteria although mysterious are non-political. Scotland has now diverged, by contrast, the process having been depoliticised under the spur of the Human Rights Act. A Judicial Appointments Committee, counting non-lawyers among its members, has taken over the power previously exercised solely by the Lord Advocate, a member of the executive. The Guigou reforms in France, at present blocked in part by the conservative majority in the Senate, are designed to make the judges of the parquet independent of the

Chancellery. Appointment of Supreme Court judges and of law officers throughout the US remains overtly political. The President chooses the former, subject to confirmation by the Senate. The oddity is that these judges stand as guardians and interpreters of the Constitution and so can overrule the laws produced by the elected legislative bodies.

The obvious argument in favour of political appointment of judges is that in effect the people are making the choices through their elected representatives. The argument of this book is that this is wrong in principle. But in any event the cycle of political alternance is often such that the political complexion of the parties elected to govern is out of sync with what were taken to be the ideological profiles of those who now constitute these judicial bodies.

The critics of the Supreme Court ruling which was possibly instrumental in the election of Bush as President in autumn 2000 believe that political partisanship tainted the decision of the majority. Dworkin pushes that criticism as far as it can go in suggesting that the five judges of the majority, all nominees of Republican Presidents, followed their own agenda when they made the decision that was expected to favour Bush's election.[11] He meant that they were moved by the anticipation that Bush's future Supreme Court appointments would aim to please the extreme Republican Right and so add to the majority of political conservatives on the bench. Subsequently, in an exchange with Fried who had been Reagan's Solicitor General, he re-iterated that he had looked at their opinions in vain for 'an ideological rationale rather than one of mere self-interest for what they did'.[12] Dworkin's use of 'ideological' in this context is significant, straddling as it does the two sides of the distinction, noted above, between the influence on law of a system of political appointments and that exerted on legal judgements by a political philosophy. Dworkin tends to speak of judges as 'small c' conservatives or 'l' liberals. The designations stand for *political* convictions. So the object of Dworkin's quest for an 'ideological rationale' in the majority opinion was reasoning based on their conservative convictions. The reason which they did give, namely that the Florida Supreme Court's order that the votes were to be inspected to determine the 'clear intent' of the voters violated the constitutional requirement of equal protection of the laws for everyone, would have counted for Dworkin as ideological, although he dismissed it as a mere cover for political partisanship. An ideological ground is one based on a (mis)reading of an abstract principle of the Constitution. For Dworkin, the conservatives and the liberals are distinguishable according to the manner

INTRODUCTION

of their approach to constitutional interpretation. Conservatives, or textualists, are those who claim (wrongly) to ground their judgements on the original intent of the framers as expressed in the constitutional text. Liberals are moved rather by a constructive interpretation of the broad constitutional principles, which in Dworkin's case he calls the 'moral reading'.[13] If we think of issues like abortion, the death penalty, euthanasia and so on, which properly belong in the political arena, it is clear that constitutional conservatism will give rise to legal judgements which will please political conservatives. The same can be said of constitutional liberalism and political progressives.

Top-down

The bottom-up approach to the validation of law, the position adopted by this book, assumes that the law produced by the political and adjudication processes in a democratic state should in some sense reflect public opinion. To the extent that a convergence is achieved, the citizen is able to *recognise* the principles, norms and rules of the law as the basis of right (disinterested) choices and judgements which he might reasonably have made for himself. As already mentioned, politicians claim to follow the bottom-up approach in a crude form by 'listening to the people'. But tensions arise for politicians where social liberalism and populist views diverge. In our times, crime and punishment, minority rights, immigration and genetic engineering are sites where strainlines appear for the bottom-up ideal of popular sovereignty. For example, if public opinion favoured retention, as it was widely assumed to do, did the postwar abolition of capital punishment by Western European parliaments offend against the principle of *representative* democracy? More generally, fear of crime, stoked up by widespread personal experiences and vivid morning-after tales of the experience of others, means that people strongly identify with victims, readily turning rage onto individual perpetrators and groups from which perpetrators are supposed to spring. Identifying itself with the public mood, the New Labour government compromised the Leftist tradition by measures in line with its 'tough on crime, tough on the causes of crime' rhetoric.

Yet on gay rights, another contested zone, a Commons majority opted for the removal of discrimination even against the tide of public opinion. In rejecting the proposed reduction in the age of consent for homosexuals approved on a free vote in the House of

Commons, the (unelected) House of Lords claimed to have the people on its side.

There are, therefore, instances where politicians behave as if people were not politically incorrigible or as if representation means something more than sensitivity to both people's concerns and their tabloid-inspired stopgap solutions. The assumption is that the public sphere can be informed and become deliberative. On that basis a top-down theory of what constitutes 'legitimate' law can be constructed.

Freedom's Law, a recent work of Dworkin, is a fine example of a top-down theory.[14] Freedom's law is the collective term adopted by Dworkin to designate those major decisions of the Supreme Court articulating rights and principles which can be read out of the American Constitution. The manner in which it should be read is crucial to the theory and is prescribed in the subtitle: *the moral reading of the American constitution*. The Constitution has the status of an overriding source of law and is difficult for the legislature to amend. According to Dworkin, the 'moral reading' not only prescribes how the judges should interpret the abstract clauses of the Constitution but also describes what they actually do, even though many judges and professors of law deny it. So in the sphere of constitutional rights in America, the theory would dissolve the distinction between what *is* the law and what counts as valid law, a distinction which is at the foundation of the argument up to now.

The questioning then focuses on whether a constructive interpretation of the constitutional text based on the approach described by Dworkin will produce principles which satisfy the criterion set for valid law. Certainly, at first sight the necessary link between the public sphere and constitutional law-making or adjudication seems to be missing. On the other hand, that linkage is conspicuous in the test formula that he proposes for state and federal *legislation*: 'the laws that the complex democratic process enacts and the policies that it pursues should be those, in the end, that the majority of citizens [if it had adequate information and enough time for reflection] would approve'.[15] Dworkin's label for this test is the 'majoritarian premise'. Here, the theory offers a bottom-up yardstick. But it is one that stops short of meeting the demand implicit in the social function of law. The law must be such as to justify the provision by the state of sanctions against a person convicted in a criminal process or the loser in a civil action. But the legitimacy of the law is not founded in the case of the minority not embraced in the 'premise' against whom the threat or use of sanctions will be oppressive. Within democracy the potential exists for a tyranny by the majority over the minority.

It is exactly on this flaw exposed in the majoritarian premise that Dworkin erects his justification for the higher authority of the Constitution when constructively interpreted by judges in accordance with the moral reading. For this approach to the text brings out the universalist principle at the core of the abstract clauses that *all* citizens are entitled to equal treatment and respect, the principle held to be constitutive of a democratic society. The result is that a top-down theory of individual rights is superimposed to counteract the defect in the bottom-up theory of enacted law. What remains problematic, however, is the position of the judges as privileged interpreters of constitutional law. The link is missing between the reasoning of the judges and the will of the sovereign people.

From an external perspective, resemblances can be picked out between the Constitution as a metalegal source and systems of law founded on religious fundamentalism. For Americans in general, the Constitution is the *fons et origo* of Law, possessing the status of a (quasi-)sacred text. In her book on the making of the Declaration of Independence, Pauline Maier includes the Constitution among the 'holy texts' of 'sacred scriptures' for the display of which a 'temple', as she describes it, has been built at the National Archives in Washington.[16] Every day, 'believers' file by the 'shrine', looking up reverentially at this document 'as if it were handed down by God or were the work of superhuman men whose talents far exceeded those of any who followed them'. The Supreme Court judges are privileged interpreters of the 'scripture' just as are the ayatollahs of the sharia.

If pushed further the comparison becomes invidious, the sharia, when put into practice, bearing the burden of notoriety in the West for its cruel punishments and alien, criminal trial procedures. By contrast, constitutionalism in the United States has underpinned the construction of an impressive edifice of individual rights sheltered from the winds of state and federal legislation. This is admirably demonstrated by Dworkin's previous writings, collected under headings *Life, Death and Race* and *Speech, Conscience and Sex* and forming by far the largest part of *Freedom's Law*. Nonetheless, a question mark must always be attached to the stability of this structure. Both the validity of Dworkin's theory and the 'progressive' character of the law critically depend on the *integrity* of the judge-interpreters.[17] Dworkin attractively equates progressiveness with 'happy endings' for Supreme Court cases on key issues. The interpretative approach vis-à-vis the Constitution, which inclines the court towards liberal or progressive judgements, is the moral reading. At the same time, it saves the law from the fossilisation through the strict adherence to the text to which the fundamentalism of the 'original intent' would otherwise condemn it.[18] But as already noted, the progressive or conservative, or conceivably even reactionary, make-up of the Supreme Court bench is variable with the political winds. Dworkin's analysis of the Senate hearings on the right-wing nominees, Bork (rejected)[19] and Thomas (approved)[20] can be read as a demonstration of the precariousness of any expectation of anything approaching a linear progression in the development of critical elements of rights-based law in the US.

The tension between Dworkin's and indeed any conceivable top-down theory on the one hand and the spirit which infuses the notion of popular sovereignty on the other cannot be better put than in Dworkin's own description of Judge Learned Hand's objection:

> Hand believed passionately in the virtues of what is often called civic republicanism: he thought that a political community could not flourish, or its citizens develop and improve their own sense of moral responsibility, unless they participated in the community's deepest and most important decisions about justice[21]

Dworkin quotes Judge Hand's words:

> For myself it would be most irksome to be ruled by a bevy of Platonic Guardians, even if I knew how to choose them, which I assuredly do not. If they were in charge, I should miss the stimulus of living in a society where I have, at least theoretically, some part in the direction of public affairs.[22]

Chapter 4 contains a close study of Dworkin's approach in the light of his key ideas of the 'moral reading' and judgemental 'integrity'. Since, as we saw, the former stands for both a description and prescription of how a (particular) legal text is and should be interpreted, it illuminates the study of legal language. The latter points to the motive force behind the *systematic* development of the law. Overall, a comparison between certain principles established by decisions of the Supreme Court and corresponding areas of British law allows us to theorise on the effects of a written as against an unwritten constitution and on certain critical differences which distinguish rights-based law.

Bottom-up

Although it shares with Dworkin's book its magisterial style and some important, theoretical features, Jurgen Habermas's recent work *Between Facts and Norms*, subtitled *contributions to a discourse theory of law and democracy*,[23] succeeds in presenting both a highly innovative bottom-up theory of democracy and a discursive alternative to the classical deductive–subsumptive pattern of judicial logic. The ideas of Habermas take up the rest of chapter 4, being carried then into the final chapter to form the foundation on which the concluding analysis is built. While Dworkin largely remains within jurisprudence, Habermas's thesis straddles, perhaps sometimes awkwardly, social study and jurisprudence, his central concern being to place law in its social context, both structurally and operationally. Dworkin's moral philosophical discourse reveals a fascination with the process by which the, so to speak, DNA of the Constitution under the husbandry of the judges germinates into a variegated crop of citizen's rights. On the other hand, Habermas is intimately involved with the normative and empirical interrelations between the rule of law and democracy.

A crucial point where the theories of the two thinkers diverge clearly emerges when Dworkin's formulation of the majoritarian premise, that the test of law is approval by a majority, is compared with Habermas's criterion:

> law ... can preserve its socially integrating force only insofar as the addressees of legal norms may at the same time understand themselves, taken as a whole, as the rational *authors* of those norms.[24]

The problem faced by Habermas is to explain how this measure, both universalist and normative, is to be interpreted and justified against a theory of democracy based on majority rule. It is noticeable that the self-understanding of citizens set as a standard in Habermas's formula comes close to that expressed as a right to participate in decisions about justice in the statement of belief attributed by Dworkin to Learned Hand. Although the quotation from Hand himself goes on to sound a note of realism, this is immediately counteracted:

Of course I know how illusory would be the belief that my vote determined anything; but nevertheless when I go to the polls I have a satisfaction in the sense that we are all engaged in a common venture.[25]

The sceptical element reflects the view of democracy that, in the very act of voting when the people's sovereignty is affirmed, that sovereignty is withdrawn from them by those it has elected.

The main thrust of Habermas's contribution is directed towards a theory of social integration which contradicts this apparent powerlessness of the people. The dynamic is provided by communicative action aiming at mutual understanding. This is possible because 'communicative acts are located within the horizon of shared, unproblematic beliefs'. We live and speak against the background of this lifeworld from which we derive interpretations and which in turn reproduces itself through communicative action. But social integration is not the only mode of organisation. We are also organised in systems, the economic system being a prominent example. Law mediates between the lifeworld and the systems. Without the language of law, Habermas claims, which acts as a transformer between the public and private spheres (where communicative action takes place) and the systems, 'ordinary language could not circulate throughout society'.[26]

Critical linguistic background

The later half of the twentieth century was taken up with, first, an all-round questioning in most subject areas, other than the sciences,[27] hand in hand with an uncritical gullibility with regard to 'know-what' studies of 'know-how' fields. Then, in sight of the millennium, thinkers began to recreate a foundation of theory out of the rubble that was left. A re-appraisal of the nature of language as the medium in which ideas are expressed was paramount. Thus Ricoeur suggested that language 'formed a meeting point for all philosophical researches' of the time (1962), and went on to specify the investigations of Wittgenstein, English linguistic philosophy, the phenomenology of Husserl, exegesis, comparative history of religion, anthropological works bearing on the myth, the rite and belief, and finally psychoanalysis.[28] The non-philosophical man at his laptop showed a similar awareness: 'How do I know what I think until I see what I write!' The notion that experience was mediated through ideas and sensations had of course been a recurrent theme in the history of epistemology, and the shift from that to the focus on language had been heralded by Wittgenstein in his later work. But it was in the 1960s among theorists, especially in France, that the tacit transition from 'mentality' to critical linguistics took place.

Critical legal theory followed the same trajectory as the other intellectual domains. Law was called in question and attacked for being autonomous, closed off from the wider social contexts in which legal problems were inevitably embedded.[29] A second, mainline criticism was directed at the lawyers' pretence that the law could offer determinate solutions to these problems. This line enlisted critical language theory. Language, by its very nature, was essentially mystifying. So, it was argued, the idea that a legal text could provide a clear, fixed meaning corresponding to what the legislator or judge had intended to convey was unjustified. Both statutory provisions and precedent-setting judicial decisions were open to multiple interpretations. Even more, language at the social level could act as a cloak for ideological pressures, while, at the personal level, it might be manipulated by unconscious forces. Despite careful draftsmanship and rigorous scrutiny, the application of a legal text could not, it was argued, be made proof against a faulty interpretation, ideological taint or personal weakness or prejudice. Academics deployed this type of linguistic theory to attack the validity of theory as an underpinning of law in general and to 'trash' individual case decisions that might act as landmarks in the development of the law. Intellectuals also, in their attitude to the legal system, tended to combine full-blown or vestigial versions of Marxism and Freudianism with a similar cynicism concerning the possibility of non-rhetorical language. The legal system was not seen as a form of democratic expression. In the 1990s, the swing of the ideological pendulum away from negativism and deconstructionism towards integrationist theory carried into critical legal theory also. Landmarks here were Dworkin's works culminating in *Freedom's Law* and Habermas's *Between Facts and Norms*, which have already been briefly discussed.

Structure

The book adapts a defensive posture in chapters 1 and 2, making a claim that the distinctiveness of legal language is such that it escapes not only the attacks of the plain English campaigners but also the challenges posed to language in general by the critical linguistic theorists. Chapter 3 presents a critical, in-depth look at theories of interpretation, both legal and general, which exposes the gap between

INTRODUCTION

theory and praxis and lays the foundation for a study of Dworkin's moral reading in chapter 4. The exposition of Habermas's ideas, also in chapter 4, leads on to the conclusions in the final chapter which proposes to show how and why lawyers' language is distinctive.

The critical language theories which are reviewed in chapter 2 include Perelman's New Rhetoric, Foucault's theory of knowledge/power and the revisions of Marxism by Althusser and Gramsci. The chapter title: 'How critical language theory seeks and then struggles against its own undoing,' sums up an observation applicable to all of these thinkers except Perelman. Each became ultimately uncomfortable with his own relativist, subjective or nihilistic conclusion and sought a way out of the barren landscape of his theory. Even the impish Derrida groped in the mists for a theory of justice. For the thrust of the theories themselves fatally undermined their implied claim to objective truth. The *re*constructive efforts on which they all eventually embarked chimed in with the pre-millennial mood. In Perelman's case he went in the opposite direction, his earlier structuralist theory of argumentation accommodating itself later to the influence of cultural relativism expressing itself in language.

Chapter 3 on interpretation balances the previous chapter. In communicational terms, it concentrates on reception whereas the theories in chapter 2 focus on the text as it is spoken or written. *Dicta* on statutory interpretation by judges at work are set side by side with general hermeneutic theory. It is argued that judges both *mis*interpret what they actually do and (mostly) fail to realise or admit that what they claim to do is in practice unachievable. At the same time, hermeneutic theory is inclined to lead to the relativist conclusion that for any passage there are an indefinite number of interpretations. This matches the contention of the chapter 2 theories that texts cannot be univocal. Intentionalist theories which imply that the hermeneutic objective is by definition the single right interpretation, coinciding with the author's intention, argue about the means by which it is to be discovered. Then, if meaning is indeterminate, it follows that the law cannot make a valid claim to be certain. Finally, the chapter abstracts from Gadamer's central position that hermeneutics *is* philosophy, by drawing on his close identification of interpretation with the history of the concepts. I claim that it is in line with *that idea only* that judges may be said to *interpret* the law in cases other than those involving the collision of rights.[30] I make the point also that interpretation is only an accessory to the application of the law. The proposal at the chapter's end suggests that legal interpretation, if not interpretation in general, is more complex than as previously understood. This links up with the reconstructive view of legal language in the final chapter.

The schemes developed by Dworkin and Habermas are set side by side in chapter 4. The jumping-off point is the former's idea that the broad sweep of the law proceeds by way of constructive interpretation of the abstract constitutional principles. This provides a bridge to the hermeneutic analysis of the preceding chapter. Constructive interpretation is scrutinised in opposition to the theory that the Constitution should be read in accordance with the 'original intent' of the founders. It soon emerges from a debate with Scalia that the latter's position suffers from the same contradiction between originalism and textualism as the self-understanding of the judges discussed above in relation to interpretation. To put the problem briefly here: if the interpretation of the law proceeds by the rigorous examination of the words of the text alone, then how can one say at the same time that the sovereign test is the *intention* of the lawmaker? From the confrontation between constructive interpretation and textualism it becomes clear that the moral 'reading' takes the reader (Dworkin) very far away from the language of the text. In effect, law proceeds by 'taking rights seriously'.[31] Starting from a basis in rights, the law is *constructed* by the use not of legal language but of a philosophical discourse.

The critique of Dworkinism provides a foundation for a thoroughgoing assessment of rights-based law. The fact that, in an actual set of circumstances, rights may collide is a central problem for Dworkin. He becomes uncomfortable because rights are theoretically unlimited and self-validating. Rights operate as trumps against other norms and there cannot be two different suits of trumps in any one game. In a book recently published,[32] he attempts with philosophical subtlety and honest directness to reconcile freedom (and the rights essential to it) with equality (and its constituent rights). The right that is rejected does not in any way lose its validity as a legal norm. The decision which to reject and which to prefer depends, he argues, on what is judged to be 'more at stake' in the given situation. The chapter follows him in his analysis of a few of the judgements creating milestones in the American legal terrain, such as the cases on abortion and euthanasia and those at the margins of free speech. His pivotal idea is that the judges in such (rights-oriented) cases are directed to choose 'the best conception of constitutional moral principles that fits the broad story of America's historical record'.[33] In deciding issues according to this criterion, judges would be engaged in the construction, rather than the application, of the law through the use of philosophical, not legal, discourse.

One can look for contrast at the overturning by the Supreme Court in 1976 of its previous decision to ban the death penalty, based on the constitutional prohibition of cruel or abnormal punishment. The constitutional provision, here, is not a broad 'moral principle' and the 1976 decision adhered to the textual meaning. The abuse of the Constitution by the Republican Party in Clinton's impeachment trial is perhaps another instance.

'Judge Hercules' is Dworkin's composite name for the judges who have the responsibility of maintaining constitutional law as a system and who, in his words, 'together elaborate a coherent constitutional morality'. The name is a measure of the task with which they are burdened. Judge Hercules, though, is a loner, a Platonic philosopher-king, a privileged interpreter of a quasi-sacred text, and certainly not a representative of the people. The conclusion that, in arriving at a judgement, judges must 'decide on their own which conception does most credit to the nation' is hardly reassuring from a *democratic* standpoint. By blowing away with one breath both the presupposition that law is able to provide the single right answer and any sense of justification that might attach to the legal presumption that everyone knows the law, Dworkin, I argue, undermines the principle that constitutional decisions of the Supreme Court can *eo ipso* 'validly' claim to override any legislation or past precedent. At the same time, Dworkin rightly challenges the majoritarian conception of democracy that the laws that are enacted 'should be those, in the end, that the majority of citizens approve'.

This perspective of Dworkin's makes a contrast with Habermas's ideal requirement for the justification of law, that it should be such that the citizens as a whole are able to understand themselves as its 'rational authors'. This marks a clear shift closer to the idea of democratic law as self-imposed. Not only that but, at the level of law taken as a text, whereas Dworkin's judge-interpreter is placed at the centre, Habermas focuses instead on the people as its supposed originator. The choice of 'authorship' to describe the nature of this agency is in line with Habermas's *discourse* theory of the law. Society is ordered in systems, for example the economic system or the political system and including the legal system, each of which develops a specialised language. These have the effect of wearing down ordinary language. Without the language of the law which acts as a 'transformer', Habermas goes on to say, ordinary language could not circulate throughout society. Habermas develops this thesis in *Between Facts and Norms*, a work that is predicted to 'remain for the foreseeable future at the centre of debates in legal and democratic theory'.[34] His *justification* of the distinctiveness of legal language is recruited as one of the supports of the analysis in the final chapter.

The final chapter begins where Habermas's analysis leaves off. Although he recognises that law, as a functional social system, has developed a specialised language and that this has the socially *benign* effect of diffusing ordinary language throughout the other social systems, he does not have to enquire into what the special features of legal language are, nor go into the details of what the relationship is between it and ordinary language. The book does both of these things.

Chapter 5 addresses the second question first. The formulation by Gunther, one of Habermas's collaborators, of the relationship between the interpretation of the facts and the application conditions of the appropriate norm in a legal judgement is adopted as a starting-point. Habermas calls this relationship 'equivalence'. Here, I propose to consider the relationship as one of *representation*. Not only is this more specific than 'equivalence', but it also carries with it the notion of integrity, which connotes a moral as well as an intellectual quality. This, as in Dworkin's proposal, plays an important part in the act of judgement. This linguistic model is a substitute for the classical deductive–subsumptive model of legal logic now generally considered to be inadequate.

Three distinctive features of legal language are presented. The first is the *re*conceptualisation of words taken from ordinary language. Through the *concept*, legal language maintains the link with ordinary language, the concept acting as a conduit by which one is transformed into the other and back again. Its use in the formulation of legal norms gives judicial decisions the ability to face both ways: to state the law, drawing on the history of past usages; and to become part of that history within the purview of future issues. Legal language possesses a complex grammar. It is fraught with intricate constructions of double and triple negatives, different types of 'if' clauses, hypothesis-piling, exceptions, reservations, declarations. What these do is to impart exact illocutionary force to legal norms. It is principally this grammar which creates the mind-boggling effect of many legal passages. The third quality of legal language concerns the pivotal role of reasonableness, often incarnated as the 'reasonable man'. Standing as he does for the addressees of the legal norm, does he correspond to Habermas's 'rational author'? Is there a uniformity in the standard set by the reasonable man in all the legal contexts in which he appears? Is he moved by long-term as well as short-term considerations? Does he take into account the interests of others? These questions are covered in this last chapter, significance being drawn from the recent appearance in legal texts of the trio: 'fair, just and reasonable'.

Out of this characterisation of legal language comes a proposal that rights-based law is not written in legal language. Dworkin's analysis of his landmark cases, for example, uses the language of moral philosophy. This is connected to the fact that they are seen, only or principally, as interpretations of abstract principle rather than as applications of the law by means of conceptual analysis. When rights collide, it can be argued that such cases become undecidable because they involve choices properly belonging to the ethical or political sphere. It is telling that Dworkin is sometimes criticised for confusing ethics, politics and law.

The chapter concludes from its analysis of rights-oriented law that the British Government made the right decision in its constitutional reform of human rights. Rather than grafting the rights of the Convention on to the developed systems of law of the UK as foundational principles, it opted to adopt them to mark off corresponding no-go areas for existing and future law. Thus all legislation is to be construed 'so far as it is possible to do so ... in a way which is compatible with the Convention rights'. (s.3)

Note on discourse

It is worth introducing the concept of discourse at this stage in the Introduction. For 'discourse' has become a central term in theory of language, although, unfortunately, it is a concept that is applied differently by different groups of theorists. Two uses of the concept are relevant to this book's argument. For Habermas, discourse is communicative action directed towards mutual understanding, a process, therefore, whose end is to harmonise the views of speaking subjects concerning the world. This resembles the way in which a judge has defined an agreement:

> The notion of the parties having 'come to' an agreement implied not merely that they were of the same mind in relation to a particular matter, but also that their minds had met so as to form a mutual consensus; and that that meeting of minds had resulted from a process in which each party had to some extent participated.[35]

An essential condition of validity is that communication takes place in the public space marked by 'the free processing of topics and contributions, information and reasons'. Speech-acts can make three validity claims: a claim to truth; a claim to normative rightness; and a sincerity claim. Discourse can be differentiated according to which of these categories of claim is in line to be justified. Discourses are also differentiated by their connection to the functional (sub)systems, the economic, political, pedagogic, legal systems and so on, into which society can be broken up. Each system develops its own specialised language code. Thus lawyers' language is the discourse of the legal system. Since such discourses are code-like, it follows that unmediated, inter-systemic communication cannot take place. The mediating role of legal discourse has already been mentioned.

In Habermas's scheme, discourse is a tool available for use in accordance with illocutionary obligations by autonomous speaking subjects. Against that, for Foucault, discourse rules over the speaking subject. Discourses or 'discourse formations' or 'discursive practices' are or form patterns of words and phrases. Language is dynamic and has a certain autonomy that it exercises through the formation of discourses. Discourses shape the way in which the social world appears to us, constitutive as they are of identities, relations and beliefs.

Foucault posits an intimate link between knowledge and power. Those who have command of discursive practices have social power. Thus, positions within what he calls 'governmentality understood as a strategic field of relations of power' are determined by distributions of discursive capital. We see in society 'the absolute right of the non-mad over the mad, competence ruling over ignorance, good sense or access to reality correcting errors, normality imposing itself on disorder and deviance'.[36] But he does not propose the converse relationship that power dictates or determines what counts as knowledge. Discursive formations are not generated and shaped by governmentality. His torrential language makes him at worst equivocal on the point. But many of those who draw on his theory see the power – knowledge (discourse) relationship as two-way or stress the reciprocal approach that discourses are shaped by or reflect relations of power.

For example, Goodrich claims not only that legal language is an elite discourse remote from ordinary speech but also that it has been developed and maintained to promote the economic interest and discriminatory values of the legal profession. The thesis that language, in general, functions in society as a structured system in the service of power is assessed in chapter 2.

Note on style

Apart from the idea that discourse is expressive or constitutive of social relations, there is little in the theory which looks at the distinctive characteristics of the particular discourses. Habermas conceives the discourse as the specialised code of a particular social (sub)system. A code has no content apart from its reference, the version that is formed when it is decoded. A code, though, may be said to have a style distinguished by the principles underlying or discernible in its design. Does lawyers' language, the legal system's code, have a distinguishable style? Barthes said that legal discourse should have no style but went on to add paradoxically that there could not be a styleless text. The sheer impressionism of assessments of style is well brought out by the contradictory descriptions of legal style cited by Klinck. According to one writer, it is 'wordy, unclear, pompous and dull'; another finds it 'precise, hortatory, impressive and durable'![37] Rather than focusing on stylistic features, the final chapter focuses on those distinctive characteristics of lawyers' language that are adapted to its function in society.

Disclaimer

Finally, for the sake of the author's and the publisher's comfort, it should be stressed that this is a book about law and not a law-book. Therefore, the extracts from reported cases and other accounts of legal principles or rules appearing in the book should not be relied upon as accurate statements of what is the up-to-date legal position or even what was determinant of the issue in the case. The material was used in the book solely to bring out the characteristic features of lawyers' language.

1
BREAKING GROUND

Does everyone know the law?

This book raises and attempts to answer some fundamental questions on the law through a study revolving around lawyers' language, taken to mean the distinctive discourse used in stating and practising the law. The questions start to come into focus as soon as the need is felt to reconcile the use of a special discourse with two foundational principles: one, that ignorance of the law excuses no one; and the other, that justice should not only be done but should also be seen to be done. In passing, it is interesting to see revealed in the language traditionally used to express the first of these principles a couple of the distinctive characteristics of legal discourse. To the lawyers of the past, the Latin version would have been more familiar in the shape of the brocard: *ignorantia juris neminem excusat*. Notice that this is the negative equivalent of the legal presumption that everyone knows the law. Indeed, it turns out to be triply negative: 'no-one' instead of 'everyone', 'ignorance' in place of 'knowledge', and the overall effect to rule out, not to rule in. Here are marks of lawyers' language, the proneness to recruit terms from dead languages and the recourse to a syntax of multiple negatives. Despite the discernible trend for today's lawyers to modernise their language rather than parade a line of linguistic zombies, lawyers' language is far from being understandable by the averagely competent speaker of ordinary language. And exactly the same problem affects the second principle that justice be seen to be done. The requirement for open justice is taken to refer to the need for manifest fairness in the conduct of proceedings in court. But the hypothetical observer of open justice finds his view obstructed by the chinese wall of an alien and alienating language.

It is in relation to the first principle that the questioning is sharper. The negative form, ruling out ignorance of the law as an excuse, fits the criminal law better than the civil. It forms the basis on which *all* participants engage in the trial. Any claim by the law-breaker that he did not know that there was a law to be broken would be inadmissible. Even the layman would be likely to greet such a defence with derision, literally speaking, to laugh it out of court. Yet the presumption in its positive form, that knowledge of the law is universal, seems just as worthy of derision. Just to contemplate the labyrinthine intricacies of the act defining the crime of theft in English law suggests that the presumption is bizarre.

CASE STUDY

A motorist had made it a condition that he would provide a specimen of breath for analysis only after he had consulted a law-book. The magistrates had dismissed the charge that he had failed to provide a specimen of breath, deciding that the condition amounted to a reasonable excuse. The prosecution's appeal against the dismissal was allowed. The motorist's response to the officer's request 'plainly constituted a refusal'.[1] A similar fate had befallen a motorist in a previous case whose legal knowledge was sufficiently extensive to allow him to make a specific request to read the Police and Criminal Evidence Act 1984 (s.66) Codes of Practice before breathalysis.[2] Ignorance of the law excuses nobody!

The presumption that everyone knows the law ('presumption of knowledge') is *itself* law. Can it be said, therefore, that everyone knows the presumption? There is no crisp answer. The best that can be hazarded at this stage in the argument is a paradoxical one: that the presumption would be recognised as *reasonable* in the sense of pragmatically indispensable, and *unreasonable* in the sense of immediately falsifiable.

Make a comparison with the widely, if not universally, known presumption of innocence. This is just as fundamental to the criminal process as the presumption of knowledge. It is in its very essence rebuttable; it only stands unless and until guilt is proven. By contrast, the presumption of knowledge is irrebuttable. If the validity of either presumption were challenged, the same initial, positivist response would be available: it has the authority of the law. But, if probed for a substantive justification, each could lay claim to a different ground for its legitimacy. The presumption of innocence would be claimed to be just. But clearly, a different claim would require to be advanced for the presumption of knowledge. Without a doubt it can be justified on grounds of expediency. Yet this seems too weak a basis to support a presumption which is not only irrebuttable but also purports to describe a state of affairs.

Does it matter if the truth-claim, which is implied by the status of the presumption of knowledge as a description of a state of affairs, is false? According to positivist doctrine, the law is the law. It consists of the rules, principles and precepts which properly issue from institutionalised law-making procedures. Its legitimacy is based on the authority of the sovereign command vested in or held by a legislative assembly or on its adherence to a constitution. Purely formal legitimacy, however, is not enough for the legal system to serve its purpose as the underpinning of a peaceful society. The law must make another and different claim to legitimacy for the aberrant individual to feel that he has been rightly sanctioned by the power, for the loser in a dispute to accept the justness of his defeat in litigation and for the parties to rest content with a negotiated compromise. The nature of this claim is that the law is fair, just and reasonable. The legal system leans on its formal legitimacy, and the additional claim to validity is not explicit. Rather, the claim to validity underlies and shapes the discourse of law, for if it were to turn out to represent (legal) fiction, the law would seem to become incapable of performing its function of opinion- and will-formation in society.

Lawyers' language not only alien but also alienating

To sum up the argument so far: the law's effectiveness as a system of justice depends on its legitimacy, which in turn demands that the presumption of knowledge is tenable as a description of the state of affairs to which it refers; the remoteness of the language of the law from ordinary speech argues against the presumption. But this remoteness alone does not account for the apparently deeply felt and aggressively expressed repugnance aroused by legal utterances and texts. Two alienating traits of lawyers' language have already been identified in the opening paragraph. My book *The Lawyer and Society* assembled a portmanteau indictment from sources which went back to Edward VI of England, west to America and east to Hong Kong:[3]

The basic deficiency of legal language is believed to be its obscurity otherwise described as opacity, impenetrability, unintelligibility. This is thought to be caused, or contributed to, or aggravated, by the use of long and involved sentences of indeterminate structure, straggling over many subordinate clauses, careless or defiant of the laws of grammar; inside these malformed sentences are some words and phrases which are superfluous and some which are semantically senile, and specialised terms, a lot of which are meaningless.[4]

Later in this chapter I review recent attempts by various self-qualified linguotherapists to force legal language to submit to a complete transfusion, or at least a course of injections, of *plain* language. I conclude that these efforts are misguided and their failure is inevitable. Certainly, as with ordinary speech or any other special language, numerous instances of bad use even by competent speakers are inescapable. In the particular case of lawyers' language, the professional scrupulousness of legal writers, conveyancers and parliamentary draftsmen works in favour of good use, while its intricacies work against it. But the felt need for therapy, together with the wide-ranging attacks on its alleged obscurity and unintelligibility, suggests a pathology. The very virulence and frequency of the criticism offer a clue to the nature of the diagnosis. After all, ordinary readers humour or tolerate the recondite commentaries in the press written in the special language of economics, and the esoterics of certain types of music and art criticism. The difference in the case of the legal text is that the ordinary person (rightly) believes himself or herself, not a select few nor a particular elite, to be its addressee. Legal language is diseased in that an irksome 'membrane' is interposed, screening off the legal text from its proper audience or readership. This critique becomes sharper and more radical in theories which suggest that the disease is fostered by lawyers themselves in pursuit of their professional interests.

'When a goat is present it is stupid to bleat in its place'[5]

Regardless of whether it is accepted that such a self-interested intent lies behind the development of legal language, the next question that arises is whether the supply of legal services overcomes the problem created by its obscurity. Is the availability of access to a lawyer for consultation and representation sufficient in itself to justify the presumption of knowledge, even ignoring the reality that 'availability' may stand for no more than a *right* of access without any implication that the (largely financial) *means* required to make the right effective are within the reach of all?

But it is the representative, rather than the consultative, role of the lawyer which by far predominates. The question on the client's lips is not: what is the law? Rather than to be instructed by the lawyer on the law, he is there to give instructions to the lawyer to act on his behalf. The lawyer's consultative role is performed largely in the course of taking instructions as a preliminary to her representation of the client. Most of most lawyers' time is spent on deeds. Significantly, the alternative meanings of 'deed' point to the nature of the relationship between legal draftsman and client. The 'deed' prepared by the draftsman on the client's behalf, when executed (signed) by the client, *represents* the legal act or 'deed' executed (performed) by the client. Deeds are always complex. They are sites at which numerous fields of law intersect. But despite the complexity, the presumption of knowledge can be considered justified since the lawyer's knowledge of the law is imputed to the layman.

It is not in the writing of documents, but as speech, that the law is dramatised for the public. In litigation and negotiation, the lawyer openly takes the place of her client. The advocate's opening words are: 'I represent …'. Moreover the interposition of the lawyer as conveyancer can be held to validate the presumption that her client knows the law in relation to the 'deed' instructed by him. Is there some equivalent in the case of the legal representative as advocate or negotiator in the resolution of a dispute? On the contrary, the difference between the two situations is clearcut. The conveyancer 'represents' the client by *acting* on his behalf. Dispute resolution, on the other hand, starts from a *fait accompli* and is concerned with its consequences. The theoretical framework of the process, the trial or the negotiation, by which the dispute is resolved, can be described in the form of an extreme paradox. It is basic that in the performance of the act giving rise to the dispute the party is assumed to know the law which will define his act and determine its legal consequences. Yet the *adversarial* nature of the process itself demonstrates that there is room for argument on this very question. For the purposes of the argument, we can ignore the uncertainties of theory and take the process of adjudication as consisting of the *application* of a rule or principle of law to a particular set of facts (an act and its surrounding circumstances). The law, that is, the applicable rule or principle, exists and is uncontestable but it has to be found. There is the paradox: side by side with the assumption that the party knew the law before or while performing the act, we have to set the revelation that the lawyer could not know the law until the very moment of the judge's decision.

The conclusion then must be that although access to professional expertise goes towards the justification of the presumption of knowledge it does so only to a strictly limited extent. In the course of the analysis we have come across the problem of the uncertainty of the law, discovering that it is in a sense unknowable. And yet, the specificity of *the* law' requires, in the ideal at least, that there is a single right answer. Again, since law is almost entirely written down in accessible statutes, case reports, textbooks and commentaries, how can the law be 'unknowable' to legally qualified and competent readers of those texts? We can see that its unknowability arises from the necessity to match a general rule or principle (an indeterminate number of which become systematised to form the law) to an individual case. The process of matching involves an act of judgement. The sense in which the law is unknowable, then, becomes clearer if one compares the statement: 'I *judge* this to be so' with the statement: 'I *know* this to be so'. In the final chapter, the process of matching general rule or principle to particular case is analysed within a semantic frame of reference. Meaning, which was highlighted at the beginning of this chapter as the problem, emerges at the end as the means whereby the contradictions can be reconciled.

The following case study is a variant on a mundane situation met every day by the motorist, where the law, so to speak, pulls back its veil and stares him in the face.

CASE STUDY

Imagine a stretch of road in a sparsely populated area, which is marked by a 30 mph sign but which to the approaching motorist is visibly free of sharp bends, roadworks and other hazards. The message conveyed by the sign is that a body to which law-making authority for the purpose has been delegated has imposed a speed limit on this stretch of road. He assumes that the conditions required to make the speed limit law have been met.

There is no doubt but that the approaching motorist knows the law: he understands the meaning of the sign. Certainly, if he were to reflect, he might well be disposed to challenge the law's validity, 'validity' in the sense already explained. Reasoning that a speed limit is justified solely in the interest of road safety, he might be tempted to argue that it would not be at all jeopardised at this particular locality if he drove at a higher speed. Although the enforcement of the law by the use of sanctions against an infringer could not be successfully resisted, it would nevertheless be counted as in some sense objectionable.

Certain deeper implications of the presumption of knowledge can be drawn from this scenario. Up to this point, the argument has proceeded on the footing that the presumption must be justified for the legal system to claim legitimacy. But although knowledge of the law has been postulated to be a necessary condition of legitimacy, it now appears from this particular case that it may not be a sufficient one. Exceptionally, here, the motorist has come face to face with a legal text (the 30 mph sign), whose language (semiotics) he could not fail to understand. He also understands the law in the additional sense that he recognises the reason for it, the ground (road safety) on which it can claim validity. But, when account is taken of the physical features of the locus, his *knowledge* of what the law *is* (derived from the message of the sign) conflicts with his *understanding* of what the law *ought to be* (that is, no speed limit, given that its rationale is the promotion of road safety). A weakening of his sense of obligation to obey the law, to keep his speed to 30 mph, is the outcome. The law suffers a loss of legitimacy.

The case study, therefore, prompts us to take a step away from the conception of knowledge of the law in its absolute sense. Reflection shows that that is unattainable, even by the lawyer. Even were the opposite to be assumed, it is not knowledge, verbatim, of a legal text, but an understanding of what the law should be to match the circumstances, that counts. It is in that sense that the presumption requires to be justified.

The case study can also be used to delineate some of the features of such an understanding. Suppose that the motorist has noted that the speed limit on this stretch of road, although seemingly vexatious, is widely obeyed by others. He will then be less inclined to defy it. He may well be motivated in this by pragmatism, by the consideration that the readiness to comply with a rule is normally linked to the likelihood of its enforcement, a likelihood in this case signalled by the line of slow-moving vehicles. Nonetheless, it is worth exploring whether patterns of what might be called 'ovine' behaviour have a binding force of their own, not being just indicative of expectations of vigilant enforcement. The standard referred to as the 'normal' is, basically, discernible as a matter of (statistical) fact, whereas the standard attributed to the 'normative' claims to be *right*. Are there circumstances in which the normal acquires the characteristics of the normative?

Neither to drive on the left nor *rouler à droite* can claim to be the intrinsically superior way to drive. Yet the former in UK and the latter almost everywhere else are both normal and normative. Normativity does not, however, flow necessarily from normality. Order in the sense of conformity with the normal does not in itself set up a (strong) validity-claim. It has to be justified by a *reason*. The reason in the case of the 'rule of the road' is obvious; chaos would be disastrous.

The parent engaged in the 'training' of his child in manners, etiquette or convention is soon made aware from the child's reiteration of 'why', his demand for reasons, that the child understands the essence of what constitutes normativity. Reliance by the parent on 'the done thing' form of justification conflates the normal and the normative, leaving the child intellectually dissatisfied. Nonetheless, much of the burden of the shaping of behaviour and expectations in society, the process of socialisation, is borne by the individual's learned ability to distinguish and conform to normality. The normativity of the normal is taken for granted. And, in the same way, the child at a later stage of development ceases to demand reasons for, and adopts *unquestioningly*, the vogues and fashions of his peer group. Still, the requirement to offer reasons to justify judgements is an essential feature of the legal process, as discussed in chapter 5.

Remoteness of legal language

> What is in effect the relexicalisation of the law, its archaic terminological obscurity and its pedagogic specialisation, are all geared to the reproduction of an economic elite and the discriminatory values that such an elite serves.[6]

This polemical package manages to squeeze into one sentence not only multiple charges against legal language and an indictment of compartmentalism in legal education, but also the accusation that these are deliberate contrivances to support the lawyers' supposed elite status and further their professional interests. For full measure, the attack reaches beyond the law to some unspecified conspiracy in which lawyers participate. It would be surprising if this passage would sit comfortably in the mouth of someone who engages in *common* speech and there is the further irony that its author is now himself a professor of law! Does he not see that the language of his own critique is just as elitist and remote, or is he using parody to underline his point?

Strangely, the adoption of *uncommon* language tends to be a shared characteristic of those levelling similar criticisms. Thus Jefferson, with his indictment of the language of post-Independence American acts and pre-Independence British statutes:

> from their verbosity, their endless tautologies, their convolutions of case within case and parenthesis within parenthesis, and their multiplied efforts at certainty by saids and aforesaids by ors and by ands, to make them more plain, do really render them more perplexed and incomprehensible, not only to common readers but to the lawyers themselves.[7]

And the Statute Law Society in a submission to the Renton Committee described statutory language as:

> legalistic, often obscure and circumlocutious, requiring a certain type of expertise in order to gauge its meaning. Sentences are long and involved, the grammar is obscure, and archaisms, legally meaningless words and phrases, tortuous language ... abound.[8]

This provokes the question: why do those who attack legal language for its shortcomings reproduce in their criticism similar linguistic features? They seem to be unable to stop themselves slipping into the *ex cathedra* rhetoric appropriate to critical denunciation or, as in Goodrich's case, into the more strident discourse of ideological warfare. A vintage example from another sphere showed up in Tony Wright's polemic against the language use of academics, politicians and journalists, headlined 'Bad language':

> This is the world of verbless vacuities, of mindless 'modernisations' ... of robotic repetition of words and phrases that have long lost any connection with meanings[9]

None of these is recognisable as *ordinary* speech. Ordinary speech, plain, pithy, up to date as it is, is not to be identified as the usage of the common man or the ordinary person but the language in use by us all for the exchanges of everyday life. If challenged, Goodrich could seek to justify the '*extra*ordinary' language employed by him as that which is appropriate or necessary for discourse with other social philosophers. In line with his critique of law, he could even admit that the language of the academic system and its 'pedagogic specialisation' are 'geared to the reproduction of an [intellectual] elite' and even also to its 'discriminatory values'. That said, both sides could maintain their positions intact. The defenders of legal language could say that it is a discourse well-adapted to its function, even though the distinctive characteristics distancing it from common speech have resulted in the creation of a preserve restricted to competent users. This is just the same claim as can be made on behalf of academic language.

But against that, Goodrich and other antagonists, for their part, could argue that it is just *because* of its function that the language of law, unlike that of academics, intellectuals or economists, has a special responsibility to be intelligible. The question of whether law written in either *plain* or *ordinary* language would be intelligible would logically then confront them. Later in this chapter I put forward some evidence to support a negative answer to the question. In any event, even if the antagonists were to prevail, they would still be faced with the problem that any gain in intelligibility would be achieved at the expense of functionally valuable features of legal language, such as precision and internal consistency.

Law made plain?

Introducing a bill in the House of Commons in 1992, a Tory MP expressed its purpose in this way:

> My Plain English Bill is designed to encourage the use of plain, clear language, and prevent the unscrupulous or the arrogant or incompetent from hiding behind legalese, jargon, gobbledygook or small print.

He made it 'plain' and 'clear' that the law would not apply to politicians and the bill was given an unopposed first reading.[10] Notice the employment of the plain English word 'gobbledygook' by the MP. Plain English campaigners show a remarkable fondness for this particular term, alternating it with 'gibberish' (another plain word) to describe 'legalese' which is perhaps plain but not English. As I argue later, the preference for *plain* language over *ordinary* language as the vehicle for reform is deceptive.

On the issue of intelligibility, start with this trivial yet cautionary example from a transatlantic conversation:

Transatlantic telephonist: 'Are you through?'
Caller: 'Yes, thank you'.

Telephonist cuts caller off.

Here, the speakers found themselves at acute cross-purposes while using the very plainest of language. Of course, the piquancy of the ending of a prospective conversation before it began, due to the near-opposition of the meaning of the identical word in the particular context, may just go to support the notion that Britain and America are but one nation divided by a common language. Nonetheless, it points to the possibility that plain language may not always be intelligible.

Laymen themselves often show a preference for legal language over plain language. In the days before the spread of home ownership and legal aid familiarised the law-abiding majority with the realities of legal practice, the man in the street might *in extremis* resort to a 'lawyer's letter' (reputedly for a standard fee of seven shillings and sixpence). His primary purpose was not to convey what was probably a transparently empty threat that continued inaction on the addressee's part would provoke court proceedings. Rather, it demonstrated his belief that lawyers' language was the right medium, given the nature and gravity of his grievance. People believed in the greater illocutionary force of certain legal syntagms. A comparison of 'use one's best endeavours' with 'try one's best', for example, shows up the grounds for their belief.

The following analyses suggest more formidable difficulties in the use of plain English.

Corresponding to the terms of the statutory encroachment on the accused's right to remain silent, a new form of police 'caution' was introduced for England and Wales by the Criminal Justice and Public Order Act 1994.[11] The caution runs:

> You do not have to say anything. But it may harm your defence if you do not mention when questioned something which you later rely on in Court. Anything you do say may be given in evidence.[12]

Researchers found that not more than half of the people who listened to the three-sentence caution thought that it made sense. More than half perceived the middle sentence as intimidatory and the effect of the caution as a whole to be 'pressuring or a threat'. This was the research paper's judgement of the caution:

> Delivering the 37-word three-element caution as a whole is an inherently meaningless process. Its length, number of clauses, and syntactic and semantic complexity ensure that it is beyond the ability of the majority of people in the street to absorb let alone comprehend.[13]

It is ironic and probably significant that an eerie echo of the strictures habitually directed at legal language is to be heard in the researchers' words. Yet the wording of the caution was obviously crafted in a form designed to earn the plaudits of the proponents of plain English. But, as the research confirmed, instead of supporting it, its effect was to undermine the claim that 'plain' can be equated with 'clear' or 'intelligible' in a linguistic context.

Why does the message intended to be conveyed by these very plain words turn out to be so unclear? One reason may be that communication involves the shared expectation that a particular speech situation will call forth a particular discourse. Thus, the interjection of an unexpected (in the case of the caution, essentially synthetic) form of words makes both meaning and significance hard to grasp. Basically, however, the cause of the difficulty is that the meaning of the caution is *unavoidably* complicated. Analysis brings this out:

> 'You do not have to say anything' [negates any obligation to say some (every) thing]. 'But' [you are cautioned] 'it may harm your defence' [threat introduced] 'if you do not mention when questioned' [description of form of inaction which will cause the threat to materialise, but the full content is suspended] 'something which you later rely on in Court' [Content is now fully defined and the information conveyed that the threat if it does materialise will materialise in the future]. 'Anything you do say may be given in evidence' [alternative threat which will materialise in the future in the event of action (not inaction)].

It is evident that, whatever the wording of the caution, its semantic complexity, involving the dizzyingly sudden change from reassurance on one's freedom of action to the horns of a predicament – damned if you don't and damned if you do – would *ensure* that its meaning was slippery. Nonetheless, it is certainly arguable that the use of a word-selection preprogrammed for plainness makes the complex message more difficult, not easier, to unravel. Is it not the case that the only word in the three sentences of the caution whose meaning *in context* is clear is 'defence', a word which, taken from legal language, fits the text?

> At the root of the Plain English Campaign is a linguistic sleight-of-hand, which depends on the polysemy, the plurality of meanings, of the word 'plain'. Among dictionary equivalents of 'plain' are 'simple', 'bare of ornamentation or embellishment', 'ordinary', 'clear'. Certainly, the caution is made up of what would qualify as simple words. But, as the study of its impact demonstrates, there is no reason to believe that verbal simplicity delivers linguistic clarity. Indeed, the diversification of natural languages into distinct discourses points in the opposite direction. Simplicity, itself, is a fluid, far from simple, concept. It is true also that the composition of the caution is bare of ornamentation or embellishment. The ordinary person, on the contrary, does not write or speak in bare language, in telegramese. Even those of impoverished vocabulary feel the urge to compensate by interlarding their sayings with expletives and profanities. The proneness of the campaigners themselves to break out of the straitjacket of plainness into the violence of words like 'gobbledygook', 'gibberish' and 'jargon' has already been noted. By contrast, the inventor of the caution, through his fixation on degree-zero (plain) language has produced a synthetic, dull, lifeless composition, at a far distance from ordinary speech.
>
> Then what the campaigners advocate, perhaps, may not be simple or bare language, but clear language. If so, the conjuring trick is exposed. 'Plain language' disappears into the hat and the rabbit that is brought out is *plain meaning*. The very blandness of the quality of plainness blinds us and the campaigners themselves to the radical difference between 'make use of plain language' and 'use language which makes your meaning plain'. Would it be an exaggeration then to say that the credo of the Plain English Campaign is reducible on analysis to the tautology that the use of intelligible language is the road to intelligibility?

In a statutory instrument of 1994 aimed at consumer protection,[14] this requirement appeared:

> A seller or supplier shall ensure that any written term of a contract is expressed in *plain, intelligible* language, and if there is doubt about the meaning of a written term, the interpretation most favourable to the consumer shall prevail (italics added).[15]

Now, the text, here, clearly implies that plain language, which, the context dictates, entails the use of simple words in preference to the *mots justes*, may be congruent with, but is not indistinguishable from 'intelligible' language. Nor, the draftsman is suggesting, can either plain language or intelligible language or even language satisfying both requirements be relied upon to eliminate ambiguity. If that occurs, it is to be resolved, he says, in the consumer's favour.

Intelligibility is related to the particular addressee; texts on quantum theory may be intelligible to other physicists but not to the ordinary person. Without doubt, it is the ordinary person who is identifiable as the addressee of the consumer protection regulation. What is the point then in adding to the intelligibility requirement a prescription for plain language if it is not merely as a sop to the politicians then in power? Making that more plausible is the fact that, oddly for a statute, the text includes no sanction for non-fulfilment of the language requirement, the purpose of the regulation being to outlaw contracts whose terms (whether plainly, intelligibly and unambiguously drafted or not) are unfair to the consumer.

It is suggestive as well as ironic that the prescription in the regulation for the 'plain, intelligible language' to be used in consumer contracts is set within a text that is unmistakably composed in legal language. This, for example, is the wording with which the draftsman chooses to define one of the terms, which, if included in a consumer contract, 'may be regarded as unfair':

> [a term which has the effect of] inappropriately excluding or limiting the legal rights of the consumer vis-à-vis the seller or supplier or another party in the event of total or partial non-performance or inadequate performance by the seller or supplier of any of the contractual obligations, including the option of offsetting a debt owed to the seller or supplier against any claim which the consumer may have against him[16]

Manifestly, this passage would fail the 'plain-intelligible' test for the language of a consumer contract. It shares certain characteristics with the police caution: syntactical and semantic complexity, absence of rhetoric, univocality. Its language then is plain in the important sense of being nonrhetorical, but what of its intelligibility? The framer of a consumer contract is directed by the regulation to make it intelligible to its addressee, the body of consumers. But, an obvious inference from its language, the regulation, itself, cannot be targeted at *its* addressee, the people within the legal jurisdiction. Instead, it is aimed at the competent *professional* user of legal language. The approach of the draftsman of the Regulation can be fairly summed up in this way: consumer contracts that are likely to be accepted by the general public without recourse to a legal adviser should be written in plain, intelligible language; the possibility of ambiguity remains and any such should be resolved in favour of the recipient of the terms, the consumer. Yet the draftsman makes no attempt to present his text in anything other than legal language, which, both on the face of it and by implication, is neither 'plain' nor 'intelligible'. If we assume that the reason for the draftsman's recourse to legal language is the high value placed on its precision, then two questions arise. The first concerns the disjunction between intelligibility and freedom from ambiguity. The other asks whether the renunciation of intelligibility for the sake of precision provides an insurance against ambiguity.

Legal language is attacked by its critics not only on the ground of its unintelligibility but also because it makes a claim to univocality which it is impossible to deliver. The true position is that precision is set up as a goal to be (almost always) striven after, but there are occasional lapses. The jibe that lawyers cheer or flourish on ambiguity is salt in the wound for the legal draftsman who has fallen into a linguistic trap. Does it make sense, however, to describe a passage as intelligible but ambiguous? Is that the equivalent of 'I understand what you are saying but tell me what you mean'? Consider this excerpt from a newspaper report of an interview with the chairman of Clarity, 'a group campaigning for the [legal] profession to replace unintelligible language with plain English'.[17] After identifying himself as an authentic campaigner by way of a fanfare of 'gobbledygook' and 'gibberish' for lawyers' language he said: 'Where a human being would say: "The house is ready", a solicitor employs a large staff to say: "We hereby give you notice in accordance with clause ..."' This sentence is intelligible and *in the context* we have a fair idea what he means. We readily discount the *possible* meaning that aliens have taken over the Law Society. But, less improbably, he might be suggesting that in order to achieve the precision necessary to safeguard her client's position under a building contract, the solicitor comes under a duty not to yield to the casual language which, as a 'human being', she uses in her ordinary life. That is what he should be saying! But, even independently of the context, one can infer from certain rhetorical devices in his language that he is not commending solicitors but condemning them.

Comparing the plain-language police caution with the chairman of Clarity's statement, we note that it is a distinctive characteristic of the former that it is devoid of rhetoric while the latter is rhetorically (over-)rich. The statement is intelligible and the caution is not, even discounting for the difference in syntactical and semantic complexity. Against that, the use of rhetoric in the statement has introduced ambiguity which requires recognition by the reader to resolve it, while the meaning of the caution, *once decoded* albeit with difficulty, is unequivocal. To unravel the meaning of the statement we focus on the text, but so far as the caution is concerned what we seek to discover is the intention of the writer. These two approaches to meaning are discussed in chapter 3.

There is something more to be said concerning intelligibility. The words used may all be plain and intelligible. Yet the whole may not be *understood* in the sense that the recipient is not able to relate it to the speech-situation, the reason being that the language of the statement is discursively unacceptable. That important point, exposing the synthetic quality of 'plain language', is graphically illustrated by a journalist's account of his jury service.[18] In his summing up, the judge told the jury to convict 'only ... if you are sure, if you are not sure then acquit'. In instructing the jury in those terms, the judge was recycling the Lord Chancellor's department's guidance to judges. Evidently, the voice of the Plain English Campaign is still plainly to be heard in the corridors of power, still prey to the inbuilt fallacy that more demotic language means more democracy. But the jury, the account tells us, had difficulty with the instruction. After deliberating for almost a day, they came back with a question they were having trouble with the word 'sure'. Could the judge help them: for example, would 'reasonable doubt' suffice instead of 'sure'. The journalist makes the point:

> whereas the concept of 'reasonable doubt' provides a pole around which juries can argue, the concept of 'sure' is highly problematic.

Now, as regards the second question (that is, whether going for precision at the cost of intelligibility ensures freedom from ambiguity), the passage quoted from the regulation seems free of ambiguity. Yet, despite the draftsman's obvious output of effort to achieve overall precision, he would seem to have lapsed or relaxed by his inclusion of the very *im*precise words 'inappropriately' and 'inadequate'. His use of 'unfair' as the term on which the entire regulation pivots is even more striking. But, far from this being atypical, legal texts are characterised by the mixing in, here and there, of such imprecise or flexible words and phrases (typically, 'fair', 'reasonable', 'just', 'due', 'proper', 'good faith' and their negative forms) like currants in the pudding of precision. In consequence, legal language can put forward only a limited claim to precision. Given the imprecision, how is a passage containing such words to be interpreted? Two interpretative approaches were noted above: in one case focusing on the intent of the text; in the other looking for the author's intention. Neither of these can provide a complete or determinate interpretation for a text in legal or any other language which includes flexible words, such as those already mentioned. Close reading of the text will not yield any new insight; again, nothing more can be divined of the authorial intention, he has said all that he intended to say. According to lawyers' linguistics, such words reach out from the text to 'find' an *objective* measure. Briefly introduced at this point, the question of the flexible in legal language figures prominently in the final chapter.

Law made ordinary?

Rather than advocate the use of plain language, equivalent, as I have tried to show, to the creation of an artificial language existing in name only, it would have been more useful for the plain English campaigners to have considered whether law might be written in *ordinary* language. From what has been said so far, the omens show up as ill for such a project, for all of those flexible words causing problems of interpretation for legal language are part of an ordinary vocabulary. Taking an empirical approach, the following case studies involving other ordinary words seem to provide a conclusive answer on this point. Far from the media headlines,[19] such cases form a substantial part of the court curriculum.

CASE STUDIES

'Keep open'

It was held that a restaurant was not being *kept open* during prohibited hours, 3.00am to 5.00am, even though the doors were unlocked and customers were eating meals at 3.45am, provided that those who were present had been admitted within the permitted hours. On the contrary, premises would have been kept open, even with a 'closed' sign, if the sign was just a token and the premises were in reality open.[20]

'Premises'

(1) Was a busker playing his guitar in Leicester Square required to obtain a licence from the Council? Under an Act of 1963 no *premises* were to be used for public entertainment without a licence. The judges decided that Leicester Square was not 'premises'. One busker could replace another, with the result that several persons would require to be licensed during one day to operate in one place. Leicester Square was not a place to which the public was invited for entertainment, the circumstances envisaged in the Act.[21]

(2) Although Leicester Square is judged not to be *premises*, any vehicle is declared to be *premises* under the Police and Criminal Evidence Act 1984. The Act empowers the police to seize as evidence anything which is 'on the premises'. The issue in this case turned on whether the police were permitted by virtue of that power to seize the vehicle itself, or only any evidentially valuable contents. Given 'premises' in its ordinary sense as designating immovable property, it would be a physical impossibility for the police to seize and retain the premises in their totality. Where, on the other hand, 'premises' denoted a car, that was not the case. The court held, therefore, that the police stayed within their powers in respect of the car under a provision in the same Act which enabled them to seize and retain as evidence 'anything' for which they were entitled to search.[22]

'Public place'

(1) Is a garden path a *public place* if a dog dangerously out of control is in the garden? The Court overturned a conviction under the Dangerous Dogs Act 1991, holding that a garden path was not a public place even though members of the public enjoyed access to it as lawful visitors.[23]

Obiter dictum: those who are led up the garden path have now been judicially warned that they are not being taken to a public place.

(2) The same Act provides that the owner of a dog, who 'allows it to enter a place which is not a *public place* but where it is not permitted to be' and where it injures any person, commits an offence. In this case, the owner had left his dog chained in an enclosure in his back garden. The dog had strained and bent the clip, so releasing its chain and escaping from the enclosure. It entered a nearby garden and bit a child.

The issue was whether the owner had 'allowed' the dog to go loose, notwithstanding the fact that he had chained it up within an enclosure. The Court upheld his conviction. The offence, it argued, had been committed through omission on the owner's part to secure the dog. Even if, although erroneously, he had genuinely believed that he had taken adequate precautions, he had nevertheless 'allowed' the dog to stray. There was no need to prove intent or negligence. The owner's failure was the *cause* of the incident.

The Court reasoned that 'on the facts it could be said as a matter of *ordinary language* and causation' (italics added) that the owner had allowed the dog to enter the prohibited place. Not everyone, however, would agree that the 'ordinary language' description fitted the circumstances. Rather, the decisive consideration should be sought in the judge's analysis in accordance with legal linguistics:

> It was impossible to spell out of the Act that Parliament intended any mental element to be part of [the subsection]. It would have been easy to add words like 'intention, desire or knowledge or foresight of the consequences' but they were not there.[24]

'Accident'

(1) The meaning to be given to the word 'accident' was determinative of the issues in an appeal where the House of Lords overturned a decision of the Court of Session. Of special interest here was the fact that the case turned on whether the word should be treated as an expression of *ordinary* language, as the Court of Session thought, or, on the other hand, should be subjected to *legal* linguistic analysis, the position adopted by the House of Lords.

Statutory benefit was payable where an employee suffered personal injury caused by *accident* arising out of and in the course of his employment. The question before the court was whether a claim in respect of post-traumatic stress disorder suffered over a six-year period by a fireman whose work involved attendance at stressful and traumatic incidents qualified for the benefit.

The reasoning of the Court of Session which persuaded it that the benefit claim should be allowed, focused, according to the analysis of the House of Lords, on the question of language. Adopting the ordinary use of language, the court below had treated the phrase 'by accident' as if it were 'adverbial and equivalent to 'accidentally''. As a result it did not require to identify a particular incident constituting the accident and separate from the injury which it caused. It thought that the injury and the accident might 'merge indistinguishably', the accident being properly said to be the cause of the injury.

The approach of the House of Lords which led it to the opposite conclusion was based on 'the scheme of the legislation and on the history of its application'. The first brings the context to bear as a guide to the meaning of the particular section. 'A correct understanding of [the section] was not to be gleaned from a concentrated study of that section alone,' the Court said. Then, the past history of the legislation was to be viewed from the perspective of the current law. Nonetheless, the earlier law was not to be disregarded as a guide to the construction of the present provision. This two-way approach to the legislative history revealed that a specific incident or series of incidents, counting as *accident*, had to be established as the cause of the injury. The two concepts of accident and injury were distinguishable.[25]

(2) A plane passenger suffering from a pre-existing paralysis was injured when he fell as he tried to leave his seat. The question was whether the carrier was liable under an international treaty providing a right to compensation for injury arising from an 'accident'. The Court said that the word *accident* focused on the cause and not the effect. It was to be contrasted with 'occurrence' appearing elsewhere in the treaty. For the claim to be successful, the cause of the injury would have to have been 'an unexpected or unusual event external to the passenger'. 'Accident' could not be understood to refer to the passenger's *peculiar* reaction to the *normal* operation of the aircraft.[26]

Noticeable, in the light of the earlier discussion on the function of imprecise words in legal language designed to appeal to objectivity, is the use here of 'normal' and its oppositional word 'peculiar'.

'Frivolous'

The Lord Chief Justice complained in this case that it was unfortunate that the expression 'frivolous' had ever entered the 'lexicon of [legal] jargon'. In a legal context, when applied to an application made to the court, it bore the connotation, 'futile, misconceived, hopeless or academic'. To the man or woman in the street, however, it was 'suggestive of lightheartedness or a propensity to humour and those were not qualities associated with most actual or prospective appellants'.[27]

It is worthwhile to analyse the grounds of the judicial disdain. Legal language and ordinary language are both drawn from the natural language and many words appear in ordinary speech before importation into the discourse of the law. Many also make the return journey or even a single journey starting from legal language to the ordinary vocabulary. In crossing over in either direction, words (and phrases) undergo semantic transformation. Why then did the judge deplore the appropriation by lawyers of the word 'frivolous' on the ground of its shift of meaning, this being the process by which legal language must have evolved?

One can reasonably speculate that it was the rhetorical use of 'frivolous' which evoked the judicial disapproval. Lawyers say 'frivolous' of a court application so lacking in merit that it could not have been intended seriously, although it was, just as outside the courtroom, 'you must be joking' or 'you can't be serious' is dismissive in the same way of an argument which both parties nevertheless know to have been seriously intended. Inside the courtroom, and more generally within the language of the law, the mystifications of rhetoric have no place. This was what Barthes probably meant when he opined that legal language should have no style.

In a case arising from allegations of malpractice against officers and members of Westminster City Council, the application of an indemnity for legal costs in such circumstances came into question. The judge said:

> [T]he indemnity was not a statute; it was the council's own policy which it could apply using common sense according to the ordinary meaning of the words without having to apply a precise meaning of a word or words prescribed by lawyers.[28]

This marks the judge's recognition of the separateness of ordinary language from the language of lawyers.

Another case worth citing for its delicious irony identified the same line of demarcation. A defendant was seeking to escape liability under a deed of indemnity. The appearance of her signature on the deed, she claimed, was due to her former husband's 'fraudulent actions and misrepresentations'. Her defence had been settled by her previous solicitors in her affidavit. In it she stated that she had studied a House of Lords decision in a case which she named. In reliance on that decision she made a number of points. So the judge at first instance had inferred from her affidavit that she was a woman not without intelligence. From there he was driven to conclude that her evidence on the circumstances in which she had been deceived into signing the affidavit was simply not credible. At the appeal, the court admitted new evidence on the defendant's level of intelligence. On the basis of that evidence, and refusing to be misled by the style and content of the affidavit, the court decided that it would be wrong to dismiss the defendant's evidence as incredible. The judgement included a warning from the court:

> Affidavits were there for witnesses to say *in their own words* what the relevant evidence was and they were not to be used as a vehicle for complex legal argument (italics added).[29]

To revert to the question put at the beginning of this section of the argument, namely whether law could be written in ordinary language, a simplistic answer would be that much of it *is* so written. But the choice of the cases presented above was designed to highlight the fact that even *very* ordinary words, ('premises', 'keep open', 'accident', 'public place'), when embodied in the context of a statute, cause trouble in the course of their application. It seems reasonable to conclude that, were ordinary language generally to replace legal language in legal texts, any (dubious) gain in intelligibility would be wiped out by the loss of precision. I say 'dubious', implying that the test statement 'I understand what you are saying, but tell me what you mean' makes little sense. On the other side, it must be said that no substitute words were available in these particular cases that would have rendered the provisions precise. So, when a judge declares that he is adopting the ordinary usage of a word or phrase, this remains contestable. A better interpretation perhaps is that a meaning corresponding to the ordinary meaning falls within the semantic range of the word or form of words when appropriated by legal language.

In a case of housing benefit, the court was faced with the issue whether 'jointly occupies' meant the same as 'normally residing with'. The judge said:

> The words ['jointly occupies'] had a legal flavour. If one said to the ordinary speaker of English: 'For the purposes of regulation ..., is this man occupying the house jointly with ..., as opposed to residing with ...?' he would be unlikely to reply that it depended on whether he had the run of the house or needed permission to use the kitchen. He would say that one should ask a lawyer.[30]

A close study of the judge's remarks just cited throws a harsh light on the problems with which we are left at the end of this chapter, viz. the justifiability of the presumption of knowledge and the relationship between lawyers' language and ordinary language, now that the spurious and simplistic solutions of the plain English campaigners and others are out of the way. These problems are carried over to the final chapter.

2

HOW CRITICAL LANGUAGE THEORY SEEKS AND THEN STRUGGLES AGAINST ITS OWN UNDOING

Law as a text

A suitable beginning to this chapter is to suggest that the law is a text. This has the clear advantage that language is brought into the centre. For if law is a text, then in order to achieve its principal aims, social control and the avoidance and last-resort resolution of disputes, the writing and reading of the language of the text becomes critical. But 'text' has to be understood in a special sense of the word. Languages other than English make a distinction in the meaning of 'law'. French *'loi'*, for example, is one of a definite number of concrete rules making up the corpus of enacted law. Therefore, *les lois* would constitute the legal 'text' in the ordinary sense. In the caption at the head of this paragraph, however, 'law' corresponds not to *'loi'* but to *'droit'*. This is the system composed of a possibly infinite but at least indefinite number of binding principles, rules and precepts of different levels of generalisation capable of being brought to bear at the normative level on *any* constellation of facts. The law as *droit* resembles in this way, at the linguistic level, the natural language from which a possibly infinite number of sentences can be drawn. Again, there is the similarity that, like language which 'materialises' as words, phrases and sentences, the law materialises in the form of the laws (*lois*), case decisions and textbooks. Unlike the text in its ordinary sense, the law is not written down, but that dissimilarity is not material in the present context. For the same reason, I have not differentiated between written and spoken versions of legal language and ordinary language throughout the book.

Statements of the law in enacted law and case decisions have a different status from those in textbooks. The first two are authoritative and the last purely informative and analytic.[1] In terms of speech-act theory, the former are declaratory and the last is assertoric: it states what is the case. A declaratory speech act produces the state of affairs that it prescribes by the very act of making the statement (e.g. 'I pronounce you man and wife' or the umpire's sign for 'you're out!'). This corresponds in the legal domain with the principle that the judicial function is to *declare* the law. Not only does the judge determine what is the applicable law, i.e. *interpret* the law, and not only does he fit it to the particular fact-situation, i.e. *apply* the law, but he also establishes by his decision an element that will become part of the law in the future, i.e. he *declares* the law. In the next chapter, the vagueness which is inherent, ironically, in the concept of *interpretation* (of the law) itself is explored, while in the final chapter the analysis focuses on the process of *application* of the law. For now, the essential point relating to case decisions, irrespective of whichever of the three perspectives is in play, as well as to the enactment of law, is that language is intimately involved in the process. Indeed, if Derrida's notorious apophthegm, 'there is nothing beyond the text', is taken (half-)seriously, *only* language is involved. The words used in the composition of the statutory provisions and case decisions *construct* the law.

It follows, then, that the critical linguistic theories in this chapter, in undermining the pretension of legal language to be precise (univocal), threaten the claim of the law to be certain and of the legal process to provide the single right answer. For language, they say, is deceptive and inescapably mystifying with its figures of speech, tropes, tricks and hidden meanings. Univocality is a false, an impossible goal. Language does not resemble a code with a system of fixed meanings, as the exegetical approach of textualism would demand with its code-breaking approach to the text.

The shortcomings of language come either from its structure or from intent in its broad sense. Deconstruction is the most radical of those theories which root the problem of the inevitable uncertainty of meaning in structural features of language. It is linked to Derrida but has been drawn on (perhaps distorted in the process) by American disciples. The other group of theories focuses on the effects of forces, such as tradition, culture, ideology, at the collective level, and unconscious motivations at the individual level, on the shaping of language. In its strong form, this body of theory views such forces as determinant not only of how we speak about the social reality but also of the way in which that reality is constituted.

CRITICAL LANGUAGE THEORY

Against that strong version stands a feature of the social reality which cannot be gainsaid. Driven as social beings to communicate, unless we believe in the powers of telepathy, we are stuck with language, warts and all. In formulating their critique, even the exponents of critical linguistics have no option but to make use of language. The instrument (language) employed for the analysis is identical with the object of the analysis itself (language). So, in constructing its *critical* theory, critical linguistics cannot but build a trap for itself. Later in the chapter, the review of deconstructionism and of the position of ideology in neo-Marxist thought, with their threats to the integrity of the legal text, reveals a mechanism whereby each seeks to escape its own trap.

Rhetoric

It is an imperative to look closely at rhetoric as an introduction or background to critical linguistics, at least in relation to law. Perhaps even, in its own terms, rhetoric is to be regarded as the umbrella term covering critical linguistics. Rhetoric is classically defined as the art of persuasion by discourse, discourse in this context being used in its non-technical sense. Speech or argument, therefore, is to be measured not by whether it is true, valid or sincere but by whether it is *effective* in persuading those to whom it is addressed. The elimination of the dimension of referentiality intrinsic to language, common to the other theories to be discussed here, emerges clearly in the definition. To call rhetoric an art inevitably imports the many facets of an art: a study or a legitimising discourse; a set of practices or techniques; and along with these a nuance of *art*fulness. Nowadays, in ordinary usage, we pick up two of these aspects in the phrases: 'rhetorical question' and 'mere rhetoric'. The use of the first is a rhetorical technique; the other exposes an utterance as artful, 'only words'.

Rhetoric as study and as the art of language use has had a long history and more than one change of focus and variation in reputation from its beginning in the fifth century BC until its revival in the 1960s. Barthes, writing in the mid-1960s, thought that, with Aristotle, rhetoric had both triumphed and become moribund. But by the decade following his writing it off, it had not only sprung in full vigour from its deathbed but had even claimed an 'empire', according to the title of one of the works of the jurist Perelman.[2] Perelman played a major part in its resurrection, packaging as New Rhetoric a theory closely based on Aristotle's systematisation of rhetoric and applying it to law. He concentrated on rhetoric as the basis of a theory of argumentation. In the legal field, he analysed the grounds used by judges to support their judgements. As a preliminary to an assessment of Perelman's 'empire of rhetoric', it is worthwhile taking a quick synoptic look at the place of rhetoric in the thought of pre-Aristotelian Greece.[3]

Classical rhetoric

Rhetoric as argumentation

About 460 BC, Corax, who lived in Greek Sicily, produced a manual called *Rhetorical Techniques*. This text can be taken to be the beginning of rhetoric as a study of language designed to inculcate self-awareness in the language-user. What Corax's manual set out to do was to instruct its readers in the techniques necessary to convince the popular tribunals concerned with property restitution. The fall of the tyrants had given rise to many claims by those who had been despoiled and banished. Somewhere between an art and a set of techniques, rhetoric could be identified, described, analysed and made the object of theory. With a basis in theory, techniques could be taught and the art honed by practice. Corax's book consisted of an assembly of practical precepts illustrated by examples, and a breakdown of advocacy into exordium, argument and epilogue. There were no pretensions at all to literary embellishment or philosophical reflection in the text. At this rudimentary stage, rhetoric and argumentation were the same. And perhaps against expectation, rhetoric began in the legal sphere, not the political.

CASE STUDY

Tisias, having heard that rhetoric was the art of persuasion, had recourse to Corax for training in that art. But once he had nothing more to learn, he wanted to deny his master the promised fee. Tisias formulated this dilemma:

> Corax promised to teach me the art of persuading anyone at will. That being the case, either he has taught me that art and so must suffer the consequence that I persuade him to forego any fee: or he has not taught me it, in which case I owe him nothing, since he has not fulfilled his promise.

But Corax, in turn, riposted with another dilemma, illustrating the rule that the best (only) answer to rhetoric is rhetoric:

> If you succeed in persuading me to take nothing, you will have to pay me, since I will then have kept my promise. If on the contrary you don't manage it, then in that case you will have to pay me, all the more so!

The judges declined to announce a decision, contenting themselves with saying, 'a wicked crow deserves a wicked fledgling'. 'Corax' was Greek for 'crow'.

Power of rhetoric

In the sociopolitical setting of the time, rhetoric now emerged to demonstrate and shape the way that the power of language could be mobilised. Persuasion by words could take the place of the tyrants' despotism. More generally, persuasion by rhetoric possessed a clear moral superiority over the exercise of force, the pressure of threats, the assertion of authority, the dangling of inducements, the lure of seduction (although the line between persuasion and seduction may not be easily drawn). But must a qualification be inserted for that form of authority inherent in the pedagodical relationship? Barthes suggests that the fundamental mode of discourse is the dialogue between the master and the pupil, involving two interlocutors where one (the pupil) concedes. So the real point of the exchange between Corax and Tisias may be that it was the master who had the last word, administering to Tisias his final lesson by turning his own argument against him. But, subject perhaps to such an exception, rhetoric was meritocratic. In learning the art, one acquired the power to persuade the other, *whomever* he might be.

Not only did one gain the power to persuade anyone, one could persuade him of anything *whatsoever*. Rhetoric represented language in its performative use. There were no theoretical limits to the matters of which a person could be persuaded. Persuasion was the fulcrum on which rhetoric turned, and persuasion subverted or ignored truth. In the forensic milieu, rhetoric became tied to the notion of probability. The trial or proof, once extricated from the yes/no decision-making of trial by combat or ordeal has, throughout its subsequent legal history, pitted persuasive argument against persuasive argument to be decided finally on the basis of probability. Only the standard varies between civil trial, judged on the balance of probability, and criminal trial, where the probability must reach beyond reasonable doubt. Probability appears again at the centre of the philosophy and jurisprudence of the New Rhetoric. As I argue later in that context, however, the concept of probability is complex and problematic.

Confronted with Tisias's argument today, we would dismiss it as 'mere rhetoric'. It proved nothing and would persuade no-one. Nonetheless, while rejecting it as empty, we would surely find the form of the composition instructive or elevating or entertaining. Barthes expresses the attributes of the orator as: follow me; esteem me; love me. What seems to happen is that we are gripped by the strength of the form until or unless we are released by our becoming aware of the sophistry of the argument. The spell cast by logical form mixed with banality of the conclusion is well caught in Paul Valery's mockery: 'It is not the hemlock which brought about the death of Socrates, it's the syllogism' (referring, of course, to the classic: all men are mortal/Socrates is a man/therefore Socrates is mortal). The conceit is to present the death of Socrates as a *logical* instead of a biological necessity!

'Lend me your ears' – rhetoric as oratory

The power of rhetoric to convert its hearers into a rapt audience by words and form signalled a route other than persuasive *argument* which rhetoric was then to take. In the same century as rhetoric, consisting of proforma arguments for pleadings before tribunals, had travelled from Sicily to Athens, the rhetor Gorgias arrived in Athens as the Sicilian ambassador. He gained celebrity status as the exponent of epidictic oratory in public speeches pronounced on set occasions to eulogise the famous dead, a city or a god. He used a carefully cultivated, euphuistic prose. It was a measure of his stardom and influence that he was reputed to have lived to the age of 107 and was also 'immortalised' in Plato's eponymous dialogue.

In passing from the legal forum to the orator's pulpit, the art of rhetoric took up a different language. In contrast to the bare and spare speech of forensic argument, the prose crafted by Gorgias was highly embellished and elaborate. It was meant to rival lyric poetry, then the mode of language in use for eulogistic display. It simulated many of the devices and ornaments of poetry, its figures of speech, assonance, sentence rhythms. Alongside ordinary speech and poetry, the art of rhetoric had developed a new form, literary prose.

Although, according to theory, the objective of the speaker's art was to *persuade* his audience, epidictic rhetoric had, instead, as its cardinal purpose to *move* the audience aesthetically, emotionally. Today we would find it flowery, ornate, 'uncool'. What is self-revealingly oratorical turns us off. Gorgias crafted his literary prose to be beautiful, but nowadays the beholder's eye and the listener's ear desire an aesthetic without contrivance. We reject rhetoric that announces itself as rhetoric, which, in Keats's words, has 'too palpable a grasp upon us'. Shakespeare made the point in Mark Antony's epidictic speech on the death of Caesar – he came to 'bury Caesar not to praise him'. Yet, by his art, he first captivated his hearers and then from behind the mask of his rhetoric swayed the crowd against the conspirators. A covert and most effective argument was woven into the emotive language, symmetries and rhythmic patterns of his oration. The rhetoric put into Mark Antony's mouth by Shakespeare aimed at the mystification of his audience. Recognisably, the prose of the pleader in court in the face of a jury has undergone a similar metamorphosis in our times. The Victorian flamboyance has 'cooled'. Now, the language is designed more to mystify than to move.

Shakespeare's account of Mark Antony's oration dramatises how speech can also be exploited to rouse an audience to *action*. Rhetoric can influence an audience on all three planes: cognitive, affective, volitional. The *audience* is central to any account of rhetoric. The evolution which we have noticed in the discourse and style of jury speeches is a response to the advocate's perception of the discursive practices and expectations of the audience, the members of the jury.

Rhetoric and political philosophy

The teaching of rhetoric merged with the teaching of the sophists; Gorgias was both rhetor and sophist. The sophists were the ethical and intellectual mentors of the time, teaching the virtue and wisdom which made for good government in both the household and the City. Sophism brought to rhetoric its general ideas, including the notion of natural law. Its basic philosophy, however, was that all our knowledge comes from the senses, therefore all is appearance. Thus opinions could vary from person to person and from city to city. The combination of the cultural relativism of sophism with the self-understanding of rhetoric as the art of persuasion corrupted both. In the course of his training in the art of controversy, the novice sophist developed a rhetorical artistry enjoyable for itself alone. Debating jousts combined with exercises in dialectic, with the emphasis on contradiction, were more seductive than the pursuit of truth (believed anyway to be unattainable) or reflection on what ought to constitute the good life or good government.

Thus sophism acquired the bad name which it still has today for specious argument used to mislead or as a display of intellectual fireworks. As for rhetoric, in its marriage with sophism it could shake itself free of the formal constraints of the forensic arena and indulge in the audacity of invention and the linguistic flourishes characteristic of the epidictic. On the one side, it regained the sense of being all-powerful, which had been associated with rhetoric at its origin. On the other side, the audience loved the ingenuity and did not mind the deception. John Locke's description of the situation towards the end of the seventeenth century would have fitted the Greece of the fifth century BC:

> It is evident how much men love to deceive and be deceived, since rhetoric, that powerful instrument of error and deceit, has its established professors, is publicly taught, and has always been had in great reputation.[4]

Socrates reacted against sophism. He influenced the young to become 'philosophical', self-questioning. They were to engage in reflection which would enable them to find the errors, contradictions and inconsistencies hiding behind their ingenious arguments and eloquent words. His disciple Plato, in the course of his project to re-found Greek philosophy on a platform of reason, attacked rhetoric. Rhetoric was divorced from philosophy, he argued, for it was not controlled by reason. Nor, in its now degenerate state, was it even worthy to be considered an art, a status accorded to gymnastics and medicine in the Platonic hierarchy. The aim of eloquence was merely to please. So rhetoric, according to Plato, was to be understood as bearing the same relationship to political philosophy as cooking did to medical practice or cosmetics to gymnastics.

In turn, Aristotle rehabilitated rhetoric by providing it with a theory and placing it within a system, in which, nevertheless, it stood no higher than the third rung of the cultural ladder. At the top were philosophy and the sciences dedicated to the search for *true* propositions. Below came subjects such as social and political philosophy, spheres in which *probable*, but no more than probable, conclusions could be reached by the use of the dialectic as the appropriate method. Only after that came rhetoric which had as its objective to persuade a given body of hearers, starting from a position which would *seem to that audience to be true*. In the Aristotelian system, the probable was no longer the concern of rhetoric.

Empire of new rhetoric

For Perelman, 2,000 years later, rhetoric was simply theory of argumentation, not an art to be practised. The object of argument was to win the *adhesion* of the hearer, interlocutor, judge, jury, audience or even to reinforce one's own convictions. Is the hearer's adhesion to be regarded as the *exact* equivalent of the speaker's persuasion? A persuasive argument can be said to succeed even in the absence of complete agreement betweeen speaker and hearer on how the speaker's words are to be interpreted. Rhetoric as oratory may move to tears or persuade into action: the test of the effectiveness of political rhetoric, for example, is whether it produces a shift, or it may be just a reinforcement, in voting intentions. In the extreme case, the rhetoric of commercial advertising aims to deliver a message that is *striking* often regardless or even because of its very obscurity, its effectiveness being measured by the urge it imparts to buy the product. But Perelman's replacement of persuasion by adhesion suggests that the outcome of effective rhetoric is the production of a change in the audience's ideas or conceptions rather than a mere shift in the perspective from which they viewed the subject at the outset. A thesis can properly be said to have gained adhesion only when an understanding has come to be shared between audience and presenter. Nonetheless, it should be acknowledged that, although adhesion is stronger than persuasion, it is weaker than conviction. Conviction (beyond belief) is the end-product of demonstration, a process distinguishable from rhetoric/argumentation. Demonstration is propelled by logic, with a starting-point in clear and distinct premises recognised as true. By contrast, rhetoric, according to Perelman, is grounded on opinions that have gained acceptability (at least with the audience) and from which it advances to its conclusion not by logic but by a 'quasi-logic'. Rhetoric then is located somewhere in the space between the rigorous proof of demonstration and the fallacious manipulation of sophistry.

It is easy to see why Perelman should say that 'the notion of audience is central to rhetoric'. Since argument presupposes that the truth is neither evident nor demonstrable, its *effectiveness* can be measured only by whether or not it evokes or reinforces the adhesion of an audience. Rhetoric, as such, is *aimed* at the particular audience. At one end of the audience range is the person, himself or herself, engaged in an interior monologue. Described by Perelman as 'intimate deliberation', this implies rather improbably that Hamlet's soliloquies could go on inside his head and bring about his adhesion to one or the other side, 'to be or not to be' instead of leaving him stuck in the same impasse. In placing the 'universal audience' at the other extreme, Perelman is proposing the possibility of an argument that would be admitted by everyone. To put forward such an argument is to 'address an appeal to reason, to utilise convincing arguments, which ought to be accepted by all as being reasonable'.[5] How does such an argument differ from demonstration? Perelman's answer is that the three characteristics of argumentation are retained: a starting-point in admitted opinion; a pattern of reasoning ordered by quasi-logic; no requirement to use only univocal and strictly defined terms. Such an argument would constitute for argumentation the ideal argument. But does Perelman do any more than propose the somewhat sterile, and arguably circular, definition of the universal as that which would be acceptable by all, if an effective argument in its favour were deployed? One thinks of human rights in this context, principles whose validity is universally recognised (albeit grudgingly and with qualifications). But do these not have their basis in intuition, requiring no support from argument? In Perelman's scheme, human rights would count as admitted opinions, the *starting-point* of argument. And arguments there are in profusion at any international conference having as its agenda to draft the *terms* of the definitive universal declaration of human rights. Such arguments can be resolved or circumvented only by the adoption of flexible terms. But in any event, it should be noted, the idea of the universal audience offers nothing more than a procedural explanation of what counts as a valid conclusion. To follow the correct procedure does not 'guarantee' the truth of a conclusion or the validity of an outcome.

Basic premises

Apart from the extreme cases of the 'intimate deliberation' and the appeal to the 'universal audience', both of which turn out on a closer look to be problematic, argument in all other cases should be adapted to take account of the social, psychological and intellectual profile of the audience. That argument should be tailored to fit the audience has implications for the character of the *premises* on which the argument is supported. These are described as 'admitted opinions', neither evident nor proven but probable. Writing in French, Perelman renders 'probable' by *'vraisemblable'* and not by *'probable'* (both of these words being available in French). The dictionary gives the meaning 'the appearance of being true or real' to the English noun equivalent: 'verisimilitude' (the derivative adjectival form: 'verisimilar' being now rarely used).

So, under Perelman's scheme, the basic premises should satisfy the criterion that they are *vraisemblable*, meaning no more than that they appear to at least the particular addressee(s) to be true. This is borne out by the single category of flawed rhetoric for which Perelman makes room, the *petitio principii* (begging the question). Otherwise, an argument is to be judged on its effectiveness alone. The question is begged and the argument flawed, according to Perelman, when those who are to be persuaded have not 'accorded their adhesion' to the thesis from which the argument departs; in other words, if the starting-point is not an admitted opinion. Presumably, even an effective argument, one, that is, which gains the audience's adhesion to its conclusion, should be counted as invalid if based on *petitio principii*. This accords with the role adopted by Socrates who, as intellectual midwife, would undermine the arguments of the sophists by bringing into the light of day the conceptions which were latent in them.

The problem for Perelman was to bend fallacious logic (*petitio principii*), flawed reasoning, to fit rhetoric that is assessable by its effectiveness alone. To beg the question is to reason by a series of steps in which the premise is only true if the conclusion is true also. He cites John Stuart Mill's criticism that the premise that all men are mortal would not be acceptable if doubt existed about the truth of the conclusion, the mortality of Socrates. The criticism is misplaced, says Perelman, because a syllogism, being demonstrative and not argumentative, is concerned with truth and not adhesion. If it were an argument, it would indeed be a case of *petitio principii*, since the conclusion, the mortality of Socrates, is already assumed in the premise of universal human mortality. But, there is quite a difference between that exemplification of *petitio principii* and its appropriation by Perelman to fit the situation where a basic premise has not been admitted by the audience.[6]

Quasi-logic

The model form of reasoning which constitutes the quasi-logic of argument, according to Perelman, is the enthymeme (an imperfect or incomplete syllogism), not the syllogism. To illustrate, we can construct an enthymeme by making a slight adjustment to the syllogism. Suppose it is contended that Socrates should have taught the Athenian youth to resist the tyrants rather than adapt to life under tyranny, and that the adversary's retort is: 'After all, Socrates was only mortal'. The rejoinder is elliptical, one of the characteristics of the enthymeme. Both the major premise: *no mere mortal can defy tyranny*, and the conclusion: *therefore Socrates could not be expected to do so by inciting resistance*, are silent. The omitted major is of course dubious, leaving the conclusion vulnerable to attack along the lines: being mortal and therefore deprived of the outlook of the gods (the immortals) who could wait for history to end the tyranny, Socrates *should* have inspired resistance. Thus, enthymematic reasoning is not only elliptical but also incapable of yielding anything better than probable conclusions.

Juridical logic

When Perelman sets juridical logic within the framework of his New Rhetoric, he concentrates on the application of his theory of argumentation to the justification and criticism of decisions.[7] The theory underpinning judicial decision-making has its beginning in exegesis. Here, the foundation-stones are precisely those from which the theory of rhetoric has been dislodged: univocity of language, demonstration, syllogistic reasoning. The overarching idea is that the law (*droit*) is nothing more than the sum total of the laws (*lois*). It was the post-1945 reaction against rigid formalism and legal positivism on the Continent, Perelman asserts, that gave a new shape to judicial reasoning, for which his New (Aristotelian) Rhetoric can be regarded as a template. Early Greek rhetoric also, it will be remembered, departed from the formalism of the model pleadings provided for the Sicilian tribunals.

In the juridical context, it is the argument presented by the judge, rather than the advocates' pleadings, which is the equivalent of the thesis addressed to the audience in Perelman's general theory of argumentation. The judge is bound to set out reasons, to specify the grounds on which she seeks to *justify* her decision. Now, if it is the judge who produces the argument, who then represents the audience at the other end whose adhesion is being sought? This audience or rather those audiences are diverse. One of them consists of the party-litigants themselves, another the professionals of the law and the last is public opinion. Certainly, the judge aims to satisfy all three audiences. Regrettably, however, as was conceded in chapter 1, the legal language in which the decision and its reasons are delivered by the judge cuts her off from (direct) communication with anyone other than the professional audience. The professionals to a necessarily limited extent will act as a filter in the passage of the decision to the parties but public opinion receives nothing but snatches of news of a few dramatic (criminal) cases. Therefore, the language factor in the juristic context calls for a modification of Perelman's test: a 'good' judgement is one which *would* gain the adhesion of the public if they were competent speakers of the language in which it is pronounced.

In this transition to the sphere of juridical logic Perelman dilutes his central idea that arguments are to be judged by their persuasiveness. He says:

> Argumentation is not aimed exclusively at adhesion to a thesis because it is true ... One thesis can be preferred to another because it *seems* (italics added) more equitable, more opportune, more useful, more reasonable, better adapted to the situation.[8]

Here he moves outside the realm of admitted opinions, common sense, consensus beliefs and so on. A thesis (although the subject of an argument, not of a demonstration) can make a truth-claim independently and irrespective of the reaction of an audience. But in the same passage he immediately adds: 'one thesis can be preferred to another because it *seems* more equitable, more opportune, more useful, more reasonable, better adapted to the situation'.

He returns in this to *semblance*, although the semblance of truth (*vraisemblable*) has been replaced by the semblance of reasonableness, equity, utility and so on.

Probable or seems to be true

The notion of probability hovers uneasily between objectivity and subjectivity. This vagueness is reflected in the apparent duplication in French language, as already noted, but is fudged by the decline of 'verisimilitude' and the desuetude of 'verisimilar' in English. Is the 'probable' that which is 'likely to be true' or 'that which seems to be true'? Argumentation theory, certainly in Perelman's version of it, hinging as it does on the audience response, inclines strongly towards the latter. The dynamic of judicial decision-making and therefore of the shaping of the law is provided by persuasion aimed at the formation of a consensus (most importantly in the long run in public opinion).

But, when the different contexts of fact-finding and legal debate in the legal trial are distinguished, probability needs a closer look. First, notice that the assertion: 'That's a fact!' is not proof but mere rhetoric. As Umberto Eco has pointed out, no one can be *sure* that Napoleon died on St Helena and was not spirited away in secret by the British Secret Service. A fact (unlike a state of affairs) cannot be the subject of a demonstration, a verity exploited by the practitioners of the paranormal. Although the judge *finds* such-and-such to be the facts (a determination involving both proof and selection based on considerations of relevance), it is implicit in the whole procedure that these are probable, not certain. The different standards of proof based on different *degrees* of probability have already been noted. Forensic fact-finding is intimately linked to the credibility of evidence. This is two-dimensional, related not only to the 'seeming' truthfulness of the witnesses but also to a (more) objective judgement on whether, based on other criteria, their testimony is 'likely to be true'.

Barthes cites this example of a premise: 'a theft committed inside a house without a break-in must have been committed by a member of the family'.[9] This proposition, qualifying as common sense, meets Perelman's standard, namely 'admitted opinions', for the basic premises of a forensic argument. It could easily find a place in a chain of fuzzy logic (enthymemes) leading to a conclusion on the probability of the guilt or innocence of an accused. Suitably, fact-finding falls within the province of the (lay) jury.

Away from fact-finding, however, in the domain of legal debate, argument aims at the presentation of the *apparent* reasonableness, equity etc. of the thesis that it supports. Here, in the realm of presentation, of appearance, of veri*similitude,* the persuasiveness of the presenter for Perelman is all. Take one of his examples: 'the friends of my friends are my friends'. This simulacrum exploits the certainty of the mathematical proof: $A = B$; $B = C$; therefore $A = C$. But with humans, unlike mathematical quantities, my friends' friends are just as likely to be my rivals or enemies as my friends. One would be disposed to dismiss analogical reasoning of this sort as mere rhetoric, depending for any effectiveness that it has on semblance. Whereas, by contrast, the inference presented in Barthes' citation is logical without being syllogistic. The comparison shows up the problem that has already been pointed out in Perelman's scheme of argumentation, masked as I have suggested by shiftiness in the notion of probability.

Barthes' critique of Aristotle, and consequently of Perelman's theory, can aptly be introduced at this point. Speculating on the meaning of *vraisemblable*, he suggested that it could be applied to that which members of the public believed that the others had in their heads (Greek equivalent: *endoxon*). So the test would be whether or not the conclusion of an argument, other than an argument in pursuit of a finding of fact, could claim to be *psychologically* true. With the *vraisemblable passionel* (Gr. *eikos*), Barthes introduced the notion of what seems to be true because it touches off shared affects in the audience. An icon (from the same Greek root) evokes the same sense of the sacred as that which it represents. Barthes built on these ideas to suggest that Aristotle's philosophy was populist, based on an appeal to the masses.[10]

Critique of new rhetoric

The critical implications for Perelman's theory are obvious. The judge must present his argument before two audiences: public opinion and the legal profession. These are the audiences which matter in relation to that function of the decision which is to lay down law for the future. The party-litigants will instead be interested in the decision as determinant of their dispute. Now, when Perelman admits that a thesis can be preferred on the ground that it 'seems more equitable ... better adapted to the situation', he too is focusing on the decision as determinant of the instant case. Vis-à-vis the parties, the decision will be justified if it *appears* equitable or reasonable etc. and is supported by arguments which gain their adhesion. As long as the argument is free of that (for Perelman) unique type of flaw, the question-begging premise, the judge's argument which persuades need not in general terms be sincere, may in fact be distorted by self-interest or tainted by class or group affiliation or prejudice.

Again, in providing his reasons, the judge not only justifies his decision, he also creates a precedent-setting framework. In relation to that task, the 'seeming reasonable' etc. criterion proposed by Perelman is inadequate. Moreover, to play to one or other audience, public opinion or the legal profession, or even to both, in order to gain its or their adhesion, will leave the decision vulnerable to challenge by a more persuasive argument. Here, Barthes' strictures concerning Aristotle's system of rhetoric can be seen to score palpable hits on Perelman's derivative theory of argumentation. The validity of an argument is to be gauged by nothing more than its psychological truth. Therefore, the judge is placed in the same predicament as the modern, democratic political executive if he is constrained, as Perelman thinks he is, to gain the adhesion of the public audience, that is, to 'appeal to the masses'. Indeed, the judge's position is worse from a *democratic* standpoint, lacking as he does both accreditation and accountability as the people's representative.

Perelman's description of his system as *New* Rhetoric is justified even though it is substantially reheated Aristotle. The novelty attached, however, not to the system *in se* but to its application to juridical logic. In that context, it belonged to the broad structuralist shading into poststructuralist movements of and around the 1960s. Here, Perelman's importance at the negative pole was to register the crumbling away of the formalist, positivist theory of juridical decision-making. Theory, representing an ideal type, found itself uncomfortably remote not only from the actual practices of judges but also from their explanations of what they were doing. The idea that the legislature ought to and could give mathematically exact instructions in the laws that it passed was increasingly seen as unreal, although some still hankered after that situation. Nor did judges delude themselves that their reasoning in their judgements fell into neat, syllogistic patterns. As greater contacts developed between legal theorists of the common law systems and students of the civilian, Continental systems, the deductive – subsumptive model conceded ground, recognising that 'a full understanding of [the] subject matter must be informed by an appreciation of the tension between two competing ideal types of justificatory argument'.[11]

On the positive side, however, Perelman proposed the substitution of another, no less formalistic, structure of admitted opinions (premises), quasi-logic and conclusion (judgement). Basic to his ideas was the need for the judge to address himself to the public audience, beyond that of the parties and the legal profession. He failed, I think, to focus on the ambiguity in the notion of probability. This failure, together with his stress on persuasion as the sole instrument and criterion of argument, pulled him logically much further than he would want to go in the direction of a populist role for the judges.

He saw that, outside of mathematics and logic, language was such that it could not be characterised by univocality, nor be free of vagueness and ambiguity. The figures of speech and style that belong to rhetoric in its sense other than argumentation constituted an arsenal on which the speaker intent on persuasion will draw. Distinctive languages (*langages*) with shared meanings evolved in particular cultural communities and professional groupings. He observed that this relativised the law's application, throwing on judges the burden of interpretation of the text. But he did not go on to work out that the development of such a special language, in law, would be antagonistic to the judges' mission to persuade the people. At the end of the study of New Rhetoric and Perelman's theory of argumentation, therefore, we find that the problem with which this book began remains unresolved.

The committee of experts as audience

The American pragmatist Stanley Fish, like Perelman, brings the audience in the shape of the committee of experts to the forefront of his theory. Fish, though, being an anti-theorist, might reject the categorisation and would certainly object to the suggestion that he has a theory. His position is that theory 'is entirely irrelevant to the practice it purports to critique and reform'.[12] Unlike Perelman, who, as we saw before, (illogically) indulges in both worlds, he rejects any idea that truth-claims make sense in the realm of belief and value systems. Neither individual judgements nor belief systems can be validated by principles, grounds or legitimising discourse. Yet Fish takes advantage of both faces of a thoroughgoing judgementalism. His foundational theory is to deny any validity to foundational theory. This amounts to a knock-down argument against all comers. At the same time, he immunises himself against challenge by denying that 'you can in some way step back from, rise above, get to the side of your beliefs and convictions so that they will have less of a hold on you'.[13] Everything is ruled out and nothing is ruled in.

Critique of Fish

Fish, a specialist scholar of Milton, bestrides both literature and law. Knowing that, one can readily see how his views could have developed in the crucible of literary criticism and then been transferred to law. Related to the legal sphere, the test to be met by the individual judgement is to find acceptability within the professional legal community which in this case displaces the body of critics, academics and biographers in relation to literature. Like the latter, its members share meanings, values and conceptions of relevance. In neither case, is it other than futile to reach out beyond the charmed circle of the expert or professional community for some foundational theory of interpretation. In the law's case, the excluded are the very people who are its addressees and subject to it.

In his defence of the politically correct ('PC'), he defines it somewhat unusually as 'the practice of making judgements from the vantage point of challengeable convictions'.[14] So his justification of PC contains within itself a justification of the right to challenge, for that 'is not the name of a deviant behaviour' he argues, 'but of the behaviour that everyone necessarily practises'. This is a reasonable, although not ideal, vantage point from which to mount an attack, like Fish's, on orthodoxy or conservatism. But by the same token it offers no shelter against a challenge to traditional freedoms from voices representing the far-Right or speaking in the name of the dictatorship of the proletariat. As he himself says of his own position: 'It follows then that anti-foundationalist thought cannot have the consequences that many hope that it will have, which is to say no more than that anti-foundationalism cannot itself (without contradiction) be made into a foundation.'[15]

Ideas and words

Stripped of its status as a system of explanation and justification, theory became for Fish nothing more than 'elevated discourse'. In this he had assimilated, knowingly or not, the mid-twentieth-century movement noticed in the Introduction.

The shift of concentration from ideas to language, stripped of its referentiality as research object, is made evident in the middle of the three projects distinguishable in the work of Michel Foucault. In *Words and Things* (translation of the title of the French edition), he set out to identify the dominant epistemes in the thought of each epoch.[16] 'Episteme' was the term he adopted for any unifying ideational structure which gave a distinctive shape to the sciences and other bodies of knowledge of a particular period. Strangely, despite the book's title, it proved not to be directly concerned either with an object-world of 'things' or even with the realm of 'words'. Instead, it was as if Foucault had set off to write the book that succeeded it, which he called the *Archaeology of Knowledge*.[17] There, *words* assembled as discourses are indeed the focal point. We are to be taken beyond 'things' to 'things said', to discursive phrases and sentences. Neither are we engaged in an analysis of thought, for that would be to approach discourse other than in the 'narrowness and singularity of its event as an utterance'. For Foucault, 'discursive practices' enabled us to analyse systems of thought, the relevant question being: what was expressing itself (*se disait*) in what was said (*était dit*). Foucault describes the progression from the first to the second of these books:

> Where the history of ideas sought to uncover, by deciphering the text, the secret movements of thought ..., I would wish to make manifest in its specificity, the level of things said ... The domain of things said is what I am calling the archive; there the archaeology is destined to carry out its analysis.[18]

Death of the subject

A second strand of poststructuralist language theory was the relegation or downgrading of the individual as speaker and social actor. Language was seen as a social enterprise and discourse as *inter*subjective practice; the subject, the 'I', was 'decentred'. More dramatically, the discourse of critical linguistics in the later part of the twentieth century reflected the death of the subject. Thus, Barthes' schematisation reversed the position of the writer and the text. In a sense, the text, he suggested, could be said to 'author' the writer. But vis-à-vis the subject Foucault might well be regarded as chief mortician. The struggle of the subject to maintain his or her individuality in the face of an all-enveloping society remained throughout his life his core concern. In the middle project referred to above, his underlying aim was to demonstrate the autonomy, first of systems of thought, then of discursive practices, so uncovering and annotating historically the means whereby society shaped the minds of its members. His earliest work was a study of the evolution of the institutional treatment of the mentally ill[19] and then of the prison.[20] He came to these as microcosms of the wider society whose members were likewise incarcerated or enclosed with no means of escape. Most graphically, Bentham's Panopticon was both a model prison and a model of society. The situation of the inmate, subjected to surveillance and correction, his every move open to observation, was just like that of the individual in modern society with its ubiquitous eye and diffuse leverages and controls. Appropriating the symbol of the all-seeing eye, the nineteenth century had founded the age of Panoptism, Foucault said. These institutions, the asylum and the prison, presented in sharp relief the homogenisation of the individual, the 'subjection of the subject', undergone by men in the process of socialisation. Of the means by which social control was exercised, it was knowledge which interested Foucault.

Foucault's power–knowledge duo

I want now to refer to a key aspect of Foucault's theory not yet mentioned in this chapter. Doctrinally, it bridges critical language theories, exemplified by deconstructionism, which tie instability of meaning to the structure of language, and those on the other side which hold that discourse is manipulated to produce mystification or falsification out of the reach of the individual or collective consciousness (psychoanalysis in the one case and theories of ideology in the other). It was his proposed linkage, power–knowledge, that was picked up by radical intellectuals, especially minority movements, in the US from his body of work, amplified by the many interviews he gave. His style of writing could fairly be diagnosed as logorrhoea and this was aggravated by his delphic responses to questions. So his conception of the relationship between power and knowledge represented by the hyphen was commonly misunderstood in America.

Foucault clearly says that knowledge is the (or at least the principal) source of power in society, a position in line with his foundational idea that individual experience is shaped by epistemes and discursive practices. He presents his diagram of power relations in society: 'the absolute right of the nonmad over the mad, competence ruling over ignorance, good sense or access to reality correcting errors, normality imposing itself on disorder and deviance.'[21] There are indications here and there in his writings of the other line of thought. He states for example that knowledge is fundamentally interested in the sense that it is produced as an event of the will.[22] 'Interested' here, though, is best understood as 'not disinterested', 'not detached'. But in linking 'knowledge' and 'will', the words he uses, *'connaissance'* and *'vouloir'*, are not the exact equivalents of *'pouvoir-savoir'*, the words used for power–knowledge. A reasonable interpretation is that the latter coupling applies at the social level whereas the purported dependence of knowledge on the will holds good for the individual. So he does not position himself with those who propose the converse relationship that power dictates or determines what counts as knowledge (although his later works place emphasis on the power of institutions). Given the intimate bond between discourse and knowledge, those boundaries which he draws in his study of discourse purely concern his self-proclaimed mission as archaeologist of knowledge.

Liberation

His final project involved a quest for an escape route from man's subjection to society. Through theory, he sought liberation, a way to release the subject, made moribund by society. His political activities were shallow and fitful. Liberation was a *personal* enterprise. Characteristically, he began his search for a route to liberation of the self by embarking on a history analysing the formation and development of the experience of sexuality through the epochs.[23] In antiquity, he suggested, a 'subject' was expected to manage his sexual affairs while maintaining his character as a free man and citizen, the constraints of a socially constructed sexual morality being absent. This showed Foucault the way to the care of the self. One process necessary for the cultivation of the self, Foucault said, was to unlearn (*'désapprendre'*). He quoted a Lacedaemonian aphorism cited by Plutarch: 'To be occupied with oneself is a privilege, the mark of social superiority, in opposition to those who must occupy themselves with others in order to serve them.'[24]

The pathway to the care of the self that preoccupied him in the final stage of his work was paralleled by a lifestyle exploration of sadomasochistic homosexuality in the San Francisco bathhouses as a result of which he contracted Aids and died. There was a poignant signal that in this process of cultivation of self he had in a way accomplished the set task of 'unlearning'; for he said of his impending death, 'You always think that in a certain kind of situation you will find something to say about it, and now it turns out there's nothing to say after all.'[25] Perhaps this marked his recognition of his failure to escape from discourse.

The theories examined from this point on in this chapter can be seen to follow a similar trajectory. They begin with a critique of language stripped of its referentiality and then attempt to find an art, technique or method whereby the theoretical inadequacies of language can be overcome and the truth-claim implicit in their exposition of their theory placed on a firm foundation. Fish is an exception; he pretends not to care. Most broadly, perhaps, this can be understood as the rejection of textualism and the search for firm hermeneutic ground. (This 'interpretative turn', as Habermas calls it, occupies the next chapter.) In Foucault's case, faced with the predicament presented by his 'death of the subject' theory and close to his own death (in 1984), reacting against the self-renunciation enjoined by religion, he saw the care of the self as the redemptive path. He said in his course in 1982 at the Collège de France:

While the theory of political power as institution ordinarily has as its reference a juridical conception of the legal subject ... the analysis of power [in general] as an ensemble of reversible relations must have as its reference an ethic of the subject defined by the relationship of oneself to oneself.[26]

The project of the care of the self or the return to oneself he contrasted with Christian asceticism which pointed the path to salvation through self-renunciation. He describes the theme in Christian mysticism of loss of identity to submersion of the self in God in a way which chimes in with his conception of the relationship between the individual and the institution. In opposition to that he asks the question whether it was possible to 'constitute, reconstitute an aesthetic and an ethic of oneself'.[27]

Deconstructionism

Derrida appears less as a thinker than as an audacious user of language, a reveller in wordplay, a verbal funambulist who never falls off but never touches base. That impression notwithstanding, he has to be taken seriously. Particularly here, for, as will be seen later, deconstructionism attacks the integrity of the distinctions on which legal analysis depends. For, after all, at the foundation of Derrida's work is the *sign*. The sign stands for the thing in its absence, the 'thing' being itself a sign. The theory makes no distinction between meaning, object, idea or concept. The sign refers to the concept which refers to the world. In semiotic terms, the signifier (*signifiant*) dissolves into the signified (*signifié*). This *deconstruction* of the sign, by presenting the signifier as exterior to the sign-system, brings to the forefront, makes primary, that which metaphysics and common sense regard as secondary. The basis of deconstructionism lies in the notion, taken from Saussure, that the linguistic sign-system works by *differences*. Derrida's manufactured variant *'différance'* stands for 'the differentiality or the being-different of these differences'.[28] *Différance* is the force which holds language together against its centrifugal tendencies.

In coining neologisms (like *différance*) whenever the need arises or fancy strikes, Derrida cannot resist the temptation to sit on Humpty Dumpty's wall. 'When I use a word,' Humpty Dumpty said scornfully, 'it means just what I choose it to mean – neither more nor less!' He certainly knows that this perch of Humpty Dumpty is precarious. For deconstructionism shares with the rest of critical linguistic theory the idea that, rather than being the masters of language, we are instead colonised by it. Anyway, *différance* nurtures paradox. Indeed, the paradox at the heart of this is that deconstructionism constructs texts in order to deconstruct language including, therefore, the language in which its own texts are constructed. Neither is *différance* itself self-immunising. It is the force which holds language together while at the same time it is subjected to its own deconstructive effects. The switch to *différance* from our habitual understanding of language as based on similarities, analogies, categories, produces three characteristic features of deconstructionism: the principle of iterability, the inexhaustibility of the context, and the interdependence of oppositional couples (binary distinctions). Each poses a problem for language in general and the third of them for legal language in particular.

Iterability

The principle of iterability refers to the fact that the nature of language is such that exactly the same form of words can be used to mean different things. There are no criteria available to enable a hearer or interlocutor to differentiate (with certainty) between a 'serious' remark and one that is meant ironically, for example. The same applies to a form of words that is cited, rehearsed or even repeated by the same person for a second time. The question 'Are you serious?' recognises this structural problem with language. The same question, indeed, has often suggested itself as appropriate in the face of some of Derrida's more 'outrageous' utterances. But he always means to be taken seriously! The principle reflects the broad idea that a text cannot dictate the manner in which it will be interpreted nor the situations in which it will be applicable. Nietzsche similarly commented from a different standpoint on the inscrutability of language. A text, he declared, reveals no distinguishing marks between error, lies and illusion.

From the po-faced character of legal language one readily and rightly infers that statements of the law are always serious. The temptation then is to dismiss the problem of this aspect of textual inscrutability so far as the law is concerned. Wrongly, for the law must concern itself not only with juridical, normative statements but also with the status in law to be afforded to our utterances. The latter involves a dual approach. One is to provide a set of solemnities which now take the form of linguistic formulae, replacing in some cases ritualistic acts. These are understood as encoding a declaration that a text is intended to be taken seriously, to be regarded as legally binding. The action of raising one's right hand, for example is a non-verbal component of such a solemnity, taking an oath.

Apart from the sign-subsystem of solemnities, the law contains principles and rules that determine when certain types of statement are to be taken 'seriously', that is, to be regarded as legally binding on the speaker. In terms of speech-act theory, these fall within the categories of *commissives* and *assertives*. With commissives we commit ourselves to doing things. Different forms of commissives express different degrees of commitment, from weak statements of intention to firm undertakings. With assertives, we say or represent how things are. 'Represent' imports the presence of an audience of interlocutors whom you tell how things are. But assertives are not just any speech but a class of speech-*acts*, with a performative as well as a constative aspect. Recognising the performative side of assertives, law treats some representations in given situations as *warranted* by the utterer.

The 'grey area' exposed by Derrida's principle of iterability was clearly shown up in the following case, reported under the headline, 'Parody, pastiche or passing off?'. The case arose from a medley of mixed messages and crossed signals.

CASE STUDY

Alan Clark (now dead) was an MP and an author of established reputation, among whose published works were his diaries. The diaries were parodied in a series of articles in the defendant newspaper. The issue was whether the articles were such that a substantial number of the newspaper's readers would attribute them to Clark's authorship and not to that of the true author. Each article contained contradictory messages: a photograph of Alan Clark and the heading 'Alan Clark's Secret ... Diary' appeared at the head; the name of the true author also always appeared in capital letters.

The content was obvious fantasy, clearly not to be taken seriously. So the articles were a parody and not a pastiche. It was the significance of the material indicative of authorship which was in question. The judge decided that 'looking at the articles as a whole and the totality of the messages and counter-messages, the dominant message in the [newspaper's] presentation of the articles was of [Alan Clark's] authorship'.

The judge said:

The law of passing off embraced the concept that one and the same representation might mean something different to different members of the public.

For the representation to constitute passing off it had to be established that 'one of those meanings misled a substantial number of people'. 'The proper approach', he went on to add, 'was to determine what was the single meaning which the ... work conveyed to the notional reasonable reader'.[29]

The judge, therefore, arrogates to himself or the jury the hermeneutic mastery of the 'notional reasonable reader' in reading out of the text the 'dominant message' and the 'single [right] meaning'.

Inexhaustibility of context

Derrida points out that each syntagm of every text has a context, each text has its context, and that context a context and so on. The condensed version of the same idea '*il n'y a pas de hors contexte*' is a variant of his notorious apophthegm: '*il n'y a pas de hors texte*'. The context, like the universe, expands indefinitely. Nothing is outside it.

Leave aside Derrida's particular usage of 'text', involving the fusion of object, idea, concept and word. In the ordinary case, text designates a piece of writing. The context, then, is the whole passage of which the text is a part. If we pass over for the moment the obvious problem in setting the limits which will define the 'whole', the whole passage can be taken as the discursive context. In a concentric circle beyond that are the circumstances surrounding the writing considered as a speech-act. These again cry out for definable boundaries. All of those together, the text, discursive context and surrounding circumstances exist within a 'galaxy', the socio-political-historical (extra-discursive) context. Sometimes, the discursive context is called the co-text. But, more persuasively, 'co-text' should be reserved (as Eco, for example, does) for the surrounding circumstances.

The problem involved in the delineation of the boundaries which will give sense to the articulation of a passage into text and various forms of context (distinguished above) can only be approached via meaning. For law, the problem is encountered as a question of relevance. Meaning and relevance are in uneasy symbiosis, as are text and context. How to determine the meaning of the text without first delimiting the relevant context; how to circumscribe the relevant context without first arriving at the meaning of the text? Now that meaning has been introduced, however, it is appropriate to postpone further discussion of the meaning–relevance dilemma to the next chapter, on interpretation. For the moment, however, it is convenient to note that the binary distinction, text/context, opens itself to deconstruction by virtue of the mutual interdependence of the terms.

Binary distinctions deconstructed: 'There's no such thing as a free lunch'

In the same way as text/context, other binary distinctions (oppositional couples) can be deconstructed by showing up their reciprocal dependence and contingent character. Examples are: fact/value, facts/norm, subjective/objective, letter/spirit, means/ends, abstract/concrete, part/whole, form/content. The meaning of each member of the couple is not 'thinkable', according to deconstructionist theory, without implicating the other. Since distinctions of this type are often, perhaps always, pivotal in legal analysis, the existence of this semantic interdependence allows critical legal theorists to use deconstruction to attack judicial reasoning.

For example, the notion of gift, claims Derrida, contains within itself the idea of exchange.[30] A gift evokes some sort of a response from the donee, a sense that *something* is due or expected in return, be it gratitude or acknowledgement or favours. There's no such thing as a 'pure' gift. It is always tainted with the trace of the exchange which it denies. Just as one cannot receive a gift *as such*, neither can one refuse it. A gift is always a poisoned chalice.

In law, the concept of donation is identified by the absence of *onerous* consideration. Gratitude or acknowledgement in exchange may indeed be called for at the level of manners or personal morality but no such obligation arises in law. When it comes to the return of favours, however, we enter the grey area of linguistic instability between gift and exchange. 'Favour', by itself, with its nuances of 'preference' and 'singling out' suffers from a similar instability of content. Witness the fact that the non-onerous nature of gift in legal documentation may be marked by the trio of terms 'love, favour and affection'. But, as brought out in the last chapter, it is the work of the users of legal discourse, rather than dancing as Derrida does on the grave of language, to reconceptualise such terms.

Deconstruction is justice

Deconstructionism has a fairly obvious problem. As a philosophy of language it produces texts which claim that texts can never make unambiguous claims. But do we conclude from this unresolvable contradiction that deconstruction self-de(con)structs? The response depends on whether deconstruction is judged to belong to linguistic philosophy or philosophy of language. The first uses an analytical theory of language as a tool to tackle the problems of philosophy. The other adopts the approach of philosophy to explore the nature and usage of language. If deconstructionism is content to take up residence in the second location, the trap which its theory sets is not sprung by its own comings and goings. Nonetheless, in summing up his theory as 'the neutralisation of communication, theses and stability of content', Derrida locates himself at the edge of a void. Very recently, he seems to have begun to feel the bleakness of his situation, an experience perhaps like that of Milton's Lucifer, who 'views the dismal situation waste and wild ... no light but rather darkness visible' (the final couple a Miltonic anticipation of deconstruction!). Thus, while law rests solely on authority, is corrupted by illegitimate sources of power and is culture-specific, and while its texts offer no determinate interpretation, Derrida has come to observe that the concept of *justice* transcends these and all other limitations. What cannot be deconstructed are, he says:

> an idea of justice – which we distinguish from law or right and even from human rights – and an idea of democracy – which we distinguish from its current concept and from its determined predicates today.[31]

And having revealed that justice is immune to deconstruction, Derrida leaves us to puzzle over the thought that 'deconstruction is justice'.

In the final chapter of this book, language is indeed intimately linked to justice. Like the 'converted' Derrida in the statement just cited, language (but not, I suggest, the language of law) can be used in a way that respects the distinctions between law and right and human rights. Against Derrida, however, I argue that the language of law is designed to recognise and build on the differentiality of the binary distinctions. If this process can be called deconstruction, all the better!

Half-life of Marxism and Freudianism

Marxism and Freudianism were the most influential and ambitious doctrines of modern times until the 1960s. Both gained the accolade of an adjective (Marxian, Freudian) and both won more than enough authority and adherents and disciples to become -isms marked by factions, schisms, and heresies. Each was so radical at the outset as to amount to a *break* with existing ideas and each then went on to become orthodoxy. This was orthodoxy not only at the academic level in their own fields, for Marxism and Freudianism shared certain characteristics which in interaction with the social changes and cultural climate of the times contributed to their historic influence. Each claimed the imprimatur of *science* with the best of Enlightenment credentials and at the same time had the conceptual range for use as an analytical tool or foundational theory in other domains of social studies and cultural critique. There were two other important, common features. Their ideas were not only wide-ranging but they also reached down to a remarkable extent through the various intellectual layers of society on a global scale. This happened despite the unfamiliar terminology, the neologisms and the intricacy of the arguments in which the founding ideas were wrapped.

It has been observed that, in general, ideas, models and patterns of thinking and evaluation 'trickle down' from the academy and high culture to civil society. The spread of the nineteenth-century theories of Marx and Freud into the thinking of the ordinary twentieth-century person can be claimed as a powerful empirical verification of trickle-down theory. Yet questions remain. Why was the ordinary mentality receptive at a particular time to these systems of belief? Why did they continue to enjoy a half-life, their vestiges enduring in the public mind even after the 1960s when, at the academic and intellectual level, they had tended to dissolve in the drift to post-structuralism? Here, trickle-down theory or top-down transmission encounters *zeitgeist* theories moving in the opposite direction. Thus Walzer in *A Company of Critics* presents a selection of 'revolutionary' thinkers including Marx and Freud as conduits for the spirit of their times. For trickle-down theory, the man shapes the time. For the *zeitgeist* theory, the times find the man.

Interdiscursiveness

If we leave aside these difficult questions in the realm of theory in order to find answers in historical, social and cultural studies, the movement involved in trickle-down can much more easily be described at the linguistic level. What it demonstrates is the interdiscursiveness of ordinary language. According to systems theory, as discussed in chapter 4, each functional system is closed against and unable to communicate with the others. Only ordinary language is open and interdiscursive. So Marxism and Freudianism are equipped to appear, given the right circumstances, interdiscursively in ordinary speech. Lawyers' language as the discourse of the legal *system* is closed against the subdiscourses of Marxism and Freudianism, although these may enter the legal process as interpretations of events or states of affairs in ordinary language at the level of the facts.

The idea of the subconscious, so crucial in Freudianism, and which has become 'naturalised' in ordinary language, is for that reason perhaps exceptional. Law concerns itself with intent and it may sometimes matter whether intent is conscious or subconscious. The House of Lords has decided that the concept of victimisation under the Race Relations Act 1976 did not require a finding that the adverse discriminatory treatment was *consciously* motivated.[32] But one of the judges dissented, arguing on the basis of the language of the relevant section of the Act that the concept of victim was inseparable from conscious motivation on the part of the victimiser.

Negative justification

As well as the positive claim to validity grounded on 'scientism', Marxism and Freudianism also embodied a form of negative justification. In the case of Freudianism, opposition to doctrine could be treated or explained away as driven by 'resistance', no matter how ingeniously these objections might be 'rationalised'. The same mechanism (the 'censor'), which is designed to protect consciousness from disturbances having their source in the unconscious desire or libido will come into play to reject the very existence of the forbidden unconscious. Freudianism itself, then, predicated as it is on the idea of the unconscious psyche, represents for the individual a threat of destabilisation similar to that posed by the libido or desire itself. So psychoanalytic theory contains within itself the means to explain the unwillingness to accept it and in so doing it disarms the opposition. Far from the Cartesian notion that truth is self-evident, psychoanalytic truth is repressed. As Ricoeur puts it: 'How does desire make the word go wrong' (the psychopathology of everyday life) 'and itself fails to speak.'

These positive and negative justifications, the claimed scientific basis and the identification of challenge with resistance, seem at first sight to be mutually supportive, but of course, logically, if the first falls the second falls with it. On analysis, therefore, all that remains of these truth- or validity-claims is the appeal to the quality of the Freudian thesis as science. But since psychoanalysis neither measures nor observes nor experiments with its object, it is hardly verifiable (or falsifiable, to satisfy Popper's criterion) by most at least of the tests appropriate to science. This is evident on a comparison with neurology, although less clear but still cogent if psychoanalysis is compared with 'normal' psychology. This leaves as the sole measure of its scientific credentials the ability of psychoanalysis to predict. Since psychoanalysis embraces a foundational theory, a method and a therapy, the therapeutic situation in which the method is applied also provides an occasion to test the theory's predictive ability.

Paedophilia is a present-day concern on the legal scene and within society at large. In adulthood, victims relate instances of childhood sexual abuse resulting later on in severe emotional disturbance. These cases have all the appearance of a classic Freudian theme: experiences of infantile sexual seduction becoming repressed and leading to feelings of adult guilt and neurosis. It is open to us then to regard Freudianism as a description of the aetiology of neurosis as proven by the frequent recurrence of the theme in actuality. The theory even accounts for the deep-seated revulsion and witch-hunting excesses of the public as itself based on guilty desire. But if the Freudian psychotherapy is successful in a significant number of cases, does that mean that the theory is proved? The evidence in favour cannot be better than anecdotal. Against that, there is a considerable room for doubt concerning the effectiveness of psychoanalysis and the durability of any improvement in the patient's emotional health as compared with other forms of treatment. Success, again, might be due simply to the confessional relationship with the therapist in itself.

But even if the doubts are sidelined, the validity of Freudian theory is still open to challenge in the same way as the verity of the recovered experiences of childhood sexual abuse. As regards the latter, debate still rages at the academic level on whether Freud believed it mattered from the therapeutic point of view whether actual events or *ex post facto* constructions or just fantasies were recovered in the analytic process. In the criminal court, on the contrary, the same issue as between fact and 'false memory' is vital. In the same way, the theory itself is vulnerable once deprived of scientific status. There is no ground on which Freudianism can be distinguished from any other mere rationalisation of unconscious drives and processes. Indeed, it may be no more than a superstructure Freud has built to enable him to cope with *angst* and feelings of guilt arising from incidents in his own early history, i.e. the early personal history of Freud himself. Alternatively or additionally, there is a historicist proposal that the doctrine happened to match the inhibitions, repressions, conflicts and anxieties peculiar to Viennese bourgeois society of the time to which Freud belonged.

What should be noticed in the critique just presented is the extent to which the use of Freud's terms appears both natural and indispensable. Even as scepticism about the theory has grown, so has the *power* of the discourse intensified and spread. Paradoxically, the Freudian discourse constitutes *per se* an effective weapon against structuralist approaches (of which Freudianism is one). But it cannot escape its own trap.

For Freud, discourse, speech-acts, what we say (unless controlled by science) is shaped and driven by the internal force of desire working at a level hidden from our consciousness. Utterance takes a disguised form determined by the internal conflicts and personal experiences of the individual. It is the individual who is at the centre of psychoanalytic theory. But from a different perspective, in the sense that he, as consciousness, is expelled from the place of origin of his own thoughts, the Freudian systematic can be seen as a precursor of the mid-twentieth-century theories involving the 'death of the subject'.

Marx and the science of history

Marx conceived his work as a *science* of history. Like Freud he looked to science for authority and to gain privilege for his own theory. For inherent in both theories was a rejection of the commonsense understanding of ourselves as independent observers capable of achieving an understanding of objective reality. Independent observer status is assumed in statements in which we embody our everyday understandings and justifications. A critique of the commonsense standpoint has most force in relation to cultural and ethical matters. For example, a thesis that our ideas and values, concerning the way in which our society is and should be organised, are culturally or socially determined will find fairly ready acceptance in our sceptical times. But there remains the problem of justifying the implicit claim that the thesis itself can escape such determinism. Marx's account of social formations and changes as determined by economic forces follows this pattern by challenging the status of commonsense statements and seeking shelter under the status of science.

From ideology to spin

As I write, it seems not too fanciful to conjecture (although some will certainly object) that the notion of ideology is fading away. Just as we have postmodernism in the arts, poststructuralism in the human sciences and a postindustrial economy, so we have postideological politics. Taking a lesson from deconstructionism, one might suggest a link between the near-abandonment or at least downgrading of the term and the absence of an oppositional term on which its meaning would be dependent. Thus, as we shall see, the diffuse connotation developed by the term. A connection can also be made with Foucault. The thinkers who struggled to rationalise the concept of ideology were Gramsci and Althusser, and Foucault was the latter's pupil. So in placing the pupil before the master in the order of exposition of this chapter, anachronism has been introduced into the linguistic history of the concept of ideology. For, in extending the notion of power from the field of politics at state or regional level to intra-institutional (asylum, prison) relationships and thence to the process of socialisation itself, Foucault found it logical to discard 'ideology' and focus on 'discourse' instead. For Foucault, the epistemes or discursive practices, although stripping the individual of his intellectual freedom, were not considered to be an instrument of deception or concealment. In that respect they occupied a neutral position. They did not correspond to any of the three wavering conceptions of ideology attributed to Marx by Thompson.[33]

Ideology as mere rhetoric

The first of these Thompson labels 'polemical'. It attacks ideology for its false view of ideas as 'autonomous and efficacious'. In this it is stigmatising the original conception of ideology as the science of the origin and nature of ideas. Ideology is also accused, at this early stage in the development of the Marxian conception of society, of blindness to the *real* sociohistorical conditions of life as lived. A parallel can be drawn between this polemical conception of ideology and the dismissive usage of rhetoric, as in *'mere* rhetoric' and *'empty* rhetoric'. If one wants an ironic comparison, one can liken Marx's condemnation as 'ideology' of the ideas of *his* enemy, the young

Hegelians, to Margaret Thatcher's dismissal of the arguments of *her* enemy, socialism in the corporate person of the Labour Opposition, as 'nothing but rhetoric'. In the one case, the ineffectiveness of ideas is being mocked, in the other the hollowness of words is being derided, without in either case specification of the epistemological high ground from which the polemic is launched.

In the next stage identified by Thompson ideas have become an epiphenomenon while the *real* or *material* dynamic in society is class relations. The interests of the dominant class at given historical epochs are the 'phenomenon' to which the system of ideas is linked in a non-reciprocal relationship. As will be seen later, Althusser worries at the nature of this linkage. The dependence of ideas (knowledge) on power is, it will be remembered, the opposite of the direction in which the power–knowledge tandem was faced by Foucault (certainly in his earlier work). But of course Marx dissociates the system of ideas from knowledge, which is reserved for the product of science. For, according to the epiphenomenal conception of ideology, the system of ideas 'represents class relations in an illusory form'.

Thompson goes on to propose a third framework for ideology which he calls latent, one reason being that Marx himself did not identify it as such. Here, ideology, although it remains a system of misrepresentation, is now *geared to* the sociohistorical process. It functions to support existing relations of class domination. It works both by concealment of the reality of class relations and by a fixation on a symbolic past. It is a breeder of prejudice and superstition, operating as a reactionary force hostile to social change.

The description in the following quotation comes quite close to the polemical conception of ideology:

> ... a specific structure of values and models of behaviour was deliberately created in the consciousness of society. It was a *perverted* structure, one that went against all the *natural* tendencies of life but society nevertheless internalised, or rather was forced to internalise it (my italics).

The system of ideas is attacked on the ground that it induces a 'false consciousness'. One can leave aside for the moment the fact that the emphasis here is on the disjunction between the 'natural' and the 'perverse' and not on that between the erroneous and the true or real, as with Marx. But, if the opening part of the quoted passage is added:

> It was a genuinely totalitarian system, that is, it permeated every aspect of life and deformed everything it touched, including all the natural ways people had evolved of living together ...

it gives the passage a completely different sense. Now it is seen as what it was intended to be, Vaclav Havel's lament on the social damage wrought by communist ideology on (the then) Czechoslovakia.[34] Yet, is there a knock-down argument against a Marxist revanchist claiming that Havel's nightmare of life as lived under actual communism just reflects what Thompson identified as the latent conception of ideology in its nostalgia for the 'natural ways' of the past and resistance to social change? Indeed, Marx's image of the *camera obscura* could be invoked to depict Havel's 'experience' as a projection in which history is turned into nature and the world appears upside down.

For Marx

While Derrida's foray into sociopolitical theory was entitled *After Marx*, Althusser called his book *For Marx*.[35] Whereas the latter sought as a good disciple to interpret the sayings of the master, Derrida saw himself as donning the mantle of the prophet. What Althusser had to contend with was the (revisionist) thesis that ideology was inescapable, that it was an organic part of every social totality. For Marx, as we saw, ideology was to be contrasted by definition with truth or reality. Now, faced with the *immanence* of ideology, still productive of false consciousness, how to escape from the resulting relativism, illustrated for us by the opposing interpretations of the Havel quotation? Like Havel, Althusser finds a pragmatic answer, a solution in terms of outcomes:

> In a classless society ideology is the relay whereby, and the element in which, the relation between men and their conditions of existence is settled to the profit of all men.[36]

And he goes on to make the (invidious) comparison with a 'class society' where the relation between men and their conditions of existence 'is settled to the profit of the ruling class'.

Arrived at that point in the analysis, however, all exits from the class society appear blocked. The class structure reproduces the ideology and, at the same time, the ideology through the instrumentality of the state apparatuses maintains the relation of the classes within the conditions of production. A blueprint of an immobile and uniform society emerges, organised by means of the

> reproduction of submission to the ruling ideology for the workers, and a reproduction of the ability to manipulate the ruling ideology correctly for the agents of exploitation and repression, so that they, too, will provide for the domination of the ruling class 'in words'.[37]

The legal system participates in this structure as one of the ISAs (Ideological State Apparatuses), others being the family, the political system, the arts and so on. Indeed, the ISAs together with the RSAs (Repressive State Apparatuses) account for all significant groupings within society, leaving no room for 'civil society'. Ideology is inescapable and all-encompassing. The legal system (as the other ISAs) exercises social control by 'relaying' ideology against the background of threatened coercion by the RSAs. The repressive institutions (police, prisons, army) are also legitimised and ordered by ideology.

From ideology to rhetoric

Ideology materialises in the form of words. This suggests that, apart from the parallel that was already drawn between their pejorative usages, a comparison can also be drawn between theories of rhetoric and ideology. Rhetoric may be conceived to be as broad as language use. In Althusser's social scheme, ideology is similarly all-pervasive in the field of ideas, beliefs and values. Likewise, ideology, its form and content dictated by economic forces (albeit, according to Althusser, *in the last resort*) is a system of false representations: 'ideology is *par excellence* misunderstanding'.[38] Rhetoric, enlisted for effective persuasion of an interlocutor or audience, abandons truth- or validity- or sincerity-claims for an engagement in effective persuasion. Change persuasion to power and rhetoric articulates ideology.

Exit

Yet both rhetoric and ideology remain slippery concepts. This is, I think, because no bounds can be set to their dominion in language and ideas. This applies to all the theories discussed in this chapter.

No space seems to be left for Foucault to escape from the grip of the epistemes or discursive practices; nor for deconstructionism to elude *différance*; nor for Althusser to dispel the illusions of ideology which, as Balibar says, creates misunderstanding of one's own 'presuppositions, in the form of 'consciousness'. Or, for that matter, Freud from the turmoil of unconscious forces. Each, however, found an exit, roughly the same way out. It was, for Foucault the care of the self, the pursuit of *connaissance de soi* (direct knowledge of the self) by the exercise of will. In Derrida's case, the *answer* was societal not individual: although law, whether *loi* or *droit,* was necessarily caught in the coils of linguistic structure and was open, therefore, to deconstruction, over and above law stood the idea of justice which he claimed to be irreducible to any deconstruction. It was distinguishable, he said, 'from law or right and even from human rights'. Again, psychoanalysis was conceived by Freud as a *scientific* process whereby the primitive underlay of the individual unconscious could be discerned and disentangled by interpretation of its language. In the same way, Althusser saw the escape route from this all-encompassing and immobile state determined in the *last instance* by the economic conditions of existence via an 'epistemological break' *out* of ideology and *into* the science of historical materialism. Out of that emerged a second science which was in essence a science of ideology. Its task was 'to act on ideology and transform ideology into an instrument of deliberate action in history'.[39]

Ideology and commonsense

Examination of the objective of Althusser's new science shows that this proposed escape is just a leap of faith. It is not difficult to see that the formula is circular. The same can be said of the struggles by the other thinkers, whose ideas were discussed in this chapter, to escape from the trap they had set for themselves. It fell to Gramsci (who wrote earlier than Althusser but was published later) to propose a different meaning for ideology and to introduce a new term, hegemony. This enabled him to do justice to the actual complexity of society and to escape from the rigidities of the Althusserian scheme. He made room for civil society.

Ideology simply represented commonsense. It was 'the philosophy of the non-philosophers'.[40] It furnishes the legitimising discourse according to which the identity of social formations and arrangements of power are taken for granted. Because the discourse, as Foucault suggested, produces 'the effect of truth', commonsense (ideology) is conservative in its effects. At the same time, in this way, everyone is a philosopher or intellectual, Gramsci declares. Here we have something like the 'admitted opinions', the starting-points of legitimate argument, which Barthes equates with commonsense. Like Barthes, Gramsci goes on to infer that its claim to validity is 'psychological'.

Hegemony

Gramsci denies that commonsense, although a conservative force, is 'a single unique conception, identical in time and space'.[41] Hegemony represents the process that is introduced to account for the possibility of movement and struggle in culture and society. It names not only the end-result in domination by the dominant class or social formation but also the process of consensus-formation through which group dominance is achieved and maintained. So it is both constitutive and constituting. Hegemony is the system of meanings, values and relevance which operates at the levels of both opinion- and will-formation. To win out in hegemonic struggles, dominant groups must take account of the interests and tendencies of the groups which they seek to subordinate. The foreground of hegemonic struggle is occupied by a challenge to the prevailing commonsense. The challenge is mounted by a homogeneous social ground that arises along with the coming into being of a coherent and systematic philosophy in opposition to common sense.

Gramsci rejected the notion that all ideology produced 'false consciousness'. So he relieved himself of the Sisyphusian labour of locating a source of 'true' consciousness. He still wanted, however, to differentiate between ideologies. Since the function of ideology was to 'organise human masses', a distinction could be made between ideology that was 'historically organic' and one that was 'arbitrary, rationalist', in other words imposed.

Authority

I want to end this excursion into critical language theory by introducing a comparison between the role of *hegemony* as understood by Gramsci and that of *authority* in the legal system. The hegemony of the court over all other means of dispute-resolution and the arrangement of power among the courts are institutionally established. This gives a basis for a proceduralist certainty viewed from a positivist standpoint, although the law remains essentially indeterminate. Enter the other idea within the concept of authority corresponding to Gramsci's notion of hegemony as process of consensus-formation. For the judgement of the House of Lords, say, not only decides the case but also provides 'authority' in the form of the court's interpretation of the meaning and relevance of a legal norm. Perhaps, then, the quest for what constitutes valid law should shift from the terrain of text-production to that of its *interpretation*, the subject of the next chapter.

3
INTERPRETATION

The scheme of this chapter is to explore a few general theories of interpretation interspersed with judicial interpretations of what constitutes the process of juridical interpretation, i.e. statements by judges of what they believe they are doing when they interpret the law. Strangely, interpretation remains an elusive concept. There is difficulty in defining its objective, in prescribing in theory the route to be followed and in recognising the destination. By the end of the chapter, the point is being strongly made that the claim that judges *interpret* the law leaves us in the dark concerning both how judges arrive at a decision and how decisions are in turn to be judged. This clears the ground for the analysis in chapter 5.

Reception

The classical definition of rhetoric as the art of persuasion by discourse suggests that the meaning and impact of the words used are under the speaker's control. Effective performance in the art is dependent on mastery of the discourse. The summit of performance would be the achievement of the magical power to persuade whomsoever you pleased of whatsoever you pleased. Humpty Dumpty boasted of such a mastery: 'When I use a word, it means just what I choose it to mean – neither more nor less!' Goodrich's polemic against the legal institution, as we saw in chapter 1, was targeted on the same (false) claim of univocity for legal language that he (falsely) attributed to it. This pretension according to his thesis was not self-adulatory, nor merely incidental, but the very basis of its authority in a modern society as an intermediary between the political power and the people. If its arrogant assumption of dominion over meaning were exposed as fraudulent, the legal system would, like Humpty Dumpty, have 'a great fall' with irremediable consequences: the political power ('all the king's horses and all the king's men') could not put it 'together again'.

Rhetoric approaches language as a medium of communication, rather than as a means of self-expression. A hearer/audience is necessarily involved. Moreover, the pivotal role played by persuasion implies the presence of a recipient. Thus, Umberto Eco says:

> The functioning of a text ... is to be explained taking account, in addition to or in place of the moment of its production, of the role played by the addressee in its comprehension, its actualisation, its interpretation, as well as the way in which the text itself foresees his participation.[1]

Reception is not passive

The instantaneity of seeing, hearing etc. as matters of everyday experience leads us to assume that perception etc. is immediate, nonmediated. In whatever sense this may be accurate, we are nonetheless aware of an important difference between seeing lines of letters on a printed page and reading what they say; there is an equivalent difference between hearing a miscellany of sounds and listening to a speech. Through the optic of the theory of rhetoric, the communicative act appears as a sort of colonisation of the recipient's mentality. But, as its counterpart on the recipient's side, a system is in place for the control of immigration. An act of interpretation corresponds to the speech-act on the speaker's side.

Reading or interpretation?

Once textual reception is recognised to be more than the scanning of lines of letters, i.e. more than a mere ocular exercise, are we to treat reading as synonymous with interpretation? 'Reading' is interchangeable with 'interpretation' when we talk of 'reading' a facial expression, or 'reading (a cryptic meaning) into' a remark, 'reading between the lines', or 'reading' philosophy at university. We 'read' a railway timetable, except for the symbols designating, for example, trains which run on Sundays only, which we interpret. We 'read' a musical score but 'interpret' a sonata (musical text) on the piano. The end of both reading and interpretation is to understand, to ascribe meaning to, or inscribe meaning in, the text. Still, to have read Joyce's *Finnegan's Wake* is an achievement significantly short of what is implied by a claim to have interpreted that work.

For a similar reason, what de Man meant by 'close reading' and Dworkin by 'moral reading' is truly interpretation.

Interpretation as concept

To make the last statement is to be committed to drawing a line of demarcation between reading and interpretation. To do that, does it entitle us, in turn, to condemn certain 'standard' usages as wrong? To 'read' a face, a fortune in a tea cup or a future in the lines of a hand are examples which would almost certainly fall on the other side of any such dividing line. Despite that, as part of *ordinary* language, these uses are perhaps metaphorical or examples of catachresis, but anyway unexceptionable. It is *catachresis* when we speak of the 'legs' of the table although the table cannot walk on them. In French, the same bits of the table are called its 'feet' (*pieds*), but that does not make either the English or French usage illegitimate. The position is entirely different when our concern is not with ordinary language but with terminology or definition. Or, as here, where it is the *concept* of 'interpretation' that is under the spotlight. These distinctions are important for the argument in chapter 5, where they are pursued.

To conceptualise interpretation, do we say that it is a two-stage process of which reading is the first stage; that reading stops at comprehension of the text while interpretation (from a foreign language) goes beyond to involve the effort to reformulate it in other language? Interpretation therefore supervenes when a 'difficult' text is being read? In line with this distinction, Ricoeur proposes two different conceptions of interpretation.[2] The first involves 'unmasking, demystification, reduction of illusions'. He cites the interpretative process of psychoanalysis in which the 'language' of the unconscious, expressing itself for example in dreams, is decoded. This idea is familiar to us from the previous chapter, based as it is on the assumption that (certain) language is of its nature deceptive or capable of being manipulated. To that first category he opposes interpretation conceived as 'the re-assembly or restoration of the meaning'.

Meaning of meaning

It is unwise to go further without asking what is meant here by meaning, what is the quarry pursued by the interpretative process. Eco proposes three possible approaches to textual meaning or intent:[3]

intentio auctoris, authorial intention, corresponds to what the author intended, had in mind, to say; *intentio operis* describes what the text actually says; and *intentio lectoris,* what the text conveys to the reader, what the reader takes it to mean, is the third approach. We are predisposed to assume that, in the reading of a text presenting no particular difficulty, all three, author's intention, textual intent and reader's grasp or comprehension, substantially coincide. With a 'difficult' passage, this assumption still lingers so far as writer's and textual intents are concerned. A competent writer is assumed to have meant what he says and to have said all that he meant to say. According to the principle of expressibility, everything that can be meant can be said. The French *'vouloir dire'* (literally 'to want to say'), which translates as 'to mean', makes no distinction between what the writer means (what he wants to say) and what the text means (what the text wants to say). Indeed, on this line of analysis, it may be argued that the writer's intent exists in an inchoate or ephemeral form only, insofar as it can be said to exist at all independently of the actual words he produces: 'How do I know what I mean until I read what I write?'

Does the reader have the last word?

The act of interpretation is initiated by the reader, most obviously where *he* senses a breakdown in communication. Ambiguity, for example, indicates that the text has distorted the intended meaning, that *intentio operis* has diverged from *intentio auctoris*. More broadly, certain expressions are essentially plurivocal, so that interpretation is required in the form of an alternative meaning to be 'read into' the primary, literal, immediate meaning. Psychologically, the process of interpretation begins, as Eco suggests, with conjecture as to the meaning on the reader's part. This can be evoked or aroused by a message which is both unambiguous and univocal. 'Will be there tomorrow, 4.00 pm', is Eco's example. The *textual intent* is to convey an innocent piece of information. But it may be received as a message heavy with threat. Another might see in it the promise of a pleasurable encounter to come. The interpretations are the outcome of conjecture on the addressee's side as to the meaning of the message in the sense of the sender's intention. Say, though, that the recipient is paranoid in the one case or over-optimistic in the other. That would suggest that the message has been misinterpreted.

Eco imagines a variety of possible responses by a living author confronted by a discordant interpretation of his work: 'I never thought to say that, so this reading is illicit'; 'I did not mean to say that, but I must agree that the text says it and I thank the reader who has brought it to my awareness'; 'Independently of the fact that I did not mean to say that, I think that a reasonable reader ought not to accept such an interpretation for it appears scarcely economical and it does not seem to me that the text sustains it'. The first comment would maintain the inviolability of writer's intent as the measure of the single right interpretation. The second admits the legitimacy of the *intentio operis* and by implication the acceptability of more than one interpretation. The third allows, but suggests criteria for the limitation of, *intentio lectoris*.

These ideas theoretically advanced by Eco coincide with actuality in a postscript written by Habermas in 1994 to his book, *Between Facts and Norms*, the original version of which was published in German in 1992:

> There is a sense in which an author first learns what he has said in a text from the reactions of his readers. In the process, he also becomes aware of what he meant to say, and he gains an opportunity to express more clearly what he wanted to say ... Certainly the interpreter enjoys the advantage of understanding a text better than the author himself, but on the occasion of a new printing, the author may be permitted to take the role of an interpreter and attempt to recapitulate the core idea that informs the whole book as he sees it.

This pragmatic response by Habermas to his readers operates as reinforcement of Eco's theoretical analysis of interpretation, maintaining the separate identity of what the writer meant to say, what he has actually said and what the reader takes him to have said. Indeed, it tends to prioritise the *intentio lectoris*. In addition, Habermas is saying that the aim of interpretation is to *understand* the text.

Hermeneutics

Hans-Georg Gadamer defines hermeneutics as 'the theory or art of explication, of interpretation'. The notion that underlying interpretation are both 'theory and art' tempts us to see in hermeneutics the counterpart of rhetoric as classically defined. While rhetoric is aimed at persuasion, interpretation has as its goal, as Habermas suggests, understanding or in other terms the appropriation of meaning. Although rhetoric is measured by its effectiveness in relation to a particular audience, it places in the forefront the author and the generation of the text. From the viewpoint of hermeneutics as interpretation it is the reader and the reception that are privileged. But, what, in the case of hermeneutics, can be the appropriate measure corresponding to persuasion for rhetoric? The goal of hermeneutic analysis, according to Genette, is the intuitive accord of two consciousnesses. This suggests that the *intentio lectoris* and *intentio auctoris* should coincide, in practice that the interpretative process should lead the reader to grasp what the author had in mind to say. This demands both more and less than the proposal that interpretation is bent on the appropriation of the meaning. It can come about only if the reader has access to the writer's intention on which to base his intuition other than via the text. On the other side, it impoverishes the interpretative process by its assumption that the text can yield no more than what the writer had in mind to say.

If the focus in interpretation is switched from writer to reader, from generation of the text to its reception, the idea that there is a single right interpretation has to be abandoned. Valéry is often quoted for his suggestion that there is no true meaning of a text. But it does not follow that the range of possible interpretations is unlimited. The state of anarchy represented by those theories labelled 'anything goes' is untenable, for, as we saw, it makes sense to speak of a 'misinterpretation'. Eco chose for his title *The Limits of Interpretation*. It was in line with his argument that a text can give rise to an indefinite but not unlimited number of possible interpretations. That would fit a theory that the act of interpretation amounts to the appropriation of meaning beginning with conjecture aimed at the understanding of the text.

Intentio auctoris

It is necessary now to revisit intentionalist theory, that being the declared basis of judicial interpretation.

The meaning of a text is what its author intended it to mean. The law is what Parliament has prescribed, written down. The single right interpretation, therefore, is the one which is in that sense *author*ised. Schleiermacher's classical hermeneutic theory focused the search for the textual meaning on the author's intention. Moreover, the meaning of any part crystallized in the meaning of the whole text. Thus, interpretation was context-driven. But the context was understood to overspill the boundaries of the text in two directions, objective and subjective. On the objective side the interpreter should be awake to the situation of the particular text embedded as it was in a distinctive genre, indeed in an ensemble which embraced the totality of the literature in the field. At the same time, the work should be seen, subjectively, as a manifestation of an individual creative consciousness, whose particularity is marked in the text. The first step in the two-step theory consists of the claim that the author's intended meaning dictates the right or authorised interpretation. Against that, the second step consists of a method for the (re)construction of that intention, taking the interpreter outside the textual boundaries. This presents a contradiction since the interpreter is not authorised to go out of bounds.

Legal hermeneutics

Armed with the results of this foray into the general theory of interpretation, we can empathise with the judges as they grapple with the same theoretical problems within the four corners of the law, creating along the way a jurisprudential hermeneutics. Always to be kept in mind is that the principles of which this jurisprudence is composed are worked out not at the level of theory but, pragmatically, in response to interpretive problems encountered in particular statutes and other documents.

As already indicated, the case reports are spotted with judicial statements describing the process of interpretation of the law in strong intentionalist terms.

The following pronouncement by an eminent judge can stand as exemplary:

> No principle of interpretation of statutes, however, is more firmly settled than the rule that the court must deduce the intention of Parliament from the words used in the Act. If those words are in any way ambiguous – if they are reasonably capable of more than one meaning – or if the provision in question is contradicted by or is incompatible with any other provision in the Act, then the court may depart from the natural meaning of the words in question; but beyond that we cannot go.[4]

The principle that it is the intention of Parliament which rules judicial interpretation has a near-theological status. The mission of the judges is to carry out the will of the democratically-elected Parliament. As with theological principle, however, it is more honoured in the repetition than in its strict observance. It is now being shaken even at the institutional level by the empowerment of supranational bodies and the extension of the umbrella of universal human rights. But even there, the principle of parliamentary sovereignty remains sacrosanct. Nonetheless, it is a matter even of judicial admission that intention of the legislature is a 'slippery' notion. A second look at the quotation explains the slipperiness. For it assumes that the 'natural meaning' of the legal text may differ from the legislative intent while at the same time what is said in the text is the sole guide, the limited basis on which that intent can be 'deduced'. Where conjecture as to the intent is aroused by ambiguity in the wording or by internal incoherence within the relevant body of law, the *context* that can be called upon as a deductive aid is narrower than in general intentionalist theory.

Context

The legal process recognises the bottomless pit or infinite regress represented in the previous chapter by Derrida's principle that the context is inexhaustible; each context has a context and so on. 'Context' in this discussion has the very broad connotation described in the last chapter. A longstanding, self-imposed limitation on the recourse by judges to contextual material was relaxed in a leading case of 1992.[5] What were out of bounds for the purposes of interpretation were the *travaux préparatoires* (legislative history), reports of parliamentary debates and so on. The barrier was lifted with reluctance and only to a limited extent to allow reference to clear (ministerial) statements directed to the matter in question. The justification for the barrier was conventionally regarded as being the practical need to keep down the cost and labour in 'combing through reports of Parliamentary proceedings in the hope of unearthing some perhaps incautious expression of opinion in support of an improbable secondary meaning'.[6]

Noteworthy for the main theme of this book was a statement by one of the judges in the case of an additional reason for the prohibition:

> A statute is, after all, the formal and complete intimation to the citizen of a particular rule of the law which he is enjoined, sometimes under penalty, to obey and by which he is both expected and entitled to regulate his conduct.[7]

This, it will be remembered, is the ground on which it was argued at the beginning of this book that justification required to be found for the presumption that everyone knew the law. The judge in the case went on to say:

> We must, therefore, ... be very cautious in opening the door to the reception of material not readily or ordinarily accessible to the citizen whose rights and duties are to be affected by the words in which the legislature has elected to express its will.

The implied premise that statutes (more than Hansard) can be regarded as material 'readily or ordinarily accessible to the citizen' is notional to say the least, but the focus on the citizen as the addressee of the law points in the right direction.

He then goes on to accept that language, in particular language adopted under timetable pressure in Parliament but also legal language in general, 'is not always a reliable vehicle for the complete or accurate translation of legislative intention'.[8] Accordingly, the ban can be relaxed in situations 'where the expression of the legislative intention is genuinely ambiguous or obscure or where a literal or *prima facie* construction leads to a manifest absurdity'.

Although the canons of construction for documents other than statutes differ in detail, the core objective is the same: to determine the common intention of the parties from what was written in the document. But judges are seen to struggle to define the extent to which they can legitimately overstep the boundaries of the document. Evidence of one party's *intention* was inadmissible since the other party had no means of knowing what that intention was other than via the written document. Similarly, evidence of negotiations, those being aspirational and not something realised, was ruled out. It is hard to escape the conclusion from these limitations on the context that the emphasis is placed on the means, that is the *intentio operis*, rather than the end, the *intentio auctoris*. This is reinforced by another *dictum* which would take the focus entirely away from the intention of the real parties:

> Subject to the requirement that it should have been reasonably available to the parties ... [the factual matrix to which regard can be had] includes absolutely anything which would have affected the way in which the language of the document would have been understood by a reasonable man.[9]

INTERPRETATION

The last statement, however, leaning as it does in the direction of *intentio lectoris*, is controversial. The pendulum swings back to support the formula that:

> Surrounding circumstances should be confined to what the parties had in mind, and what was going on around them at the time when they were making the contract.

CASE STUDY

It is an offence for a person to drive a motor vehicle on a road 'without reasonable consideration for other persons using the road'. At a hearing against a bus driver charged with this offence, the case against him was limited to complaints by passengers travelling on his bus. The issue, therefore, was whether the statutory words 'other persons using the road' included passengers in the motor vehicle itself. The judge decided the case on the footing that 'other persons using the road' clearly meant 'persons other than the driver'. '*Prima facie*', he said, 'any passenger uses the road just as much does the driver'. He then supported this reading of the words with the reasoning that:

> if one was going to construe those words [to exclude the passengers] ..., one would have to insert some such words as 'without reasonable consideration for other persons using the road other than such persons using the road as passengers in the vehicle being driven by the person concerned.'[10]

He concluded that:

> there seems to me no warrant for inserting words of that sort or for giving the words other than their natural meaning.

After noting that the plain English campaigners could not fault the statutory language, one can observe that the case is instructive too because the judge has made explicit his interpretative strategy. First, he considers the textual intent on the basis that a passenger and a driver are, equally, road-users. He then engages in a process of 'deduction' from the words to arrive at what he judges to be the legislative intention. So he reasons that if he were the writer of the text intending to exclude the passengers in question, he would have used different language. This method of exegesis is resorted to because legislative intention, as such, is usually rendered in effect inscrutable by the foundational principle that the intention is to be gathered only from the words that are used. Judges are prone to advance as justification for their reading of a statute that, if Parliament had intended something different, 'it would have said so'. On the principle that everything that can be meant can be said, Parliament must mean what it says since it can say what it means.

'Natural' meaning

As exemplified in the case study, judges assume that words have a 'natural' meaning. This can be ranged with other descriptions of the semantic qualities of language, such as 'literal' meaning, 'plain' language, 'primary' meaning, 'immediate' meaning, 'core' meaning. Eco considers that utterances do have a literal meaning. But an example readily shows that the literal meaning is not necessarily the natural meaning. 'You're standing on my foot,' taken literally, is a statement of fact, while 'naturally' it is to be understood as a request to get off it. What judges seem to have in mind using 'natural' meaning is the meaning which is 'unforced', where the sense of the words is not *distorted* to fit the Procrustean bed of an argument. As was evident in the case study, the problem is that, where the meaning is in dispute, the sense of the words constituting the 'natural' meaning emerges only as the outcome of an adversarial argument. For example, it has been held that, where the particulars of a charge simply alleged conspiracy to supply a controlled drug to 'another', then, *as a matter of language*, that meant supplied to someone other than a co-conspirator.[11] The question which then arises is whether it is valid to interpret a principle of law by means of semantics alone. If the criterion of the single right interpretation is based on theoretical reference to the will of Parliament and the Parliamentary will is inscrutable, then is legal hermeneutics, as promulgated by the judges, not ensnared in the same trap of non-referentiality as the linguistic theories paraded in the previous chapter?

The golden rule

I want now to juxtapose to the 'core principle' with which this analysis began a statement of what is judicially considered to be 'the golden rule':

> in construing ... statutes, ... the grammatical and ordinary sense of the words is to be adhered to, unless that would lead to some absurdity or some repugnance or inconsistency with the rest of the instrument, in which case the grammatical and ordinary sense of the words may be modified, so as to avoid that absurdity and inconsistency, but no further.[12]

Now, the rule may shine like gold but gold does not make the sharpest instrument. Of the rule a judge has said:

> I agree in that completely, but unfortunately in the cases in which there is real difficulty it does not help us much, because the cases in which there is real difficulty are those in which there is a controversy as to what the grammatical and ordinary sense of the words used with reference to the subject matter is.[13]

When the golden rule is compared with the core principle, a significant change is the addition of 'repugnance' to ambiguity and incoherence as a textual flaw sparking off the need for interpretation, but, although ambiguity and incoherence may properly be described as linguistic defects, repugnance is a state of mind occasioned in the reader by a tension or conflict between the ordinary meaning of the text and some matter *extraneous* to the text. In the same vein, the expression of judicial cynicism just quoted concerning the golden rule points to a disparity between the sense of the words and the 'subject matter'. To refer to the subject matter in order to interpret the words must again take us outside the confines of the text. Where does that lead us?

CASE STUDY

Under the Street Offences Act 1959 it was made an offence for a prostitute to solicit in a street. An issue arose where prostitutes were attracting the attention of passers-by from balconies or windows. Nonetheless, they were found guilty of a 'street offence'. The judge made the statement: 'everybody knows that this was an Act intended to clean up the streets' and went on to reason that '[v]iewed in that way, it can matter little whether the prostitute is soliciting while in the street ... or at a window, or whether the window is shut or open or half open; in each case her solicitation is projected to and addressed to somebody walking in the street'. Since the act of soliciting represents an (attempted) communication between prostitute and client, there is ambiguity in the Act as to which of them or whether both must be 'in the street' for the offence to be committed. To resolve the ambiguity, the judge's approach is made explicit in his opening remark where he proposes to consider 'what is the mischief aimed at by this Act.[14]

Purposive interpretation

The case illustrates the path of purposive interpretation. It seeks 'to identify the social or juristic defect which is the likely subject of remedy'. To arrive there it may have recourse to 'examination of the social background' and 'a conspectus of the entire relevant body of the law'. These routes (*inter alia*) were authoritatively declared to be open in the context of this case where it was strongly affirmed that the court's duty was 'so to interpret an Act of Parliament as to give effect to its intention'.

Yet the following case study points up the problem.

CASE STUDY

A male prostitute was charged with being a common prostitute under the same section of the same Act (the Street Offences Act 1959). An appeal was lodged against the magistrate's dismissal of the case. The basis of the appeal was that the language of the statute was not gender-specific. The appeal court agreed with the magistrates, holding that a male prostitute could not be a common prostitute within the meaning of the Act.[15] It is hard to think of a reason which would justify the argument for a purposive interpretation in the first case and its absence in the other, except that the term 'common prostitute' has been conceptualised and absorbed into legal language. By contrast, the architecture of the street in the first case is referred to in ordinary language. Conjoin that with the judge's invocation of the people as (universal) audience: 'everybody knows that this was an Act intended to clean up the streets'. Therefore, the recourse to the intention of Parliament in the first case was buttressed by the judge's insight into the way that the law was popularly understood.

The shift of focus to purposive interpretation reflects a fine difference in the meaning of 'intention'. In the other cases, where interpretation was exegetical, the trace of the legislative intention was discernible only through the statutory language; it was shadow to the substance of the words. The words said what Parliament had intended (had in mind for) them to mean. In the first street offences case, on the other hand, the words become the trace and it is the intention, in the sense of will or purpose, which is substantive. This leads us to the second feature. The intention of Parliament, now become substantive, is to be sought by other means, the literal or natural meaning of the language being relegated to a purely indicative status. The judge leans in this instance on the general or public understanding: 'everybody knows that this was an Act intended to clean up the streets'. Does this case not leave us with the suspicion, however, that the very nub of the problem lies in the circumstances which call for or permit this switch from exegesis or literal construction to purposive interpretation?

Repugnance

Other than ambiguity and textual incoherence, it is declared to be repugnance which impels judges to desert the text and pursue the intention of Parliament. Once at that point, the legislative history, other than exceptionally, having been ruled out, 'intention' resolves into, not the legislature's intention, but the intent of the legislation. It emerges that it is the judge's insight, as a member of the public, into the social situation to be remedied by the body of law, of which the statute forms part, that both stirs up the repugnance and indicates how it can be resolved. Thus, the referent is to be understood not as the people's representatives but as the people itself. More than that, from the linguistic standpoint, it is public discourse and not the discourse of parliamentary debate which counts. Yet the interpretative process, judicial deduction in pursuance of the core principle, must always negotiate with and ultimately accommodate to the words of the text. Put another way perhaps, the meaning of a legal text is determined by *intentio lectoris*, what its addressee would be reasonably expected to understand by it.

Where a conflict between the meaning of the words and the *suspected* legislative intention proves to be irreconcilable, the judge will not always, as we shall see, opt for the latter.

CASE STUDY

Most, if not all, commercial leases provide for the landlord to have a power to terminate the lease prematurely if the tenant breaches any of the conditions or obligations imposed on him by it. The conditions of supply–demand determining the power-relationship in negotiations, as well as the relative socioeconomic status reflected in the descriptions land*lord*/tenant, have resulted in a proliferation of such obligations, ranging from the obvious to the trivial. Exercising the option to remove the tenant in a rising market, the landlord may gain greatly by the recovery of his property free of the tenant. So its exercise, although authorised by the lease, may nevertheless contravene the metalegal principle of proportionality. This can be formulated as the notion that an innocent party is not entitled to be compensated by the wrongdoer to an extent greater than the loss sustained by him as a result of the wrongdoing.

English law has largely resolved the tension. Judges are empowered to intervene to give an opportunity to the tenant to rectify the default, so overriding the stark provision of the lease. But until 1985, Scottish judges had effectively no such power. The rationale behind the difference: in England the option to terminate prematurely was seen as one of a range of measures designed to enable the landlord to *enforce the performance* of the tenant's obligations; in Scotland, the same provision, written in the same or equivalent wording, is considered to have as its purpose the provision to the landlord of a means to *rid himself of a tenant* who has proved himself unsatisfactory by his default. The case now about to be examined turns on the interpretation of the statutory qualification of the landlord's power put in place in 1985.[16] This was to the effect that a landlord would not be entitled to terminate the lease 'if in all the circumstances of the case a fair and reasonable landlord would not seek so to [do]'. In framing the wording, the legislature had adopted a report by the Scottish Law Commission which had preceded the enactment.

An event counting as default under the lease by the tenant of property in an industrial estate having occurred, the landlord served notice to terminate. It was accepted that substantial advantages would accrue to the landlord on regaining possession of his property while at the same time the tenant would suffer a corresponding loss. 'To a significant extent the tenant's loss would be the landlord's gain', said the judge.

The nub of the case emerged in the judge's analysis of the 1985 provision. It was reasonable to assume that the legislative intention had subsumed the Law Commission's statement of the juristic defect which the clause was to rectify as well as its having been expressed in the Commission's recommended phraseology. On that basis, the judge considered that what would be called for would be 'a comparison between the prejudice occasioned to the landlord by the event which provided the ground for exercising the option to irritate and the prejudice which would be suffered by the tenant if the option was enforced'. In effect, that would provide the appropriate foundation for the application of the principle of proportionality. The judge said, however, that he was 'not wholly confident' that what he conceived to be the legislative intention had been achieved by the 'language used in the section'. But, despite his doubts, it was the latter, *the actual words used, not the suspected legislative intention*, to which his decision gave effect.

The Human Rights Act has further complicated the tension between the actual language and the legislative intention which should rule. This case leans in the opposite direction from the one last cited.

In this chapter, I want to examine the basic assumption that what judges do is to interpret the law to uncover the intention of the legislature. In that way their judgements acquire a derivative authority flowing from the sovereignty of Parliament. Their work of interpretation provides the right answer when it gives effect to the will of the people's representatives. The question which runs throughout the chapter, therefore, is whether interpretation in general, and so judicial interpretation in particular, can fulfil its aim to find the single right answer.

Constitutional and legislative intention

The intervention into the interpretative problem of a constitutional text or one that sets out overriding rights is long familiar on the US scene. There, twin debates go on between originalists and others like Dworkin in relation to the Constitution (a debate sketched out in the Introduction) and between textualists and proponents of legislative intent in relation to ordinary law. The positions taken up in these debates are not always mutually consistent.

Purposive interpretation demands that the legislative intent is a matter of common knowledge or can be inferred convincingly enough to be imputed to the legislature. This makes it surprising at first sight that, as we saw earlier in the chapter, the court is barred from looking at the raw material from which such an inference might obviously be constructed. These materials roughly constitute the legislative history of the statute consisting of official reports, Hansard, *travaux préparatoires*, etc. In *A Matter of Interpretation; Federal Courts and the Law*,[17] Scalia, a Reagan appointee to the US Supreme Court, strongly argues for textualism, the position that wording of the text must rule. 'I object to the use of legislative history on principle,' he says, 'since I reject intent of the legislature as the proper criterion of the law.' A moment's reflection, however, will show that this strong textualism is effectively not far removed from the *doctrinaire* intentionalism manifested in the preceding quotations from the UK judges. Where the judicial duty is to fulfill the legislative intention and the legislative intention is to be drawn from the words used in the legislation the two become as difficult to distinguish as identical twins.

The book includes a commentary by *inter alios* Ronald Dworkin and a reply by Scalia. Dworkin 'forces' Scalia to re-introduce what the former calls 'semantic intention' and the latter prefers 'import' as something separate from the actual wording. Both, I think, Dworkin in his challenge and Scalia in his apparent concession are at cross-purposes. By 'semantic intention' Dworkin means what the legislature intended to *say* in using the words it did. Now the whole point of strong textualism is that it does not allow us to go behind these words to look for that intention. So Scalia's 'concession' that 'the import of language depends upon its context, which includes the occasion for, and hence the evident purpose of, its utterance' is in effect unforced. Not only that, but it is scarcely a concession at all since even strong textualism gives importance to context. Add in Scalia's definition 'import' as 'what the text would reasonably be understood to mean,' his reflection that 'those two concepts [semantic intention and import] chase one another back and forth to some extent' and it becomes apparent that the same confusion in the approach to statutory interpretation reigns in the States as has already been noted in the UK. This is hardly controversial, for the 'hard truth of the matter is that American courts have no intelligible, generally accepted, and consistently applied theory of statutory interpretation', according to two law professors.[18] Indeed, the problem is complicated in America, as we will see in the next chapter, by the looming presence of the Constitution and the attendant conflict between those who seek only the original meaning of the text and their opponents, among them pre-eminently Dworkin himself, who advocate a different interpretative stance. Scalia finds it impossible to reconcile his 'originalist' position in relation to the Constitution and his textualism in the case of modern statutes.

Application

By this stage, one is driven to conclude from the inconsistency between the canons of interpretation, whether these are seen as descriptions of what judges actually do or normatively as rules defining what they ought to do, that a wide gap exists between the theory and the art of legal hermeneutics. The problem is compounded by the introduction into the theory of 'repugnance' as a stimulus to depart from the ordinary meaning of the words. The difficulties, it should now be stated, come from the idea that adjudication involves no more than the interpretation of the law in the same sense as a traditional text is interpreted by a reader. Judges are not engaged on a quest *in vacuo* for the single right *interpretation* of a statutory rule or principle. Instead, their business is the *application* of a form of words of varying flexibility to a subject matter consisting of a fairly rigid set of facts. The facts are, themselves, a 'set' of states of affairs and events which have, on their side also, been the subject of interpretation. To apply the law requires an *understanding* of the reasons which would justify its enactment in the words used in the statute. The judge's understanding is not significantly different from the general understanding which, as argued in chapter 1, underpins obedience of the law. It also shapes the interpretation of the facts.

In chapter 5 the function of the language of the law in the transformation of this understanding into the legal text and in its application to the particular facts is examined.

The case decision which develops or articulates the law presents a Janus face: looking back, it states what the law is; looking forward it establishes what the law will be. In this way the judicial process functions as a continuous commentary, or like an encyclopedia of applications as contrasted with a dictionary of synonyms. The concern is not with what the words mean but with how they are to be applied. Each decision, in order to perform its lawmaking role, must give reasons which justify it as a valid application of the law. The use of that decision as precedent, in turn, involves a critical evaluation of the reasons provided for its justification.

Judicial discretion

The habitual reiteration by judges of limiting words, such as 'beyond that we cannot go', which appear as a coda to the canons of construction, is designed to mark the boundaries of judicial discretion. They oppose the idea that there are an indefinite number of possible, or at least permissible, interpretations as well as the 'anything goes' school of critical legal theory. It goes with the function that judges recoil from the need to exercise discretion. In the ideal, law should resemble a set of mathematically exact formulae available to be picked up and applied to the facts. This pushes the judges towards strong textualism, that the wording of the text should rule. The problem is that, doctrinally, the unique right interpretation is that which gives effect to the legislative intention. But textualism is in a state of cold war with intentionalism, which would admit into the process as guides to intention matters extraneous to the textual wording. How is the tension resolved?

The phrase, 'intention of Parliament', is not itself clearcut. The initial complication is that the actual author, the legislature, is collective. In the case of legislation, as with deeds, intention is equated with the consensus. Therefore it is to be sought in the words which issue forth and not in the statements of *individuals*. The exclusion of the legislative history (other than clear ministerial statements) conforms to the logic of collective intention. Once 'intention of Parliament' becomes 'legislative intention', or 'intent' or 'import' (terms which are also in use), a subtle change of significance takes place. The site of the intention then switches from the actual to the hypothetical author. A critical, evaluative element then enters into

INTERPRETATION

the process aroused by 'repugnance' at the ordinary meaning. The place and nature of such a critical element in interpretation in general are discussed later in this chapter. Repugnance and then critique lead the judge to purposive interpretation. Purposive interpretation corresponds in an interpretative framework to judicial discretion from the standpoint of application of the law.

Robert Post provides a framework which can be used to illustrate the interplay between textualism, intentionalism and judicial discretion.[19] He proposes a rule-making paradigm in which traffic control takes the place of the judicial process and the traffic policeman represents the judge:

1 Traffic should be regulated as the police officer on duty sees fit;
2 Traffic should be regulated so as to avoid congestion;
3 Traffic should be regulated so that it alternates between two minutes' movement in a north–south direction and three minutes' movement in an east–west direction.

Rules 1 and 3 represent the extreme positions. Rule 1 entrusts traffic control to the discretion of the police officer, while rule 3 strips the officer of discretion. The effect of rule 3 is to render the officer 'a mere machine' by imposing upon him purely administrative duties. Here we have the mathematically exact formula, set out unequivocally in the text, apparently eliminating the scope and need for discretion. But, although there is no problem of interpretation, the strict *application* of the rule will inevitably end up in gridlock. The close texture of the rule leaves no room to give effect to the *understanding* of the purpose or reasons for its adoption. Nor will the road user, who must be understood to be the addressee of the rule, recognise its validity. For, as was argued in chapter 1, underpinning obedience is an understanding of the law. Even if he, the citizen, appreciated that traffic flows should be alternated, he would, by virtue of the critical component in the process of interpretation, reject as unreasonable the *rigidity* of the timescale for movements in each direction. While the road user will behave flexibly, i.e. exercise discretion on his own part, in front of traffic lights, he will expect discretion (justice or fairness) from a traffic policeman.

In direct contrast, rule 1, as Post suggests, 'liberates the officer to carry out his personal vision of social order'. That being the case, the so-called rule, being essentially nothing more than the delegation of coercive authority, is not a rule at all. Although situated at the opposite pole, the fact that it draws its binding force solely from authority has the result that it lacks validity in the same way as rule 3.

Examination of the intermediate formula stated in rule 2 shows that this, like rule 1 but for the opposite reason, is not a rule in the strict sense either. A rule, as compared with a principle, specifies the typical situational features that constitute the conditions of its application. The applicability of a principle depends on *general* conditions which require interpretation. Therefore, 'rule' 2 possesses the defining characteristic of a principle. For, according to Post, it 'requires the [judge] to determine the meaning of "congestion"'. The process of interpretation, however, is not driven by the difficulty of the text. Rather, it arises in the application of the rule. That calls for the exercise of judgement, unlike rule 1 which licenses unlimited discretion or rule 3 which imposes rigidity. Rule 2 can be taken as exemplary of legal discourse.

The nature of interpretation within the judicial process turns out to differ from the way in which it is conceived by the judges. As is evident from the cases, the meaning is scarcely ever encrypted in the text. On the contrary, problems arise with the clearest of language and disappear when language is at its most complex. Everyone knows the *meaning* of 'congestion' in the context of rule 2 even if those at the margin of linguistic competence do so only through the medium of their understanding of the traffic policeman's role.

A lead can be taken from Post's proposition that judges 'determine' meaning, as exemplified by rule 2. Not in the sense that they fix it in stone but that their decisions, their applications, play a part in its establishment over time. For that reason, a 'body' of law, as the metaphor suggests, is often said to be a 'living instrument'. In the descriptive phrase is the idea of a dynamic balance between change and continuity. The 'living' of the law, its development, is manifested in the evolution of legal *concepts*. The concept is multi-aspectual, its extension measured by the range of cases in which it is applicable.

Critical element

Before going on to end this chapter with a mention of the key role that I attribute to the concept in the interpretation and application of the law, I want to show the place of the critical element in Habermas's theory of interpretation in general.

For him, the goal of interpretation is comprehension. The point of departure on the psychological plane, which takes the place of 'repugnance', is the 'confusing realisation' that his initial understanding of the text was inadequate and will have to be revised. This state of mind of the reader represents a 'disturbance of communication'. The interpretative process consists of the effort to understand *why* the author felt justified in putting forth certain propositions as being true, in recognising certain values and norms as being right, and in expressing certain experiences (or attributing them to others) as being authentic'. Built into the process is the projection on to the hypothetical (not the real, empirical) writer of a belief system drawn from a particular cultural situation defined by the three dimensions of background knowledge, values and psychology. To the extent that the interpreter possesses insight into that cultural situation, he is able to set the author in his time and place, so becoming in Schleiermacher's words an 'immediate reader' of the text.

Contemporanea expositio is a similar approach adopted by judges for the construction of 'old and obscurely drafted legislation'. There, it was permissible for the court to have regard to reliable and contemporaneous observations as to how a statute was operated and understood at the time. This was declared in a case where reference had been made to Trollope's *An Autobiography* to assist in the interpretation of statutes of 1834 and 1859 governing superannuation allowances for civil servants.[20]

But Habermas claims that the interpreter not only aims to understand, but in the process of gaining understanding, must also become involved in an evaluation of the *reasons* for the author's factual assertions, value recommendations or disavowals, and expressions of inner states. Thus, a critical element is built into an interpreter's understanding.[21] Habermas adds that the interpreter 'has to clarify the context that the author must have presupposed as being common knowledge in the audience he was addressing', Again, this comes close to the contextualisation by judges of the law within its social background.

Concept

Hans-Georg Gadamer developed hermeneutics into a distinctive philosophy.[22] At the heart of his theory was the history of concepts, the concept being not only an instrument and means of communication but the very *subject* of philosophy. In chapter 2, I pointed out a turn in the focus of mid-twentieth-century theory from ideas to discourse. Gadamer postulates that it is the relation between words and concepts which determines our thought and that there are no words to describe that relationship.

His idea of our historicised understanding is that we can only affirm tradition as such if we place it within the social and cultural framework in which it was formed. At the same time, we must be aware of our own perspective from which we are receiving the tradition. What is accomplished is a 'fusion of horizons'. But his history of the concepts, because of his fondness for Greek sources and roots, tends to have the two-dimensionality of etymology. What should be occupying the missing dimension is the interpretative work of history. Each interpretation is a *re*-presentation, not only a reproduction of the original text, its interpretandum, but also the potential for a new text, just as each case decision is both a declaration of what the law is and a precedent for what the law will be. Packaged in the concept is the narrative of its historical encounters in the situations referred to by Gadamer as text, commentary, dialogue or reflections. A recurrent theme of his is the duality of interpreter and text, or parties to a dialogue, or even an individual with himself, to which can be added judge and legislator, between whom such encounters take place.

Where the concept has it over terminology is in its possession of a history. Terminology is arbitrary as Gadamer says, arbitrary and prone to obsolescence. It has no history; it changes inexplicably like fashion. Certainly, with the use of terminology, regular relationships can be established between things. These relationships, however, are important only insofar as the 'things' have significance, something which depends on their being identifiable ostensively or within the experience of others through the use of non-terminological language. Another clear difference: the usage of terminology cannot be challenged. Because its adoption and definition are arbitrary, a defining characteristic is its univocity. But it makes sense, on the other hand, to claim that a particular *concept* has been misused. Responsible for the difference between concept and terminology in this respect is the continuity of the tradition within which the concept is embedded.

Does Gadamer's elevation of interpretation into hermeneutic philosophy, in particular his analysis of the history of the concepts, go further to the extent of solving the central problem of what counts as a valid interpretation? As was already apparent, the problem of definition dissolves if the meaning of a text is taken to be the equivalent of what was preformed in the author's mind as he wrote it. But then, the difficulty shifts to method. Is not the text itself the sole, the definitive, the only reliable, the uniquely valid, index to what the author intended to say? The distance between interpreter and text, due to the interposition of authorial intention, which creates the essentially insoluble problem for the intentionalist, provides instead, according to Gadamer, a vantage point from which the text can be understood. It becomes a space in which a 'dialogue' can take place between the interpreter and the virtual author, where understanding comes about through the 'fusion of horizons'.

Nonetheless, the problem of validity remains: what difference does it make to conceive of misinterpretation as a misunderstanding or absence of 'true accord', rather than as an error in identifying the writer's meaning? Swift in *On Poetry* remarked: 'Learned commentators view in Homer more than Homer knew'. He *meant* (intended) that as a jibe, and an intentionalist would agree with the underlying sentiments. Gadamer would detect the same ironic meaning, but would *understand* Swift's saying in a different way: those commentaries which drew on a knowledge of the society and culture of the world in which Homer wrote, shaping his experience and reflected in his metaphors, terms and concepts, form, so to speak, vertebrae in the spine connecting the Homeric narrative to the versions of our times.

Judgement

What emerges is the need for judgement. Gadamer uses the domain of aesthetics to emphasise the decisive role played by the judgement in interpretation. If the work is to gain 'accord' in the artistic ensemble to which it belongs it must command in the viewer a sense which he recognises as an assent, as expressible by the phrase 'that's it'. The same assent is evoked by the 'convincing argument' (*eikos*) which consummates the dialogue. The use of the faculty of judgement, he concludes, pervades the whole of our lives and experience, everywhere indeed where 'it is a question of the reasonable application of rules'. Judgement cannot be learned, it can only be exercised; for example in speaking, when we apply, employ and understand the words that we have learned. In engaging in communication, we work at the formation of concepts and at our orientation in the world. He alludes to the distinction between two usages of the concept of 'measure' in the politics of Plato. One use refers to the application of a standard measure. The other is that sense of measure which is the qualifying attribute of a beautiful object. The latter is the foundation for the reasonable application of rules, for the exercise of the act of judgement.

One tends to be charmed by the elegance of Gadamer's prose together with its classical references into seeing his hermeneutic philosophy as representing the closure to the search for the criterion of the single right interpretation. But this is to treat it as itself a work of art. Experience and judgements of courts of appeal contain reminders that the sense of 'that's it' can turn out to be illusory. The 'convincing argument' which seemed to lead up to the sense of consummation is revealed to be a legitimising discourse that in reality came afterwards. For Gadamer's description of the act of judgement in interpretation is just that, a *psychological* reconstruction of a state of mind. What is lacking is a test. In the next chapter, I will explore the proposed test that emerges from Dworkin's reconstruction of the process of judicial decision-making with its implications for the determination of many of the major issues of today.

4

CONSTRUCTIVE INTERPRETATION

Dworkin

Dworkin is a commanding figure in legal theory. No radical, philosophical analysis of the realm of law (law's empire)[1] can reasonably fail to build on or distinguish itself from his system of ideas. That apart, his distinctive approach to juridical interpretation is a necessary annex or epilogue to the previous chapter. In the introduction to his recent work,[2] in which he collects previously published material on what he describes as 'almost all of the great constitutional issues of the last two decades', he sets out his conception of what is involved in interpretation as the keystone of his theoretical system. Against the background of Dworkin's theory, I continue the argument of the last chapter that adjudication is steered by the application, rather than interpretation, of the law, showing that his emphasis on interpretation is driven by the focus of his work on rights-based law. This, I suggest, leads to the use of philosophical in place of legal discourse. In the chapter's later section, I introduce Habermas's theory in which the central position is given to communicative action and particularly legal language.

The argument of the previous chapter showed that the individual case decision went beyond the basic text in the process of applying it to a novel set of circumstances and interpreting it to set a precedent. For Dworkin, this process demands construction rather than construal. Construal, which textualists and often judges consider to be accurately descriptive of the methodology of interpretation, Dworkin stigmatises as 'that arcane and conceptual craft'.[3] By contrast, in a constitutional frame, Dworkin speaks of 'elaborations' of the text. To be admissible, he says, an elaboration must have the generality of a principle. In addition, that principle must count as a principle of political morality. But two questions arise: what breadth of generalisation should such a principle possess; and where do we look for a guide or a model for political morality? Dworkin responds to the first question, illustrating his thesis by restating the 'equal protection' clause of the Constitution, describing it as 'a principle of quite breathtaking scope and power: the principle that government must treat everyone as of equal status and with equal concern'.[4] The formula he proposes to attain the single right interpretation constitutes his answer to the second question.

His example of *constructive* interpretation undoubtedly qualifies as a principle of *political* morality. Does it, however, require the *authority* of the Constitution as support? Principles present themselves as essentially self-validating. Everyone is against *sin* in principle. Rather than audaciously being far-reaching and powerful, the principle would be accepted by all as a sovereign duty. Indeed, it may be considered to be constitutive of law or of the sense of justice underpinning law, shared by judges and laymen alike. That said, the irony is that some at least of the framers of the US Constitution were and continued to be slave-owners. But, apart from the quality of self-validation, principles, unlike rules, do not specify the situational circumstances in which they apply. Nor do they dictate the way in which they are interpreted. Once slaves are defined as chattels and not as persons, they can be excluded from the scope of the universal.

Dworkin's approach to interpretation appears to be entirely detached from authorial intention. Ranged against Dworkin are the holders of the originalist position. Extreme originalism would tie law to the Constitution interpreted as the framers would have intended its abstract language to be taken to mean. Dworkin could himself concur with a proposition along those lines but only if 'intention' were to be understood in a significantly different way. He would make the argument pivot on the distinction between 'what someone means to say' as against 'what he hopes or expects or believes will be the consequence for the law of his saying it'. The latter is, other than in exceptional circumstances, unknowable, although, as we saw previously, Habermas supplies a formula by which it can be constructed. In any event, Dworkin rules it out as a mistaken approach to the original intent and with it the originalist interpretation of the abstract clauses of the Constitution.[5] He can now conclude that the framers simply said what they meant to say, each clause containing a clear statement in accord with their intention.

There are two possible reformulations of Dworkin's position that link up with themes in this book. Based on the widespread conception of the Constitution as a living instrument, the original intent could be said to be that its abstract clauses should be read in accordance with *intentio lectoris*, that is, as its addressees would understand them. Or, in accordance with a main theme to be developed in chapter 5, that terms such as 'free speech', 'due process', 'equal protection' and so on undergo a process of reconceptualisation when embodied in legal language, evolving systemically over time. But the problem remains: does the 'equal protection' clause, for example, in the terms adopted in the US Constitution, sustain the construction placed on it by Dworkin as the uniquely right interpretation, rather than an alternative version dismissed by Dworkin to the effect that everyone is equal before the law?[6] Armed only with that understanding of the principle, amounting to nothing more than the protection of the interchangeability of the legal subject, the judge would not be empowered to override enacted law. Against that, Dworkin's claim is that constructive interpretation entails a 'moral reading' which constructs the *best* possible meaning out of the object of interpretation.

Integrity

Take the US constitutional judge of today engaged with a contemporary issue, such as a state law restricting abortion or the claim by a pornographer to be exercising his right of free speech. The judge would seem to confront a vast gulf of indeterminacy stretching back to what he judges to be the appropriate constitutional clause. How is it to be filled in, so that, on the one hand, the judge's discretion can be reined in and, on the other hand, he is able to make a reasoned claim of validity for his decision? Law in its nature is a structured *system*, demanding not only textual but also decisional or intertextual coherence. The 'body of laws' describes the legal system in this sense while French has *loi* for a particular law and *droit* for the system, and, correspondingly, German differentiates between *Gesetz* and *Recht*.

Integrity is Dworkin's apt term for the demand, both intellectual and ethical in nature, on the law-maker to maintain the integrality of the system. This imposes a twofold constraint. First, the principle which comes out of his or her interpretation and elaboration of the appropriate constitutional clause must fit in with the structure of the Constitution as a whole. Second, he or she must respect its history. Here, this refers to legal history, the succession of precedents and commentaries out of which has developed the current understanding of the principle. Dworkin recognises, of course, that the abstract clauses, even when elaborated to accommodate to a holistic view of the Constitution and in consonance with precedent, would still leave too much power to an arrogant judge and too large an area of doubt for a conscientious one. Left in doubt, the judge must seek out the 'best conception of constitutional moral principles ... that fits the broad story of America's historical record'.[7]

In the process of constructive interpretation, history is invoked by Dworkin at three stages: initially, in the shape of the historical circumstances generative of the Constitution; then, as legal history regulated by the doctrine of *stare decisis*, the principle that preceding decisions should be followed or at least respected; and third, in the form of the history of the nation. But, the indistinct guidelines offered by these histories, along with the language appropriate to value judgements and moral discourse, are ominous indications of the difficulty which faces any claim that the 'moral reading' delivers determinate answers. Of course, once the strict originalist position, eked out by historical research into original intention, is given up, as exposure to facts and cases shows it must be, the doctrine of the *certainty* of the law is in any event placed in jeopardy. What Dworkin proposes amounts to coherence plus morality, under the auspices of Judge Hercules.[8] His choice of name for the ideal constitutional judge measures the heroic dimensions of the task of constructive interpretation informed by the moral reading. The name works also to point to the counterfactual status of Dworkin's proposal that the moral reading is not just what judges ought to do but what they actually do.

The determining factor, the 'best conception', translates as the judge's estimation of what will do most credit to the nation. Note parenthetically that the process of constructive interpretation as so outlined inclines in the same direction as a judgement which aims explicitly to 'put the best construction' on its object, although the latter usually operates at the other end of the scale of value. In Dworkin's theory, the 'best' identifies what is the single, right interpretation, the correct resolution of the legal issue. The claim of 'rightness' implicit in the judge's decision leaves room for Dworkin's necessary concession that mistakes are possible. Real judges fall short of Judge Hercules's heroic stature and lapse into misinterpretations. This matches the status of precedents in American constitutional law, which have authority to the extent that they command consideration and respect but are not binding. In the metaphorical chain novel, to which Dworkin compares the line-up of case decisions,

Constitutionalism and fundamentalism

In the Introduction, I discussed the relationship between fundamentalism and the originalist view of the law. There are, I want to suggest, two defining characteristics of fundamentalism: one is the belief in certain tenets, principles, values which are the object of strict interpretation; the other, that there is a duty to use the institutions of the state for their enforcement. Strict interpretation allies itself with social and legal conservatism, punctuated by interludes of regression. In the context of the US Constitution, the school of *strict* interpretation is represented by the theorists of originalism, arguing that the text is to be understood as the founders ('prophets') would have understood it. This argument is used to undermine the strength of the case for the constitutionality of positive discrimination, namely that state institutions should compensate for the oppression and deprivation historically suffered by minorities by such means as 'head starts' and favouritism in the award of contracts. The second feature of fundamentalism, that state institutions should be informed by certain belief systems and used for the enforcement and protection of appropriate patterns of social behaviour, is shared by Dworkinism and originalism alike. But these push in opposite directions. The interrelationships among the three, fundamentalism, originalism and Dworkinism, show up clearly in the abortion debate which gave rise to a series of Supreme Court cases responding to constraints imposed on abortion by state legislation. Much of the pro-life movement is animated by religious fundamentalism. It finds support in the right to life enshrined in the Constitution. The pro-abortion case extricates itself from the constitutional coils by the (successful) argument that a foetus does not qualify as a 'person' whose right to life has constitutional protection. This, though, represents no more than a shift back to neutrality; it provides no ground to override the state laws restrictive of abortion that were in issue. It is the moral reading of the Constitution that tilts the other way: the principle that all persons should be accorded equal respect extends to a woman's right to control her own sexuality. It amounts to a recognition of her moral 'personhood'. Dworkin cites with approval the Court's view that certain decisions merit constitutional protection because they involve 'the most intimate and personal choices a person may make in a lifetime'. So the 'moral reading' drives towards liberalism and away from fundamentalism.

Paradoxically, *pro*-lifers in relation to abortion are often retentionist in relation to the death penalty for capital crimes. Paradoxically also, pro-choice protagonists, though basing their position on the high value to be placed on the principle that the individual human being, as a free moral agent, must take responsibility for his actions, are inclined to be abolitionist. These contradictions no doubt find their most cogent explanation at the psychological, or social psychological, level. The concern here, however, is to observe the impact of the Constitution as an originating text on the development of American law in these areas. The abortion question was answered in the first place by interpretation, in the sense familiar to British judges, of the concept of 'person' in a specific, legal text. The determinant was the meaning of the words used. After that, the argument, as we saw, turned *philosophical* rather than legal, but still rested on an 'interpretation', the 'moral reading'. Most in the contemporary Western world would agree that the freedom of a moral agent to choose abortion satisfied Dworkin's criterion of the 'best' conception, that which does 'most credit to the nation' (although a strong, vocal and sometimes violent minority in the US takes the opposite view).

The opposite applies to the situation prevailing in the US, where, alone among the Western democracies, the exaction of the death penalty is a normal incident of the criminal justice system in several states. It is a matter of fact that fundamentalism and capital punishment go together, one of the links between them being no doubt the primordial concept of talion justice. Unlike the abortion issue, where the Constitution proved to be an effective counterweight, here it has been unavailing. The provision of the Constitution that bears directly on the question is the Eighth Amendment forbidding punishments which are inherently 'cruel and unusual' in the practices of civilised nations. If the fundamentalist theory of the original understanding is adopted, the effect of the clause would certainly not be to proscribe capital punishment. Two centuries ago, death sentences were everywhere commonplace; even in doubtful cases, 'he'll be none the worse of a good hanging' was a thought firmly rooted in the social consciousness. Now, however, it carries conviction to say that a sentence of death qualifies as an 'unusual' punishment among civilised nations. Similarly, any argument to the effect that the death penalty did not amount to 'cruel' punishment would seem cerebral and remote from today's cultural standpoint in face of the harsh contrast between the programmed brutality of the actual execution and the refined, juristic distinctions on which life and death decisions turn. The issue of the constitutional legitimacy of the death penalty today hangs, therefore, on hermeneutics. When interpretation follows the route to original intention familiar to us from the self-understanding of the judges as expressed in the last chapter, then laws permitting capital punishment will not be struck down. Also, interpretation, in general, demands that a text should be read as a whole. Here, the Constitution, in its entirety, represents the context that bears on the import of each individual clause. So indirect support for the inviolability of death penalty legislation can be sought in the constitutional provision that no-one should be deprived of life without due legal process. If the death penalty is already forbidden, this is robbed of its content.[9] The argument in defence of the death penalty may then conclude that since the framers at this point had capital punishment in contemplation they could have taken the opportunity, if that was their intention, *expressly* to forbid it. That they chose not to do so deprives the abolitionist of recourse to constitutional authority.

When Dworkin contends that the Constitution should not, indeed cannot, be interpreted according to the established canons for law made by legislatures, he is surely right. It is dubious logic to infer from the conjunction of two principles, whose clear meaning is to afford constitutional protection against cruel punishment in the one case and against lynching in the other, that their combined effect is to sanction the use of capital punishment by the state. Yet to reject that inference is far from amounting to endorsement of the moral reading as the basis of the uniquely right interpretation of the law. On the one hand, the Constitution has proved to be a powerful defence against fundamentalism in one area (abortion) by providing a foundation on which the value of the individual freedom to make moral choices can be grounded. But before that case could be made, it had to be established by the ordinary means of legal discourse analysis that the concept of 'person' did not apply to a foetus. Disappointingly, on the other hand, it has been deemed not to speak on the basic question of whether the state has the right in any circumstances to take the life of one of its citizens. Indeed, it has shown itself open to be misused to bolster the retentionist case. The condemnation of the United States for its everyday use of the death penalty is sufficiently widespread in Europe to suggest that the Court's decision in 1976 to allow its re-introduction cannot be judged to meet Dworkin's criterion as a judgement that does 'most credit to the nation'. This can be explained away in two ways. One, the decision was a mistake, a wrong interpretation. Or two, it may be held to be the right interpretation, one dictated by obedience to the constraint introduced by Dworkin in the requirement for constitutional case law to *accommodate to* 'the broad story of America's historical record'. That points up the battle in the process of constructive interpretation between the progressivism of the 'best conception' and the conservatism of traditional practices. To see how the theory proposes that the outcome of the battle should be decided, we can look at two critical areas, freedom of speech and euthanasia. As preamble, I want to suggest that whereas Dworkin underlines the problems attached to interpretation as that is normally understood by the judges, the moral reading cannot at all usefully be understood as a process of *legal* interpretation.

Freedom of speech

Freedom of speech is protected in the US by the First Amendment. As for the UK, even apart from the European Convention (of which Britain was an original signatory), now incorporated into British law, the right of free speech existed under its unwritten constitution. An unwritten constitution can be taken to describe an indefinite number of principles which are broadly understood across the political spectrum (other than among those regarded as extremists) as having self-evidently high value. Is any difference to be detected in the force attributed to, or the scope of, the right of free speech depending on whether it is embodied or not in a written text? Semantically there is no difference, they are indistinguishable; everyone knows what is meant by a right of free speech, whether it is put into writing or not. Clearly, for example, 'speech' is understood in this connection to include written and other forms of public expression, as well as the spoken. Legal protection of free expression is afforded against not only oppression or censorship by the state but also against attempts at suppression (including actions for damages) by other individuals or groups. Liberty of political expression is so fundamental that it is now rarely or ever put to the test. But that apart, relying on the principle, people have a legal right to lie, talk nonsense and filibuster, or, on the other hand, say nothing interminably. At the margins lie contested areas: pornography, hate speech, forms of commercial speech, the impact of defamation law on press freedom. The illustrations chosen by Dworkin in conceding that there must be limits to the application of the principle of free speech are 'fighting talk' designed to provoke a violent response (even if what is said has a basis in 'truth') and a *false* alarm of 'fire' in a crowded enclosure. Therefore, his theory of constructive interpretation can be tested by its explanation of the basis on which these situations are excluded. Either free speech has limits which can be justified or decisions can be reached by interpretation of the constitutional clause in cases where liberty of speech collides with another constitutional right.

Dworkin believes that rights are 'trumps' against other interests. The proposal that free speech has limits is therefore inadmissible. Free speech always fulfils the criterion of what will do 'most credit to the nation'. Dworkin accepts but considers inadequate J.S. Mill's justification of the institution of free speech as necessary for free exchange in the 'marketplace' of ideas. Rather it is to be justified non-instrumentally as a good in itself, as a value 'constitutive' of a just society. Whenever it is curtailed, for example in wartime, or to save a life, a loss is entailed; the denial of the right counts in each of these cases as a 'necessary evil'. The 'necessity' arises from the interest in survival, collective or individual. Yet such cases of exclusion are not to be understood as beyond the bounds of the principle, to be defined in writing, as if in a tenancy document, by way of exceptions, qualifications and provisos. In these situations, the principle is displaced while remaining intact without any loss of validity, and that for the reason proposed by Dworkin. For the same reason, he is also right to take up position against Stanley Fish's view, encapsulated in the pugnacious title to a collection of his essays: *There's No Such Thing As Free Speech and It's a Good Thing Too*. What Fish means by the title is that free speech does not exist since it is not the case that *anyone* is regarded as having the right to say *anything* he wants to *anyone* he chooses in *any* circumstances. The truth of this statement depends on one's interpretation of 'exist' and the rhetoric of his title. Would Fish not have deprived himself of any defence if his university tried to prevent the publication of his essays as academically subversive? Indeed, it is only in response to a challenge or threatened constraint that the right 'materialises'. Otherwise, it is like the air, taken for granted.

This illustrates, I think, the advantage of an unwritten constitution or, rather, the handicap of a written one. Where a written constitution with a *quasi*-scriptural status conferred by history exists, as in the United States, it comes to represent *authority*. *Contra* Dworkin, judges are drawn to harness authority *wherever they can* by strict interpretation of the text. We have already seen textualism at work on the relevant provision and context in relation to the death penalty in the US. It distorts the process of judging between colliding rights. Say, for example, that 'speech' when inscribed in a legal text is broadly construed as a form of social action, as it is in speech-act theory. What would then be lost by this blurring of the line between speech and action is the defining characteristic of speech as the use of a symbolic system. A legal consequence might then be, for example, that flagburning would not then be judged to be constitutionally protected, as it has been in the States, as a form of public protest.

How else is a judgement to be made in a competition between rights? Rights resemble values in that they cannot be prearranged in a hierarchy. In the desert a bottle of water is more valuable than a bar of gold. In analysing fighting talk, Dworkin employs the discourse not of values, but of competing rights. It is the right to physical security that is infringed by fighting talk. In the competition, it is the right of free speech which falls to be 'compromised ... in deference to [the right to physical security which is,] in context, more urgently or centrally at stake'. There is a false ring to this explanation of how the collision between the two rights is resolved. As in any 'collision', both rights are at risk. As in any competition, one will gain, the other will lose out. The addition of the words, 'urgently' and 'centrally', makes no difference. The point is that interpretation of the constitutional text gives the judge no guidance whatsoever. Furthermore, even if one invokes as a basis for the decision Dworkin's own standard, judging that to stifle talk which is 'very likely to produce immediate violence' is creditable even in a democratic society, then, in the absence of any interpretative link-up to the authority of the Constitution, this will amount to a *political* and not a *juridical* judgement. Significantly, perhaps, Dworkin himself resorts not to that criterion but instead to the purely instrumental argument of urgency.

None of these analyses, the deconstruction of the notion of legal right *à la* Fish, the introduction of limits to the category of constitutionally protected speech or the weighing of political values, explains in a fully satisfactory way the decisional process in a case where rights collide. Move from the individual plane to the collective, from 'fighting talk' to what has come to be called 'hate speech'. Hate speech can be defined by its intention to engender, or to manifest publicly, attitudes of hostility towards identifiable minority groups within a multi-ethnic, multi-faith or multi-cultural society on the grounds of their difference. In response, minorities feel excluded and society becomes divided. Nonetheless, the courts in the US have held that the protection of the

First Amendment extends to speech of that sort. Dworkin cites two extreme cases of racist manifestations held by the federal courts to be sheltered by the First Amendment: a statement by a person, wearing a hood at a Ku Klux Klan rally, that 'the nigger should be returned to Africa, the Jew returned to Israel', and a march by a small band of neo-Nazis displaying swastikas in a district where many Holocaust survivors lived.

Dworkin finds wanting the instrumental justification for upholding the right of free speech in the instances just mentioned. Succintly put, it can only debase the marketplace of political ideas to allow free commerce in such tainted 'goods'. But the 'constitutive' argument, he judges to be decisive. He says: '[W]e are a liberal society committed to individual moral responsibility, and any censorship on grounds of content is inconsistent with that commitment'.[10] That position also serves as a defence against the suppression by law of pornography.

At this point, one is led to wonder what has happened to the transcendent, constitutional principle that all citizens merit equal concern and respect. Should it not follow that the state of law should intervene in situations where hatred is being stoked up against a vulnerable target group by a discourse marked by intimations of violence and strong exclusionary language? Note that the most powerful argument for the legal suppression of pornography adopts a principle along similar lines, based on its degradation of women which has the effect of hampering their full participation in the institutions of a democratic society. Again, Dworkin himself proposes that the same broad constitutional principle is applicable in the different context of positive discrimination to justify favourable treatment aimed to catch up on the constitutional objective by compensating for a historical backlog.

But, in relation to hate speech and pornography, Dworkin deploys a generalisation of his pro-choice argument with regard to abortion:

> [M]orally responsible people insist on making up their own minds on what is good or bad in life or in politics, or what is true and false in matters of justice or faith. Government insults its citizens and denies their moral responsibility, when it decrees that they cannot be trusted to hear opinions that might persuade them to dangerous or offensive convictions ... [M]oral responsibility has another, more active, aspect as well: a responsibility not only to form convictions of one's own, but to express these to others, out of respect and concern for them, and out of a compelling desire that truth

be known, justice served and the good secured. Government frustrates and denies that aspect of moral personality when it disqualifies some people from exercising these responsibilities on the grounds that their convictions make them unworthy participants. So long as government exercises political dominion over a person, and demands political obedience from him, it may not deny him either of these two attributes of moral responsibility, no matter how hateful the opinions he wishes to consider or propagate, any more than it may deny him an equal vote.[11]

I have quoted Dworkin's truly noble language in full in order to set it side by side with what Lord Bonham Carter said in support of the diametrically opposite position in the first report of the UK Race Relations Board:

> A law is an unequivocal declaration of public policy. A law gives support to those who do not wish to discriminate but feel compelled to do so by social pressures. A law gives protection and redress to minority groups. A law provides for the peaceful and orderly adjustment of grievances and the relief of tensions. A law reduces prejudice by discouraging the behaviour in which prejudice finds expression.

Bonham Carter's words set out the pragmatic justification for the sharp contrast between the UK and the US positions in relation to hate speech. In the UK, the Race Relations Act outlaws speech that insults people on the ground of race, religion or gender and section 82 of the 1998 Crime and Disorder Act provides for higher sentences for racially aggravated crimes. It is significant that behind the deviation in the approaches to hate speech lies a difference in the law-making process. As we saw, liberty of speech in the States is preserved against such encroachments by sheltering it within the protective embrace of the Constitution. A specific piece of legislation went through Parliament in the UK defining abusive discourse against minorities as an exception to speech safeguarded by a traditional freedom. The difference provides an opportunity to compare parliamentary law-making in the UK with judge-made law based on the interpretation of constitutional rights in the US. Begin with the criticism of Dworkinism that constitutionalism guided by the moral reading confuses law, morals and politics. On the contrary, as is shown by the passage just quoted, he draws a clear line between the law and (individual) morality. Although he reads the Constitution as protective of racist speech and pornography, he would judge both of these to be 'loathsome' from a moral standpoint. The responsibility of the moral agent is sharply differentiated from the duty of the legal subject. That apart, Dworkin agrees that judges make *political* decisions. This, of course, flies in the face of the doctrine of the separation of powers.

Beyond formalism, however, consider the signals that are given in each case to the people by the law-making processes. On the one hand, the *authority* of the Constitution as a law-making text is neutralised by the clash in this instance of rights which flow from it. Freedom to indulge in racist speech is then *preferred* to the protection of minorities by a tenuous chain of judicial argument linking the judgement to the Constitution. Of great significance is the fact that the discourse in which the argument is conducted is philosophical, not legal. At the level of discourse, this puts, although it should not, a patina of legitimacy over racist and other forms of hate speech. Again, the use of an argument to justify the *principle* of free speech where what is in issue is whether or not the principle should be applied to a particular form of speech lends support to the accusation that political decisions are being made by unelected and unaccountable judges. This critique highlights some of the virtues ascribed by Bonham Carter to the making of a specific law. People understand the law by appreciating the reasons for its enactment. On the other hand, they do not readily engage in the moral reading of constitutional principles and, when they do, their perspective is easily overwhelmed by populist discourse.

Once a law is promulgated, *legal* discourse comes into play. The sub-category of *hate* speech has to have strict definition. For example, should homophobic speech be included by extending the protective reach to those marked out by difference in sexual orientation?[12] Or, the other way, is a law forbidding in school education the recognition of homosexuality as a permissible form of human relationship incompatible with the principle underlying the law protective of minorities? Again, although less seriously, lawyers are almost universally attacked or at least sneered at in the media; anti-lawyer jokes by the man in the street adopt a rhetoric just as virulent as racist jokes. Yet, the idea that lawyers should be protected by law would be 'laughed out of court'. They are not an endangered minority and so far as known, no one since Shakespeare has seriously suggested: 'Let's kill all the lawyers'.[13] The judge's power to punish for contempt of court is to be regarded, rather, as a shield for authority.

The following case shows that, once a legal norm (other than the enunciation of a right or liberty) is established by legislation or judicial declaration, legal language ousts philosophical discourse and comes into its own. In this instance, what occupied the court was the exception made for provocative language.

CASE STUDY

The appellant in the case was one of three women who had been preaching on the steps of a church to passers-by in the street.[14] A crowd in excess of a hundred people had gathered around them, some among the crowd showing hostility towards the speakers. Fearing a breach of the peace, the police had asked the women to stop preaching and, when they refused, arrested them. The appellant was appealing against her conviction for breach of the peace by the magistrates and against the Crown Court's decision to uphold the conviction.

The court's approach was two-fold. In view of the crowd's size and the hostility aroused by the preaching it had to determine whether the policeman's intervention was justified. It was for the court to determine whether the circumstances prevailing at the time were such as to give rise to a reasonable assumption that violence might ensue. This amounted to an objective test, from an observer's standpoint, distinguishable from the subjective question of whether the action of the policeman as a participant in the situation was a rational one. Applying the test, the court ruled that it was unreasonable to anticipate violence and so the arrest was unjustified.

There was a second question: on the assumption that violence *was* threatened, was the arrest of the preacher the right form of intervention to lift the threat? If the preaching fell within the range of free speech, the policeman's duty, if he had a reasonable apprehension that violence was going to erupt, was to intervene against the hostile element in the crowd to protect the right to speak. On this point, the court drew a boundary:

> Free speech included not only the inoffensive but the irritating, the contentious, the eccentric, the heretical, the unwelcome and the provocative provided it did not tend to provoke violence.

Now, not only does this indicate the extension of the concept of free speech but it also defines 'fighting talk'. That is not only provocative but is such as to tend to provoke violence. Although some in the crowd may have found the preaching offensive, the speaker nevertheless had the right to protection for her liberty of speech. It did not arise as an issue, but difficulty will attach to any judgement of whether the interpretation of speech tending to 'provoke violence' should be ruled by speaker's intention, textual import or the construction put on it by the audience.

The case also demonstrates, I want to suggest, a discursive gear-change by the court in moving from the first to the second issue. On the reasonableness of the policeman's intervention, the court said *inter alia*:

> Thus, although reasonableness of belief, as elsewhere in the law of arrest, was a question for the court, it was to be evaluated without the qualification of hindsight.

Here, the discourse, logic and parameters of relevance are characteristic of the law. But, in upholding the preacher's liberty of speech, the court's language was philosophical:

To proceed as the crown court had done from the fact that the three women were preaching about morality, God and the bible, ... to a reasonable apprehension that violence was going to erupt was, with great respect, both illiberal and illogical.

As I proposed in the last chapter, philosophical language is characteristic of arguments deployed in rights-based law.

In the same elevated argument for free speech the court also referred to the condemnation of Socrates and the historical refusal by a jury to convict two Quakers for preaching ideas which offended against state orthodoxy. But the speech in question in the case was not challengeable as being offensive or provocative to the state or the authorities. At bottom, it involved individuals, the preacher and the hostile members of the crowd. Logically, the latter could move away if they found the speech offensive. Is that aspect of the situation a factor in the determination of whether provocative but permissible speech has turned into violence-provoking talk?

Politically correct

Away this time from the context of constitutional law, the notion that speech might be correct or incorrect gave rise to highly-charged clashes in the campuses of the American universities, again centred on race and gender. The fulcrum of the dispute was Foucault's linkage of power and discursive practices. The minority groups within the university communities argued that the modalities of representation embodied in discourse not only reflected and identified but also maintained and reinforced actual power relationships of domination and subjection, privilege and deprivation, respect and low esteem, elitism and exclusion. Instances were easy to find in the lexicon: '*man*kind' for what should have been '*human*kind'; words descriptive of woman as sexual object; the signification of 'christian' and 'jew' when spelt without an initial capital; the misappropriation of the eulogistic 'white' for 'men' (i.e. men and women) who happen not to be black, brown or yellow; the designation of homosexuals as 'queers'. In consequence, action groups, such as student power, black power, the feminist and gay movements, could be mobilised to exert political, social, cultural and pedagogic pressure for the sanitisation of the discourse by the suppression of discriminatory language. While aiming at equality, such groups sought at the same time to reinforce for the purposes of the struggle their collective identity or particularity. To an extent, these aims are contradictory and tend also to arouse in turn in the others, the outgroup, a sense that it is they who are the victims of exclusion or discrimination. In Fish's words: 'You can only fight discrimination with discrimination.'

Politically incorrect speech in the university was a paler version of, but involved the same conflict of rights as, hate speech in the national sphere. The highest value had to be accorded to both the freedom to develop and express ideas and the right to equality of respect and concern. There is always a potential conflict between these two rights at the discursive level and, with the admixture of ideas of cultural relativism, this broadened into 'culture wars' in the multi-ethnic and multi-cultural world of the American universities.

It is clear that either to impose censorship or to allow signifiers of racial, religious, gender, sexual preference, superiority or inferiority in accepted language is equally hard to justify. The existence of the problem provides some support to Bonham Carter's argument in favour of a law against hate speech within society as a whole as an 'unequivocal declaration of public policy'. In the case of politically incorrect speech, however, the only reasonable way to delegitimise it is to discourage it. Pressure for any stronger measure appears as extremism and is readily mocked. The 'war' against the 'politically incorrect' remains a struggle for hegemony in Gramsci's sense between 'politically correct' and long-established discursive practices. It made a public appearance in the 2001 parliamentary election campaign in the UK when Hague (paralleling, no doubt unintentionally, Gramsci) proposed an opposition between 'political correctness' and commonsense. This opposition was woven into a populist discourse.

Individualism

Dworkin's approach to law is to 'take rights seriously'. As already pointed out, the flaw appears in situations where rights seem to require curtailment or are incompatible with one another. Here, it is worth exploring the connection between rights-based law and individualism. Bear in mind Isaiah Berlin's well-known distinction between positive and negative liberty. Rights resemble negative liberty, that is freedom from interference by others in one's actions and choices. So legal rights are observed as obligations on others to refrain from encroachment on one's liberty. The 'others' include collectivities and particularly the state. For example, the constitutional *right* to 'due process' is constructed out of the *obligation* on states under the Fourteenth Amendment not to 'deprive any person of life, liberty or property, without due process of law'. If an *entitlement* can be distinguished from a *right* by a requirement for a *positive* form of action on the part of another or others, then, outside of contract and apart from the obligation undertaken by the state to provide social security (and measures aimed at positive discrimination in the United States), one has to look to Continental systems for the enshrinement in law of obligations of such a nature as to represent the counterpart of someone else's entitlement vis-à-vis another adult person. There, non-assistance to a person in danger is a breach of the criminal law. Reflecting a similar sense of community, the scope of the criminal responsibility of political executives in France for mishaps within their jurisdiction is amazingly far-reaching as compared with administrative responsibility flowing from the British law of negligence. Resistance to the extension in the same direction of British negligence law finds expression in the judges' recoil from 'the nursemaid school of negligence', which would extend liability into the grey area between reasonable care and responsibility.

The same individualistic tendency, leaning on the pejorative sense of the same metaphor, appears in the reaction against the 'nanny-state'. Dowrkin expresses it more positively in the notion of the 'liberty interest' to make one's 'own decisions about matters' involving intimate and personal choices. Each of these might be recruited, for example, to support an argument against seatbelt legislation. Similarly, the 'whose life is it anyway' position can be advanced in order to claim moral and legal legitimacy for *suicide* in any, or at least in narrowly restricted, circumstances. In all of those instances, the individual's right or liberty cannot be promoted without balancing it against the impact or repercussions that its exercise would have on others.

Euthanasia

The thrust of Dworkin's intervention in a recent euthanasia case in the Supreme Court demonstrates the sort of twist which, I believe, tends to be imparted to legal analysis by the individualist focus of the rights-based approach. In addition, the problems associated with his approach to the application of the law by way of constructive, constitutional interpretation are encountered.

Euthanasia, according to its etymology, means a good or easy death, translated by its proponents into a death with dignity. Analysis reveals distinct uses of the concept: death resulting from the withdrawal of life-preserving medical equipment from a person whose life is dependent on it (situation 1); death resulting from the administration of pain-relieving drugs to terminally ill patients even though this will bring about certain, or almost certain, death (situation 2); and medically-assisted suicide (situation 3). It is situation 3 that raises a sharp issue. Medically-assisted suicide takes two forms: the provision of a lethal prescription to patients requesting it or the injection of lethal drugs by the doctor or under his instructions. Lethal injection would count as assisted suicide and be differentiated from situation 2 by being *aimed* at death and initiated by a demand to that effect from the patient. Of the three situations, it is physician-assisted suicide (situation 3) whose legitimacy is now at the centre of the euthanasia debate.

The Supreme Court in 1997 refused to recognise a constitutional right to medically-assisted suicide even in the case of a patient who is terminally ill and experiencing great suffering or is condemned to a life he regards as intolerable. Dworkin, along with five other distinguished moral and political philosophers, had submitted an *amicus curiae* brief to the Court urging it to 'recognise a limited constitutional right of terminally ill and competent patients to the help of a doctor in ending their life, in order to avoid further pointless suffering and anguish', a right which would be limited by appropriate safeguards.[15] In support, Dworkin mobilised the same broad principle as referred to above in the context of the abortion debate. People had a (constitutionally protected) *liberty interest* 'to make their own decisions about matters "involving the most intimate and personal choices a person may make in a lifetime, choices central to personal dignity and autonomy"'. In the aftermath of the case, Dworkin argued in a careful analysis of the judges' opinions that, because of the parameters of the issue in the form in which it was laid before the court, the unanimous decision not to recognise the right masked a reservation on the part of five of the judges that they did not reject medically-assisted suicide 'in principle'. But when the opinions are examined from a less committed viewpoint, it looks as if the reservation attached to the administration of analgesia even in cases where death would be the foreseeable outcome (situation 2) rather than to medically-assisted suicide (situation 3).

In the jurisprudence on this side of the Atlantic, however, it is the corresponding duty or freedom of the other party to the relationship (in this case, the physician) to render *assistance* which is in question. Should the medical attendant have a professional duty (subject to an opt-out on conscientious grounds) or at least be free to assist in the termination of his patient's life in response to the patient's request but only in certain defined circumstances and subject to certain safeguards? That would require in the first place a revolution in medical ethics to extend the concept of treatment from the prevention and cure of illness and the alleviation of pain to include active participation in the termination of the patient's life. The attitudinal changes that would ensue to the doctor–patient relationship should not be underestimated if the doctor is transformed from a carer into an executioner. Next, physician assistance to suicide would have to be decriminalised. Doctors would have the freedom under the law to provide pills or administer injections *aimed* at the patient's death. This would be both a licence to kill, on the one hand, and at the same time a responsibility to make the complex judgements concerning mental competence, authenticity and strength of the indications of consent, absence of moral coercion and so on (judgements which a court is fitted to make) as well as a crucial prognosis. Viewed from the doctor's side, the change would be tantamount to the recognition of, not a right, but an *entitlement* of the patient, to treatment aimed at death.[16]

CONSTRUCTIVE INTERPRETATION

Dworkin casts an incidental glance at these aspects in recognising that the right is only a right to the help of a 'willing doctor'. His argument is that the right of the patients is *against the state*, that it 'not forbid doctors to assist in their deaths'. He therefore separates the two sets of adversarial interests: one, the patient's 'liberty interest' in having the doctor's help in hastening death versus the legitimacy of the burden that would consequently be imposed on the doctor; two, the patient's liberty interest versus the state's interest in preserving life. It is the assertion of the patient's liberty in the form of his request for euthanasia, underwritten by the constitutional 'due process' provision which, for Dworkin, ought, in given circumstances and subject to given criteria, to prevail against state laws protecting life.

Consent

So Dworkin virtually ignores conflict one between the patient's right and the ethical burden on the medical profession. While focusing instead on conflict two, he invokes the Constitution to set aside the state's interest in protecting life. This approach represents, it seems to me, a clear example of the individualist bias of rights-based law. And again, the brief by the self-styled 'moral and political philosophers' presents itself unsurprisingly in philosophical language appropriate to rights-based law. But once euthanasia is legalised, as it has just been in the Netherlands, legal language takes over, as demonstrated below. For a contrast with Dworkin's argument for euthanasia, we have the following House of Lords appeal.[17]

CASE STUDY

The issue was whether consensual sadomasochistic practices occasioning actual bodily harm to the parties fell foul of the criminal law or not. Was *consent* an effective defence in that the assaults had been carried out on willing victims?

The judges pointed to the parallel with the situation in assisted suicide. Suicide had been decriminalised but, they said bluntly, 'a person who assisted another to commit suicide was guilty of murder or manslaughter.'

On a preliminary point, the judges considered that the

supposed consents in the case of some of the participants were dubious or worthless. This reminds us aptly of the difficulty that would attach to the interpretation of the meaning and meaningfulness of the expression of the request for death uttered by persons in situations of extreme suffering in the case of assisted suicide.

Even had there been no doubt about consent, however, a majority (three to two) of the judges held that consensual sado-masochistic practices were unlawful if actual bodily harm was inflicted. An argument based on the right to private life protected by the European Convention on Human Rights (now incorporated into UK law) was rejected. Against the individualism of rights-based law, one of the judges took the view that '[s]ociety was entitled and bound to protect itself against a cult of violence'.

Once resort to the right to private life was rejected, it followed that, as another of the judges said, 'it was for Parliament with its accumulated wisdom and sources of information to declare [such practices] lawful' and not injurious to the public interest. This is directly opposite to Dworkin's assessment in which rights are trumps. I will return to that in order to round off the examination of Dworkin's legal philosophy, but in the meantime, as regards euthanasia, things have moved on.

Dutch courage?

In April 2001 the Dutch upper house approved a bill to legalise euthanasia. The devil, though, is, as always in the law, in the detail. The bill focuses on the circumstances of the doctor's role rather than on the patient's right to control the timing and manner of his death. Its purpose, as stated in the preamble, is to grant 'immunity to a physician who, acting in accordance with the statutory due care criteria laid down in [the] Act, terminates life on request or provides assistance with suicide'. Therefore, a *willing* doctor who participates in the patient's death is protected provided that he complies with the 'due care criteria'. The particular criterion that I want to pick out is in 2.1.b, which provides that 'the attending physician must be satisfied that the patient's suffering was unbearable, and that there was no prospect of improvement'. Now this introduces a strictly *objective* standard, independent of both the patient's wishes or fortitude and the doctor's sensibilities.[18]

The effect is to place a double lock on legitimate intervention by the doctor to terminate life or assist in suicide: one, the patient must make 'a voluntary and carefully considered request'; two, the patient must be *in extremis*, defined as above. It is generally recognised that the patient *in extremis* is entitled to palliative treatment or intervention to ease his suffering even though there is a high risk or near-certainty that death will eventuate. The effect of the statutory double lock could well be an increased reluctance to use 'risky pain-relief' techniques without complying with the formalities imposed by the Act. On the other side, there is little movement towards the position where the request by the patient would be paramount if, for example, he believed his life to be worthless or otherwise intolerable.[19] The motivation behind the imposition of the statutory double lock arises, I think, from confusion on the moral issue. This is not whether a person has the *right* to manage the timing and manner of his own death but whether he is *entitled* to call on another person to involve himself in it. Even Dr Kevorkian, the pathologist known as Dr Death for his widespread practice of euthanasia in the US and now in prison following conviction in an exemplary case, claims that it is the intention to ease suffering which justifies euthanasia. He does this in a comparison with the intent behind the near-public Federal execution of McVeigh, the Oklahoma bomber. He said:

> A physician's *only* aim is to end the subject's suffering (positive result) which unfortunately entails death (negative result) ... The executioner's *only* aim is the subject's death (totally negative).[20]

My contention is that Kevorkian's assessment of the physician's intent applies exactly to the administration of risky palliative relief while that of the executioner fits the administration of euthanasia as Kevorkian understands it.

Political law

Apart from the moral issue of whether euthanasia is justifiable and, if so, what principles should govern its scope, the more general question is whether judges do or should have the power and responsibility to decide them when they enter the legal arena. As we saw in the sadomasochistic case in UK, the court's stance was that the 'liberty interest' to inflict bodily harm in pursuit of sexual pleasure on a willing victim was a matter for Parliament to decide. In contrast,

Dworkin bases the patient's right to euthanasia on constitutional principle. Since such principles are general and abstract, they require interpretation when applied by the judges in individual cases. By means of interpretation, the US constitutional courts produce superordinate law capable of striking down enacted legislation. Not only do judges then take political decisions but these decisions tend to form constellations of a particular political or ideological character.

This characterisation in turn depends on whether a 'historicist' or an 'interpretativist' approach is taken to the reading of the abstract constitutional clauses. For example, the 'due process' clause is generally understood to protect those liberties that are 'deeply rooted in [America's] history and tradition'. On the face of it, this deeply conservative formula appears to express a pure 'historicist' approach and to work to make legal change the prisoner of history. For a right to be applied it would require to have already been recognised as derived from the Constitution. But against that, the interpretativist approach decrees that what is unearthed from tradition are not rights as such but the 'basic values' which they reflect. Basic values express themselves in 'general principles of political morality'. The problem is that there is no order of values and, therefore, no hierarchy for the principles which they generate. So, when principles collide in actual cases, judges who incline towards the interpretativist tendency come to make political choices. The following case illustrates how a clash of principle might be approached in an UK context.[21]

CASE STUDY

The issue was whether a press report of a trial should be postponed until after a second related trial had been concluded. There is a public interest in the reporting of proceedings in court. There is also a public interest in the avoidance of any risk of prejudice to the administration of justice. In this case these interests clashed. The judges proposed a three-stage test for the resolution of the conflict, of which the third is germane to our discussion. The first question was whether reporting would give rise to a substantial risk of prejudice. If so, the second question arose; whether a ban would eliminate the risk and, even if that were the case, whether a less restrictive measure might achieve the same purpose.

If the conclusion was that there was indeed no other way of eliminating the perceived risk of prejudice, the third question remained:

> whether the degree of risk contemplated should be regarded as tolerable in the sense of being the lesser of two evils. It was at that stage that value judgements might have to be made as to the priority between competing public interests.

It is instructive in the light of that formulation to return to the area of competition between the freedom of expression on the one side and 'fighting talk' and 'hate speech' on the other. Dworkin was disinclined to regard these as exceptions or limitations on the right of free speech. Instead they presented a context within which two basic rights opposed each other. With fighting talk, freedom of speech must defer to the competing right to physical security which was 'more centrally at stake'. In the other example, hate speech, the introduction of a higher level of principle, namely that a good society was one in which great scope was allowed for individual moral responsibility, won the day for the liberty interest in even 'loathsome' speech.

Why is Dworkin averse to the idea that principles should be limited by exceptions that are spelled out in relation to particular factual configurations? His reluctance flows, I think, from his focus on the great constitutional issues of the day, issues of life, death, equality, joined to his essentially *philosphical* approach which he has identified in his recent work as the moral reading of the Constitution. At an earlier stage, I suggested a connection with fundamentalism. More accurately, in operation, it works as a counter-fundamentalism. Whereas religious fundamentalism produces laws and codes of behaviour containing prohibitions and obligations which deprive individuals of moral autonomy, the product of Dworkin's counter-fundamentalism is a set of rights designed to free the individual to be morally responsible. Nonetheless, Dworkin's doctrine shares certain key features of fundamentalism. One is the never-severed umbilical cord stretching back to the written text. The brahminical caste having sole authority to interpret the text is another. A third is the menu of principles or rules, independent of context, resistant to factual configurations, which brook no exceptions.

Not only does the third question in the last case study demonstrate, in line with Dworkin's position, that a judgement, based otherwise than on the interpretation of constitutional words, is necessary to resolve a competition between principles or interests, but it also gives a clue as to why this is so. For the article of the European Convention on Human Rights which declares the right to freedom of expression is itself (as are other Convention rights) made subject to express limitations, *viz*:

> 10.2 The exercise of … [freedom of expression], since it carries with it duties and responsibilities, may be subject to such formalities, conditions, restrictions or penalties as are prescribed by law and are necessary in a democratic society

Because the exception evokes principles that are themselves highly abstract, it does not serve in itself to lighten the task of adjudication between competing public interests. This is an inescapable problem with rights-based law. Still, as I argue in the last chapter, legal language, replacing philosophical language, can offer solutions in the process of adjudication; that is, of the application of the law in an adversarial context.

Habermas

Habermas in *Between Facts and Norms* devotes a generous amount of space to Dworkin's theory. It commends itself to him primarily because of its emphasis on *principle* as the foundation of juridical interpretation. That provides an avenue whereby a legal norm can escape its context-dependence. To locate law, at least at one level, on a system of principles avoids the weaknesses underlying positivist and realist theories of law, as well as the artificialities of textual exegesis, referred to by Dworkin as that 'arcane and conceptual craft'. But, in moving away from the domination, and at the same time from the support, of the authoritative command as the sole legitimising source of law, Dworkin places great power in the hands, and a heavy burden on the shoulders, of the judges who apply it. This picture of the judges' constitutional role leaves the legal system vulnerable to the criticism that law is made and (against the will of democratically elected and accountable law-makers) unmade by judges who are themselves unelected and unaccountable.

On the other side of the argument, Dworkin brings up the domination of the majority in decision-making. In the absence of the interpretive role of the constitutional judges, the best that can be looked for from democratic institutions is that the laws enacted are 'those, in the end, that the majority of citizens would approve ... if properly informed and given enough time for reflection'.[22] Instead, Habermas's position is that at the post-traditional level of justification only those laws count as legitimate that emerge from the discursive opinion- and will-formation of equally enfranchised citizens'.[23] 'Post-traditional' because traditionally, Habermas says, laws are justified by the authority conferred by their source in kingly, priestly or charismatic power. Here, Habermas begins to diverge markedly from Dworkin's theory. Legitimate law must be such that it is *capable* of *universal* acceptance within the jurisdiction. Thus, law imposed by a majority on a minority would not pass Habermas's test. Dworkin entrusts to the 'moral reading' of the Constitution by the judges the application of those principles aimed at all-round equality of treatment and respect that serve to counter majority domination. But that has the effect of decoupling the citizens from active engagement in the process of interpretation that is necessary to articulate the content of their basic rights. Insofar as the judge can be said at all to be a representative of the people, it would be as their stand-in in the interpretative process. His fidelity to the role depends on the quality of 'integrity' as elaborated by Dworkin. According to Habermas, however, the judge acts for the community in relation to law conceived as a medium that sustains the 'self-understanding' of the legal community as a whole.[24] It is this conception of the law which binds the judges to the people.

Dworkin is a jurist. For him, Judge Hercules, as suggested by his pseudonym, is marked off as a hero with privileged access to the commands of the gods through the interpretation of the Constitution. In dispensing the law, he is also its sole depository, carrying in his head, so to speak, all the laws ever written and decisions ever pronounced. As so depicted, the problem for him and for Dworkin's theory is that he is a 'loner'. But if law is to be justified, it cannot, says Habermas, be anchored in a 'monologically conducted theory construction,' 'monological' being here the critical term.[25] Set against it in his theory is the key term, 'intersubjective'. This is in line with expectations since Habermas is a social theorist, not a jurist. He has already pointed out elsewhere that modernity has ousted 'the traditional notion of the solitary subject that confronts objects and becomes reflective only by turning itself into an object. In its place [is] put an idea of cognition that is mediated by language and linked to action. Moreover, ... the web of everyday life and communication surrounding 'cognitive' achievements [is emphasised]. The latter are intrinsically intersubjective and co-operative.'[26]

It follows that the interpretative process, if it is to validate law in the sense used here and adopted from Habermas, must reach beyond the immediate judicial tradition to the lifeworld engagement of citizens. The 'lifeworld' is depicted as an 'unshakeable rock of assumptions, loyalties and skills', so occupying the fields of knowledge, morality and practice. The so-called 'objectivity' of the judge–interpreter, founded on the requirement or practice of justifying decisions by reasons, reflects in reality the intersubjectivity of the citizens constituted as a community of interpreters. It is the reference, for the justification of laws and their application, to communicative action taking place against the background of the lifeworld which forms the root of the discourse theory of law developed by Habermas. 'The lifeworld forms both the horizon for speech situations and the source of interpretations, while it in turn reproduces itself only through ongoing communicative action'.[27] He deviates from Dworkin's emphasis on society as a mass of disparate individuals identified by their disaggregation from the collective. From the same starting-point in the recognition of liberty of speech, he finds its ultimate justification in what Dworkin played down as the 'instrumental' argument that free speech was needed to create a marketplace of ideas. The business of the state was not principally to ringfence a private domain but to underwrite the public realm.

> The state's *'raison d'être'* does not lie primarily in the protection of equal private rights but in the guarantee of an inclusive opinion- and will-formation in which free and equal citizens reach an understanding on which goals and norms lie in the equal interest of all.[28]

Thus, for Habermas, law is legitimate to the extent that it achieves some kind of match with the understandings as to goals and norms reached in the public sphere by way of communicative action. In this way the presumption that everyone knows the law will be justified. In addition, Habermas provides, as will emerge later in this chapter, the link between legal language and the ordinary medium of communicative action that satisfies the hypothesis with which this book began, that the language of the law plays an essential part in the process.

Social integration

The mutual understanding brought about by communicative action provides a basis for the co-ordination of actions. So communicative action or discourse is a major mechanism of social integration. Communicative action is assumed to be rational. Any speech-act makes one or another of three claims to be justified: a claim to propositional truth; a claim to normative rightness; a claim to personal sincerity. These claims, implicitly advanced, open up statements to criticism. They require, therefore, the back-up of reasons. It is this interplay between criticism and reasoned justification which offers the possibility of the rationality of communicative action. The goal of mutual understanding is presupposed by the communicative act and its achievement is accompanied psychologically by conviction. So if the criticism necessary for the rationality of communicative action is muted or altogether silenced by personal domination or coercion, the goal of mutual understanding is blocked. Habermas's theory substitutes that goal, represented by *conviction*, for *persuasion* in theories of rhetoric, as the aim of discourse. Although persuasion in common with conviction is incompatible with means such as bribery, threats and force, Habermas makes a clear distinction between the two, based on the claim to sincerity: one cannot make the statement 'by telling lies, I *convinced* him'.

Mutual understanding would be unachievable without the shared background of the lifeworld. We live and speak within the horizon of the lifeworld from which we derive interpretations and which in turn reproduces itself in communicative action. The status of the lifeworld is that it is certain, unproblematic. The epistemic advantage of assumed certainty has as its counterpart a deficiency, the absence of awareness of falsifiability. When reproduced in communicative action, the lifeworld does not become the subject of a criticisable validity claim. The constitutive characteristic of the lifeworld is that it *is* background. If called in question it 'disintegrates'. Within the legal system, the lifeworld is 'within judicial knowledge'; no proof is required.

Systems integration

But *social* integration, as so depicted by Habermas, is not the sole mode of organisation. He also invokes the schematisation of society developed by systems theory. The economic system, political system and the legal system are exemplary. The co-ordination effected by systems is, essentially, neither planned nor intended by the participants. It works 'behind their backs', says Habermas, alluding to Adam Smith's 'invisible hand'. Interactions between strangers are mediated by the particular system in which they are operatives and not by values, norms and mutual understanding, as is the case with the face-to-face encounters of social intercourse. Each system is 'autonomous', having all the other systems as its 'environment'.[29] This autonomy is intimately connected with the development and maintenance by each system of its own code. Each is 'encapsulated in its own semantics,' unable to communicate with, but only to observe, other systems.

Using these concepts, Habermas provides a working drawing of society in which law has a mediating function. Language, as the medium of communicative action by means of which action can be co-ordinated on the basis of mutual understanding, is placed in the forefront.

Systems closure

The legal system is attacked on the ground of its closure. What is meant is closure not only within its special language but also against other forms of knowledge. Systems theory, however, underwrites the suggestion that closure is no more characteristic of the legal system than of any other system. Indeed, it is the price to be paid for systematisation. But the argument remains that closure matters in the case of the legal system, whereas it does not or at least it matters much less so in the case of the others. With the economic system, for example, the fitness of its organisation and its operational success are, arguably, to be measured by its efficiency in the production and distribution of goods. Given a successful economy, it would not matter (much) that, as a result of its systematisation, it was closed off from, and could not (because of its and their special codes) intercommunicate with, the other systems. Nor would it matter, either, for the legal system, if that were to be regarded purely as a machine for the avoidance (by means of agreements with performative effect prepared by lawyers) and resolution of disputes. The use of a special language (code) would be pragmatically justified insofar as it conduced to the effective working of the machine. Legal judgements would then be reached and justified in accordance with the deductive–subsumptive theory. A decision would be right if it were demonstrated by the judge to be arrived at by a process of *deduction* leading from a general principle or rule of law to the salient circumstances of the case (decoding), or, conversely, if the particular circumstances could be *subsumed* within a legal principle or rule (encoding). Law would then achieve the certainty which, in a sense, it implicitly claims and to which, in another sense, it aspires. But the legal system would fail to fulfil its function in society if it truly conformed to the mechanistic model.

The process of social integration makes two demands. On the one hand, discourse aimed at reaching understanding based on the advancement of reasons must be curtailed, so that consensual opinion can be more readily arrived at and expectations of the behaviour of others more confidently formed. Otherwise, discussion will be endless and the risk of dissension unlimited. The answer which emerges to this requirement for curtailment is enacted law. As well as enacted law, the legal system adopts customs and traditions, patterns of ethical life followed from 'time immemorial', giving them binding force. Law underwritten by the threat of coercion shapes expectations of the way in which others will behave. This limits the need to convince others by discourse. The expectation of compliance with the law takes over the burden otherwise borne by communicative action. Within its territorial jurisdiction, man-made law has the same quality of universality as sacred precepts and the dictates of spell-binding authority. Against these others, on the other hand, law is understood as being open to change. What gives rise to and underpins this understanding is the implicit claim of law to validity. The facticity of a legal rule or principle, that is, the fact that it is the law, stems from its authoritative source. But its claim to validity depends upon the presumed 'acceptability of the reasons supporting its claim to legitimacy'. The rational acceptability of enacted law:

> takes into account the unleashing of communication, that removal of restrictions that in principle exposes all norms and values to critical testing. Members of a legal community must be able to assume that in a free process of political opinion- and will-formation they themselves would also authorise the rules to which they are subject as addressees.[30]

Thus, law lightens the burden of social integration carried by communicative action, while at the same time freedom of discourse assumes its revisability, its constant openness to change.

The role of law is to act like a 'transmission belt' between the lifeworld and the systems by establishing the procedures and a medium by means of which 'structures of mutual recognition are picked up from the lifeworld and transmitted to the systems'. The systems operate within forms provided by the law.

These structures of mutual recognition are symbolically represented in language. According to theory, however, as already mentioned, each system is 'encapsulated in its own semantics'. Their specialised codes present a version or picture of society as a whole which is particular to it (each system); that is, one not shared by other systems. The power of ordinary language, Habermas argues, resides exactly in its lack of such specialisation. Law (social integration), in common with certain other functionally specialised systems, such as education (cultural reproduction) family (socialisation), also utilises the shared code of ordinary language. These are systems which touch on the totality of the lifeworld. It is significant from this point of view, while symbolising denial of the charge of closure laid against the legal system, that 'nothing human is alien' was adopted as the motto of the Law Society of Scotland. Finally, on lawyer's language:

> The language of law brings ordinary communication from the public and private spheres and puts it into a form in which these messages can also be received by the special codes of ... systems – and *vice versa*. Without this transformer, ordinary language could not circulate throughout society.[31]

We should not leave the grand mansion of Habermas's theory without crediting him with the insight, as a footnote to the previous discussion on hate speech that 'in complex societies law is the only medium in which it is possible reliably to establish morally obligated relationships of respect even among strangers'.

5
CONCLUSIONS

At the outset of the concluding chapter, it is fair to bring out again that the venture initially undertaken by this study, as laid down in chapter 1, was to justify the use by lawyers of a distinctive language in the formulation and practice of the law. By the end of the previous chapter, I had enlisted for the defence the heavyweight support of Habermas's grand project, the construction of a theory of law on the foundation of his notion of communicative action. Legal language functioned, he said, like a two-way transformer between ordinary language and the special language codes of the economic system and other specialised systems. So he forged the link, on which social integration depended, between those texts recognised as laws and the networks of speech-acts in which society ordinarily engages. Beyond the metaphor of the transformer, however, he tells us nothing of the special characteristics of the language of the law nor of the nature of the transformation undergone by ordinary language to produce it. Since Habermas's theory, as he recognises, is proceduralist, absences of this sort, that is of description and analysis of substance and content, are appropriate. But, of course, it is a vital task for a book such as this on lawyers' language, to present those matters concerning legal language, which Habermas can legitimately omit, and so carry on the discussion for some distance from where that magisterial work leaves off. This chapter undertakes that task in exploring in what ways lawyers' language is distinctive as well as the nature of its nexus with ordinary language. At the same time, it rounds off the book by drawing together various concepts, such as representation, concept itself, rights-based law and so on, introduced during the excursions of the previous chapters.

CONCLUSIONS

'Illegitimate' law

The first chapter explained why the link with ordinary language is fundamental. That explanation started from the inadequacy of the positivist view that what counts as law is a question of fact, to be tested by whether a particular text has passed through certain parliamentary procedures or more generally has issued from the edict of a sovereign power. The rule of law is one of the pillars of democracy. This must refer to more than the ideal that the laws should be universally applicable, the principle that no one is above the law. If we were all *without exception* subject to an unfair, unjust and unreasonable regime, that principle would still be satisfied. Despite being obliged because of his origins to flee from the Nazi terror, Hans Kelsen, founder at the beginning of the twentieth century of the positivist school of Vienna, believed himself forced by the logic of his own doctrine to grasp that very nettle:

> From the point of view of juridical science, the law under the Nazi regime was the law. We can regret it but we cannot deny it was the law.

But such a theoretical stance does not account for the general sense that law *should*, rather than *must*, be obeyed; nor indeed that if a particular law is 'illegitimate' or 'invalid' or cannot be justified by reasons, it may therefore be demonstrated against, challenged or defied. Even though we may not accept them, the arguments of extremist environmentalists or animal rights campaigners in support of their breaches of the law make sense. At the other end of the scale, we appreciate the nature of the further step that is taken if someone passes on to tax evasion, which (we feel, rightly) infringes the criminal law, from tax avoidance, which does not. Tax avoidance exploits the legal principle that every citizen has the right so to conduct his affairs as to minimise his liability for tax. It is pursued through schemes designed to exploit loopholes in tax laws. The notion of a 'loophole' is interesting from the point of view of discursive analysis for it exists only in the space between interpretation (more properly, application) and law-maker's intention. The analysis has be pursued further by invoking Dworkin's distinction between semantic intention; that is, what the law-maker intended to say given the words he actually used on the one hand and, on the other hand, what he hoped to achieve by saying what he did. But, as we saw in chapter 3, writer's intention falls to be assessed by textual intent. So tax avoidance remains a matter of personal morality, which, arguably, should be (but is apparently not) a problem of ethics for the professional makers of tortuous avoidance schemes.

'Reasonable' law

From the side of the law, a legal decision is judged to be invalid if not supported with reasons. This principle was underlined in the two marginal cases below.

CASE STUDIES

(1) The Criminal Injuries Compensation Board had refused to exercise its discretion to waive the time-limit for a particular claim.[1] The question in the appeal was whether the Board was under a duty to give reasons for its decision. Its functions could be classified as administrative or quasi-judicial. The judge decided that the particular function to which the discretion was attached fell into the quasi-judicial category.

That being so, the Board became subject to the duty, 'as a matter of fairness and natural justice' to state reasons for its decision. It had to establish that it had applied proper criteria in its judgement not to exercise its discretion. The judge equated the circumstances here with those in a case where there was an express statutory obligation to give reasons but the reasons actually given were unintelligible. He cited the judge's observations in the latter case:

> If the reasons are so stated as to be unintelligible, the parties cannot tell whether the decision has been reached according to law. The evils are the same as if no reasons have been given when the statute requires that they should be given, and the defect in the expression of the reasons is as much an error of law as would be a failure to give them.

(2) In the second case, an appeal court ordered a re-hearing in the absence of any statement of the reasons for a magistrate's decision.[2] Even though magistrates were not required to state reasons when refusing an application to vary a maintenance order, any appeal from their decision could only be determined

by reference to the reasoning behind the decision. In the absence of reasons, the case had to be re-heard.

'Understanding' the law and the reasons

Besides or indeed rather than the appeal court, everyone within the jurisdiction of judicial decision-making bodies makes up the audience to whom the reasons are addressed. Perhaps the right way to portray the relationship is that the appeal court receives the decision and the statement of the reasoning of the lower-tier body as a representative of the people. The emphasis on reasons assumes that the commonsense of the people as addressees, direct or indirect, not only demands reasons but also provides the capacity to *understand* the reasoning. 'Commonsense' here is nothing other than the shared sense of 'fairness and natural justice' which, according to the judge in the first case, called for reasons to be stated. 'Understand' corresponds to something less than the meaning of 'persuasion' in the theory of classical rhetoric or 'accession' in New Rhetoric or 'agreement' in the case of a subject confronted by political or religious coercion. And to something more than 'comprehend' as well. When Habermas says that 'addressees of legal norms must understand themselves as their rational authors,'[3] he has the same conception of 'understanding' in mind. A similar sense is encapsulated in the legal term 'consensus ad idem', which describes the intersubjective meeting of minds constituting the basic condition of a legal contract.

Comprehension, however, although insufficient in itself, seems to be a necessary step on the way to the 'consensus' in question. Once that point is accepted, the language *problem* asserts itself. Because of the barrier thrown up by the special features of legal language, the legal text, including the 'reasons', are open to condemnation as incomprehensible by the citizens. Not only that, but their sense of 'natural justice' conveys to them that *they* are intended to be at least the real addressees of the law, even if they do not perceive themselves as its 'rational authors'. It was to the children of Israel that Moses, their representative, presented the tablets of the law. The sense of violation, of usurpation, is aggravated by the frustration that the language of the legal text is irritatingly just out of reach. Another stratum, a cognitive overburden, has been superimposed. The question then emerges in its sharpest form: how can the people understand themselves as the rational authors of the law when they cannot understand the legal text?

Conclusions

Application

From this point of view alone, that is, in not directly addressing this irksome question, Habermas's work does not live up to the promise of its subtitle: *contributions to a discourse theory of law and democracy*. Although, of course, as brought out in the Introduction, 'discourse' for Habermas is a term of sociological or sociopsychological import, equivalent to communicative action, and does not have the close linguistic connection that it has with Foucault. Dworkin's compendium of his work subtitled: *the moral reading of the American constitution* similarly stops short. Certainly its approach to law is hermeneutic. It lays down a theory of interpretation and elaborates on how the theory works in practice. This ought to throw light on the quest to discover the nature and operation of the distinctive features of the language of legal texts. But, as already pointed out, Dworkin's 'discourse' (in Foucault's sense) does not display the characteristics of legal language. Dworkin's customary language draws on what is recognisably a philosophical discourse. Moreover, it fits not only his approach based on the moral reading, but also the task he sets himself to take rights seriously. This is none other than to articulate the law in terms of rights grounded on moral principles drawn in turn from the words of the Constitution. The legal system, in the sense of the body of laws, materialises rather around more complex constellations of facts. Dworkin comes close to endorsing a description of those adjudications, inevitably the majority, in which the moral reading has no place, as 'technical exercises in an arcane and conceptual craft'.[4] Thus, his theory divides off constitutional issues from other legal issues. Hence, his focus on rights modelled on areas of individual freedom, hence also his promotion of moral over conceptual arguments,[5] while at the same time he appears to nod, to slur over the distinction, when justifying the use of philosophical discourse in legal writing:

> [The] proper business [of legal doctrine] forces it to use the concepts of will, intention, meaning, responsibility, justice, and other ideas that are frequent sources of philosophical complexity and confusion.[6]

So we find that Dworkin draws on philosophical rather than legal discourse. As a direct effect, he misses the distinction between an argument which justifies the validity of the legal norm and one which validates its application in a particular case. This, in turn, is responsible, I think, for the argument in his recent collection that the moral reading, otherwise his special hermeneutic approach, that is, *interpretation* rather than *application*, is the key that unlocks the right answer in adjudication. We saw before that this deprives him of armament to cope with cases where rights or principles collide. Judges are directed 'to find the *best* (my italics) conception of constitutional moral principles ... that fits the broad story of America's historical record'.[7] Later in this chapter, alternative criteria are proposed which have the advantage over Dworkin's formula that they fit an application argument instead of an argument in justification of a norm.

The next step, however, is to explore what Habermas, following Gunther, derives from the shift of emphasis to application. Legal norms consist of principles and rules. The distinguishing feature of rules – for example, 'The park will close between June and September at 8.00pm each day' – is that they specify the conditions and situations in which they apply. Principles are, on the other hand, indeterminate in reference to their application conditions. A legal norm in the form of a principle presents itself as *prima facie* valid but does not by itself determine whether it is the applicable norm in the particular case. So *prima facie* applicable principles can collide and one of them be discarded as *inappropriate* without loss of its *validity*. For example, confidentiality is a norm in legal professional ethics. Where a client confesses to his lawyer that he has just run over a person who may be bleeding to death nearby, the lawyer's moral obligation to save life will override the ethical principle of confidentiality. The latter's validity remains unimpaired.

Discourses of application involve two processes. Habermas explains:

> Because each norm selects only specific features of an individual case situated in the lifeworld, the application discourse must determine which descriptions of the facts are significant and exhaustive for interpreting the situation in a disputed case; it must also determine which of the prima facie valid norms is the appropriate one once all the significant features of the situation have been apprehended as fully as possible.[8]

Here it should be pointed out that, according to this description, it is the facts which undergo interpretation, not the norm, not the law.

CASE STUDY

The application discourse can be studied in the following case.[9] A 90-year old motorist who had killed two people pled guilty to a charge of causing death by dangerous driving. After 73 years of driving he had a hitherto unblemished record. The judge thought that his poor eyesight might have been the cause of the accident. According to the methodological model just described, the issue in the case would be whether the legal norm which declares the criminality of dangerous driving was *appropriate* to the circumstances. Did the circumstances constitute a 'concretisation' of the norm? At the factual level, as the judge said, those circumstances which usually underlie charges of dangerous driving, such as recklessness, speed or taking a risk, were not involved. Instead, the relevant interpretation of the situation here was that it was a case of driving when impaired by age. Had the 'impairment' been due to sudden cardiovascular deterioration which the aged driver had no reason to anticipate or to an unexpected side effect of medication of which he had not been warned, the dangerous driving norm would not have been appropriate. By contrast, in an earlier case, where a diabetic driver, who was aware that there was a real risk that he would have a sudden hypoglycaemic attack, suffered such an attack when driving and killed the driver of an oncoming vehicle, this was held to be a case of dangerous driving.[10] Where the facts are disputed, the judge's task is to find them by an interpretation of a complex lifeworld situation. That is the nature of the process whereby a state of affairs is transformed into the facts to which the law is applied. At the same time, additional specification is provided to the application conditions of the dangerous driving norm, over and above those of recklessness, speed and risk-taking, without exhausting its semantic content.

But we do not yet have a complete understanding of the basic problem of the relationship of the law and the facts. The process of selection from the situation (including its relevant context), and the like process applied to the semantic content of the *prima facie* applicable norm, aim to produce a *match* to be recognised in the judgement as a *case* of the legal principle or rule. But the facts must not be twisted to fit the rule nor the meaning of the rule perverted to match the facts. One way of describing it is that the facts must meet the criterion of relevance and the rule must express the appropriate norm. But the problem lies exactly with the chicken-and-egg interdependence of relevance and appropriateness. Not all the features of the situation are relevant. Yet the determination of which features are significant depends on the outcome of the competition between the norms which present themselves as applicable. The difficulty is that, in turn, the appropriateness of the norm depends on the features which are included in the description of the situation. Recognition of this interdependence plays an important part in Scottish civil actions which are based on full written pleadings. A plea to the relevancy of an action or of a defence to an action takes the form of an argument that the plea-in-law (the legal rule relied on) is not supported by the condescendences (the statement of the facts deemed to constitute the situation) even if these were assumed to be proven.

Instead of the traditional deductive–subsumptive model, a linguistic description of the relationship is proposed. 'What finally decides the issue,' suggests Habermas, 'is the meaning equivalence between the description of facts making up part of the interpretation of the situation and the description of facts that sets out the descriptive component of the norm, that is, its application, conditions.'[11]

One side of the 'equation', the selected circumstances, will be presented in ordinary language, the other, the articulation of the legal rule, in legal language. Therefore, we are concerned not strictly with an equation but with an equivalence. A statement in legal discourse will correspond in significance with a narrative in ordinary, everyday language. At this point, it is worth revisiting the distinction between rule and principle. A rule, at one extreme, such as the times of closure of the park, is application-specific and does not give rise to cases. But rules in general, although of narrow application, such as 'No loitering' or 'Vehicles are not allowed in the park', may well do so. For example, do roller blades or park maintenance machinery come within the definition of 'vehicles' for the purposes of the latter rule? Now the application-specific rule, which cannot give rise to cases, is expressed in ordinary language. But the language of the others, when they do, takes on the characteristics of legal language. Specifically, a process of *reconceptualisation* takes place.

To return to Habermas's test for 'legitimate' law: judicial decisions should be such that citizens can understand themselves as their 'rational authors'. 'Equivalence of meaning' between the description of the facts and the description of the articulation of the norm turns out to be necessary to satisfy Habermas's test. So to accomplish the task initially set in chapter 1 of this book, to vindicate the distinctive features of legal language in the teeth of persistent and widespread criticism, it must be established that its salient characteristics are well-adapted to produce this equivalence of meaning. For this purpose I propose the following as key features of legal discourse without suggesting that they are either exhaustive or even from some other standpoint the most striking: (1) the reconceptualisation of words taken from ordinary language; (2) a highly intricate grammar; (3) the recourse to words of extreme flexibility of meaning within passages of extreme complexity.

Reconceptualisation

To say that a decision both states what is the law and declares what will be the law, that it acts as a precedent, shows that the meaning of a legal norm is flexible. When a judge points out that his decision is determined solely by the 'facts and circumstances', he is discouraging its citation as a precedent. It is tantamount to saying that nothing is added to the semantic content of the appropriate legal norm in consequence of the *singularity* of the decision. In this way it is different from the ordinary case where the meaning of the norm varies with each situation. Moreover, the system, as a whole, is geared to coherence. The subtle change to the meaning of the appropriate norm by its concretisation in the particularity of the case produces a knock-on effect that reverberates throughout the system. This effect is noticeable in legislation where a statutory amendment to existing law often requires to include a list of consequential deletions, substitutions and additions to associated, already enacted, law.

Concept

The hermeneutic category that operates in this way is the concept. Gadamer reminds us that the formation of concepts is constantly preconditioned by previous language use.[12] Put that together with the idea that the concept is the key to the semantic content of the norm. Then it can be argued that it is the use of concepts in the formulation of legal norms which gives judicial decisions the ability to face both ways: to state the law, drawing on the history of past usages; and to form part of that history within the purview of future issues. A legal concept has its source in a concept of ordinary language. It maintains a link of sorts with its origin, that being part of its history or perhaps prehistory. So changes in the ordinary usage of concepts taken up into legal language will still have an impact on their meaning in legal language. Nonetheless, the demands of coherence exerted by the system of laws operate sometimes as a drag, sometimes as a reinforcement or even accelerator, on the forces for change.

To speak of legal *terminology*, as is commonly done, as the sum total of the reconceptualised words taken from ordinary language, is a misnomer. The nature of concepts differs radically from the terms of terminology. A term has a fixed semantic content. It is intended to mean nothing more than what it denotes. When Gertrude Stein said 'a rose is a rose,' she used 'rose' as a term. 'Superego', 'ego' and 'id' on Freud's map of the psyche are terms just like heart, lungs, brain, on the anatomical map. Words in law which function performatively, such as 'dispone', 'bequeath', 'consent', bringing into effect in the real world the state of affairs which they describe, are properly terms. Typical of the legal text, more a quirk than a characteristic, are the near-synonyms clustering around these performative terms. With these, the legal writer tries perhaps to compensate for the fact that terms have no connotations. Again, unlike concepts, legal terms are distanced from their homonyms in ordinary language. 'Assignment', for example has nothing to do with an appointment.

CASE STUDY

In this study, I provide an example of the process of reconceptualisation through an exploration of the role and dynamic of the legal concept of provocation.

The case of Sarah Thornton was probably the first to highlight publicly the part that might be played by provocation in a charge of murder. In 1990, Thornton was convicted of the murder of her violent, alcoholic husband. In 1996, in response to feminist pressure, the charge was commuted to manslaughter on the ground of provocation. The cumulative effect of violence on battered women giving rise to the killing of their tormentors was recognised.

A preliminary point to make is that this recognition reflects a shift in public sensibility towards women's rights. It was to be viewed not as a licence to females to kill (Thornton's killing of her husband under provocation being still judged to be a serious crime). Rather, the admissibility of such a defence, along with other changes such as the acceptance that a husband can commit the crime of rape when his wife is the victim, and the closely-set limits on the parental right to beat children, mark a radical movement away from the conception of the patriarchal family. Concomitantly with this, perhaps a forerunner of it, was the emergence of a feminist discourse. This shows up vividly against the background of a recent report by the World Organisation against Torture. Battering women is still not considered a crime in some countries, in South Africa, Asia and Latin America, the report said, adding that even in countries where beating women was considered a crime, police often regarded complaints as a private matter.[13]

The defence of provocation has been given a general statutory definition:

> Where on a charge of murder there is evidence on which the jury can find that the person charged was provoked (whether by things done or by things said or by both together) to lose his self-control, the question whether the provocation was enough to make a reasonable man do as he did, shall be left to be determined by the jury; and in determining that question the jury shall take into account everything, both done and said, according to the effect which, in their opinion, it would have on a reasonable man.[14]

As a defence, provocation is sandwiched in between *self-defence* and *diminished responsibility*. Its distinguishing mark is the loss of self-control. Self-defence, on the other hand, assumes that there is no loss of self-control, that the degree of defensive force employed is reasonably proportionate to the threat and that the response is immediate and designed to ward off the danger. These conditions of application of self-defence present their own problems.

A defence of diminished responsibility was admitted as a result of a successful appeal in circumstances where a battered woman had stabbed to death her abusive and alcoholic partner. The mental condition classified as battered woman's syndrome was recognised to be capable of sustaining such a defence.[15] The line of demarcation between provocation and diminished responsibility was drawn by the House of Lords judges sitting as the Privy Council. A defendant's mental infirmity, it was argued, had the effect of reducing his powers of self-control below that to be expected of a reasonable man. But the defence of provocation was rejected. To accept it, the judges argued, would be to incorporate the concept of diminished responsibility indirectly into the law of provocation. If the impairment of self-control was attributable to mental infirmity, this would produce inconsistency with the 'objective test' for provocation based on the power of self-control of the reasonable man.[16]

A fundamental analysis of the concept of provocation was necessary in a case where the House of Lords overruled the Court of Appeal. The appellant, who was addicted to glue-sniffing through the voluntary and persistent abuse of solvents, had killed the person who had taunted him with his addiction. On the pivotal question of whether such a self-induced addiction could be the subject-matter of provocation, the Court of Appeal thought not, but the House of Lords disagreed. For the former court, self-induced addiction to glue-sniffing was wholly inconsistent with the concept of the reasonable man on whom the test of provocation was focused. But against that, the House of Lords judged that the reference to the reasonable man had the purpose only of setting a standard for the power of self-control that was to be taken as the norm.

Whether the reasonable man's self-control would snap or not in the given circumstances was an objective test to be applied by the jury. Self-control required to be related to the strength or gravity of the provocation. The concept of provocation fell within the province of the law. Thus the legal reconceptualisation of the concept of provocation involved the admissibility of subjective characteristics of the person who was the target of the provocation. Although the judges below appeared to have assumed that the provocative taunts must be directed at a personal characteristic which was not repugnant to the concept of a reasonable or ordinary person, that was to objectify the test in the wrong way. The reasonable man standard governed the exercise of the power of self-control. Examples of relevant characteristics that might affect the gravity of the provocation could include some shameful incident in the past, as well as age, sex, race, colour, physical deformity and so on. The House of Lords saw no reason to exclude the addiction in this case as a relevant factor in assessing the gravity of the provocation.[17]

CONCLUSIONS

In a recent case the House of Lords further developed the concept of provocation, extending its embrace to additional categories of subjective characteristics of an accused person.[18] This time the attribute was not, like the glue-sniffing addiction, the target of the taunts but instead was a mental or emotional state which might affect the exercise of self-control. Specifically, the accused according to the evidence suffered from clinical depression which made him more 'disinhibited', less able to control his reactions. So the focus was on a personal factor which might sensitise the accused to provocative words rather than a personal characteristic, such as an addiction, *about* which he might be sensitive. By a narrow majority (three to two), the court decided that a defence of provocation based on a mental abnormality such as depression was admissible. In so doing, it undoubtedly came close to encroachment, if it did not make actual inroads, into the concept of diminished responsibility. The majority recognised that the decision downgraded the reasonable man standard:

> Judges should not be required to describe the objective element in the provocation defence by reference to a reasonable man with or without attribution of personal characteristics.

The evolution of the concept of provocation was responsive to social changes. A judicial statement that 'as society advances it ought to call for a higher measure of self-control' was endorsed by the judges, who also said:

> the jury represented the community and decided what degree of self-control everyone was entitled to expect his fellow would exercise in society as it was today.

The case study on provocation demonstrates that the outcome of the process of matching the appropriate legal norm to an interpretation of the factual situation is a (subtle) shift or development in the semantic content of the norm. It is the concept that drives this movement. It is in the nature of the concept that it is multi-aspectual; that is, it takes on different shades of meaning depending on the different contexts in which it is used.

Grammar

Everyone is against sin. If 'sin' had been adopted as a legal concept, its semantic content would have been developed by the application or rejection of the norm in which it made an appearance after consideration in different fact-situations. Sin having been excluded, perhaps because of its history of use in religious discourse, 'crime' filled the role instead. The point to be made about 'sin', however, is not about its function as a concept, but that it includes its own valency within its connotation. By 'valency' I mean that attribute of a word or phrase that corresponds to illocutionary force in speech-act theory. Legal discourse is marked, instead, as compared with ordinary language, by intricate grammatical constructions of double and triple negatives, types of 'if' clauses, hypothesis-piling, exceptions, reservations and declarations. It is principally these which, as was pointed out in the first chapter, are responsible for the 'mind-boggling' effect of many legal passages.

CASE STUDY

The purpose of a lease is to parcel out the property rights between the landlord and the tenant. In the case of certain rights, their exercise by the tenant is made subject to the control of the landlord who has an interest in the way these rights are exercised. An example is the tenant's right to transfer the tenancy by assignment or sublet. The landlord has an obvious interest here, since the result of the transfer might be to burden him with an objectionable tenant or subtenant whom he would never had countenanced at the outset.

This is a typical clause used for the purpose:

> The tenant shall not without the prior consent of the landlord, which consent shall not be unreasonably delayed or withheld in the case of an assignee or subtenant who is respectable and responsible and of sound financial means and demonstrably capable of performing the tenant's obligations under this lease, assign or sublet the premises in whole or in part.

The grammar instanced here, designed to provide exact illocutionary force at the cost of complexity, well justifies the stigma of mind-boggling. But this is necessary in a language which exalts reasonableness and therefore eschews rhetoric. In ordinary language it is *rhetoric* that expresses the sense of violation and unfairness by which rights and claims are defined. Hence the conceit of Barthes that legal language should be without style.[19] Perhaps, however, it is its style, characterised by the absence of style, whose distinctive colour, so to speak, is colourlessness, but that nevertheless exudes at the same time great power, which is responsible for the hostility to legal language.

Fair, just and reasonable

Those complex constructions, characteristic of legal language, that endow it with precision are often interspersed with flexible words, such as 'unreasonably' in the example, which have the opposite effect. The trio, 'fair, just and reasonable', has recently been noticeable in legal texts. This of course eliminates the dubiety which attaches to the meaning of 'reasonable' standing alone, for example, to the question of whether it includes considerations of fairness. Not only that, but the criterion of justice has been conjoined for good measure. But when the triple test comes to be applied to a particular set of circumstances can a judgement one way or another be justified as being the right answer?

CASE STUDY

The trio has been invoked in two disparate cases to justify the imposition on a solicitor of a duty of care to a third party, not his client. In the earlier case, a testator had executed a will disinheriting his two daughters after a family row.[20] Following a reconciliation he instructed the solicitor to prepare a new will containing legacies to his daughters. Because of the solicitor's negligence, the will was never drawn up. The question was whether the solicitor was liable in damages to the intended beneficiaries, with whom he had no professional relationship. The court decided that it was *fair, just and reasonable* to impose liability on the solicitor to compensate the beneficiaries.

CONCLUSIONS

In the later case, the court also came to the conclusion that it was *fair, just and reasonable* in the particular circumstances to impose a duty of professional care on a borrower's solicitor in favour of a lender.[21] This applied despite the obvious conflict of interest between the lender and his client, a factor which, the court considered, was overridden by the circumstance that the solicitor knew, or ought to have known, that the lender was not obtaining independent legal advice but was relying on him to put in place an effective security for the loan. The solicitor had failed through negligence to provide an effective security.

It is worthwhile asking why the judges believed it necessary to mobilise the multiple criteria, 'fair, just and reasonable' in this particular context. Remember that *all* three standards must be satisfied for liability to be imposed. I suggest that there are two significant elements in the situation that push in opposite directions in relation to the stringency of the conditionality. One is the reluctance in British law to place responsibility on a person for loss sustained by another with whom he is not in contractual relationship. The triple criterion is invoked only after and provided that those conditions, relating to tort or negligence claims, of foreseeability and the relationship characterised as 'proximity' or 'neighbourhood', had been seen to be met. This negativism in comparison with French law has already been pointed out in the discussion of the distinction between *right* and *entitlement*. The obligation to render assistance to a person in danger does not exist in British law. The other element in this situation, which operates to counteract the negative tendency, is the solicitor's position as representative. Would the law have imposed liability to compensate the intended beneficiaries on someone who had instructions from the testator to deliver the will to the solicitors but had lost it? Representation is a complex and distinctive relationship to be examined later in this chapter. In the meantime, I want to explore the separate ideas of the fair, the just and the reasonable in that order.

Fair

Both Ricoeur and Fish, coincidentally, begin their analysis of moral and legal questions by exploring what is suggested by the exclamation, 'that's not fair'. They then go in rather different directions. In

Ricoeur's case, his book is a philosophical reflection on the eponymous *Le Juste*.[22] With Fish it is a collection of essays taking a sceptical look at 'the invocation of high-sounding words and phrases like "reasons", "merit", "fairness" ...'. He argues that 'when such words and phrases are invoked, it is almost always as part of an effort to deprive moral and legal problems of their histories so that merely formal calculations can then be performed on phenomena that have been flattened out and no longer have their real-world shape'.[23]

Ricoeur's aim is to argue that the sense of justice, which is pacific, is just as primordial as the proneness to violence in human societies. He goes back, therefore, to the memories of childhood, when our first entry into law's region, he claims, is marked by the cry, 'that's unfair'. This is a cry of indignation aroused typically by experiences of unequal shares, promises not kept, punishments unmerited. He points to the clearsightedness behind such exclamations compared with our hesitation when as adults we are called on to pronounce on issues of fairness.

Can meritocracy be unfair?

Fish cites a film, *How to Succeed in Business without Really Trying*, a comedy. The main character succeeds in finding a post with the firm of his choice where he is assigned to the mailroom. There he finds just one other worker who turns out to be the boss's nephew. One of the two is to be promoted to be head of the mailroom. The manager who is to take the decision announces with due solemnity: 'I've been told to choose the new head of the mailroom on merit alone.' To this the boss's nephew (like Ricoeur's child faced with the unequal slice of cake) immediately responds with indignation: 'That's not fair.' The audience is supposed to laugh.

Fish knows this, of course, but proceeds to take the episode seriously for didactic purposes. He invites us first of all to look at the situation from the boss's nephew's perspective. This is of course the wrong stance from which to form a judgement about fairness. Ricoeur, for example, proposes the opposite, the treating of 'oneself as another' as the key to a philosophy of morals.[24] Anyway, from this 'solipsistic' position, the boss's nephew's indignation, Fish intuits, does not attach to the introduction of a system based on merit, as such. Rather, his sense of unfairness is aroused by the fact that the rules are suddenly being changed late in the day. Thus, he takes the situation with its overturning of 'a tradition, a set of expectations' to represent a change in a 'way of life'.

From this, he draws the moral that while 'notions like "fairness" are always presented as if their meanings were perspicuous to anyone no matter what his or her political affiliation ... gender, class, institutional history etc., in fact [they] will have different meanings in relation to different assumptions and background conditions.'[25] Elsewhere he makes the same general point in a similar way:

> [F]airness is itself a contestable concept and will be differently defined depending on what assumptions inform those who brandish it as a measure. Fairness for everyone would be possible only if everyone's interests were the same ...[26]

Against Fish I want to argue that in laughing 'out of court' the nephew's judgmental exclamation, the audience offered the right comment. For Fish's misconception lies at the very root of his analysis. The *meaning* of 'fairness' is not in question. It is valid usage for a person to designate a situation where he has received too *large* a share as unfair. Subjective motivations, considerations and calculations may of course at the conscious or unconscious level underlie judgements of fairness but, to the extent that they do, their effect is to distort the judgements. What is *meant* by fair is unaffected. The child, when exclaiming 'that's unfair' understands the meaning of 'fairness' only if he expects, if challenged, to be able to defend his statement other than by invoking personal interests. The same argument lies against Fish's idea of relativism which makes the definition of 'fairness' depend on background assumptions. It is just not possible to *define* 'fairness' at all. Indeed, I would want to go so far as to deny that 'fairness' is a contestable concept. Perhaps not a concept at all, merely an abstraction derived from the corresponding predicate, such as 'greenness' from 'green'. I put that forward for the reason that the semantic content of 'fair' or 'fairness' is not enlarged by, nor does it change or vary with, the multifarious constellations of circumstances to which it can be applied. 'Concept' is itself a concept and it makes sense to contest Fish's view that 'fairness' is an example of it.

The point is that the predicate 'fair' is imported into legal discourse from ordinary language. The noun 'fairness' is not (re)conceptualised. This applies to all of the words previously identified as flexible words. They cannot be (re)conceptualised, that is, defined in a legal context, without their replacement by one or more similarly flexible words. Some lessons were drawn in chapter 1 from the Unfair Contract

Terms Act. It was noted that the attempt to pin down and replace the central notion of 'unfairness' by a catalogue of conditions, whose appearance in a contract regulated by the Act would constitute unfairness, was self-defeating. In the example cited, a judgement of fairness or unfairness was dispensed with, but the cost was the introduction into the definition of the words 'inappropriately' and 'inadequate'.

The argument can be underlined by refocusing it on a discussion in the Court of Appeal.

CASE STUDY

This was an appeal against a conviction of being drunk on an aircraft.[27] One of the grounds was that the relevant regulation contained no definition as to what was meant by being drunk or by drunkenness. A broad principle was invoked:

> A norm cannot be regarded as a 'law' unless it is formulated with sufficient precision to enable the citizen to regulate his conduct.

The Court made the point that the Strasbourg court in a human rights case had upheld the English domestic jurisprudence in relation to such a concept as 'obscenity', but only because a body of domestic law had identified it sufficiently clearly. The term 'drunkenness' was distinguished by the absence of any definition. The appeal court rejected the argument, holding that 'drunkenness' had a clear meaning in ordinary language.

Whereas 'obscene' had been reconceptualised in legal discourse, 'drunk' had not undergone, nor was there any need for it to undergo, that process. Moreover, when the attempt was made, lo and behold in the definition that a person is drunk 'when she is so affected by the alcohol in her body that she is without proper control of her faculties or behaviour,' its conceptualisation is seen to pivot on the flexible word 'proper'.

Just

Take 'equitable' as a synonym for 'fair'. Then Aristotle differentiates 'fair' from 'just' in this way:

> The equitable, while being at the same time just, is not what is just according to the law, but a corrective of legal justice. The reason for that is that the law is always something general and that there are specific cases for which it is not possible to lay down a general statement which applies to them with certitude ... Thus one sees clearly what the equitable is, that the equitable is just and that it is superior to a particular sort of the just[28]

Significantly, Aristotle does not seek to define either 'equitable' or 'just' in any other way than by their interdependence.

We prosaically describe our courts as courts of law while the French grandiloquently call theirs the *Palais de Justice*. Furthermore, confusingly and boastfully, they use *le juste* to mean both the just and the fair. This is an indicator of the problem met in any attempt to discover a semantic space for the just between the fair and the reasonable. What comes quickly into view is procedural justice. But just as correct methodology does not necessarily lead to valid propositions or true descriptions of states of affairs, so procedural justice seems to leave a gap for a justice which could be identified as substantive justice. First, see what procedural justice entails and then look for substantive justice on the horizon.

Procedural justice

Law in the form of statute is authorised as law by its passage through the established procedures of a representative, legislative body. In the same way, law in the form of judicial decision will be nullified on appeal if it is not the outcome of due process. The judge understands himself as presiding over the procedural requirements that due process entails. This self-understanding is defined from the observer's standpoint in the form of the core principle of procedural justice: 'Justice must not only be done but must also be seen to be done.' What constitutes due process appears in an idealised form in Alexy's version of the assumptions underlying rational discourse.

> In rational discourse, we assume that conditions of communication obtain that (1) prevent a rationally unmotivated

termination of argumentation, (2) secure both freedom in the choice of topics and inclusion of the best information and reasons through universal and equal access to, as well as equal and symmetrical participation in, argumentation, and (3) exclude every kind of coercion ... other than that of the better argument ...[29]

Habermas prefaces this presentation of Alexy's proposal by pointing up the idealised character of the conditions, summing them up as 'endless time, unlimited participation and perfect freedom from coercion'.

While blaming lawyers for the slowness and expense that result from the effort of complying with a workaday version of these conditions, the public would be forced to acknowledge that they represent a fair system of justice. In other words, they set the parameters of an ideal procedural justice. But they tell us nothing of what might be meant by substantive justice.

Substantive justice

The silhouette of what constitutes justice in the substance is discernible in the following case:

CASE STUDY

The defendant newspaper in a libel action had continued to maintain its defence after the claimant had offered to settle at a certain figure.[30] When the court awarded damages at a higher figure, the claimant applied for payment of his costs on an indemnity basis plus interest for the period of the litigation attributable to the defendant's maintenance of the action after the offer to settle. The indemnity basis steps in to cover costs which would not be recoverable on the standard basis. When indemnity costs were refused by the court, the claimant successfully appealed.

The purpose of the power to award indemnity costs, the Court of Appeal reasoned, was to 'redress the element of perceived *unfairness* (my italics)' arising from the fact that part of the successful claimant's whole costs were otherwise irrecoverable. But the power to make the order was ruled out where the court considered it *'unjust* (my italics) to do so'. The judge below had rested his refusal to make the order on the injustice that would flow from the presumption that indemnity costs carried 'punitive overtones'. The appeal court, disagreeing, did not believe that indemnity costs implied any condemnation and to award them would not, therefore, be unjust.

Here, substantive justice made its appearance, even though in negative guise, to set a boundary to the court's power to redress unfairness. I can take it no further.

Reasonable

'Reasonableness' in its ordinary sense is a vague term. As a standard of behaviour, it is unclear whether it applies to short-term, or only to long-term, calculations of one's individual interest, or whether it also includes considerations of fairness to others. Fairness may be instrumental to a person's long-term interest by earning for him a good reputation or otherwise 'paying off' in the long run, although it may also represent a value *per se*. A similar uncertainty attaches to what is required when 'reasonable' conduct is prescribed in a legal text. In Scots law it went no further than behaviour that was not irrational, impulsive, quixotic. But in English law on the contrary, an element of regard for the interest of the other in the relationship forms part of the standard of reasonable behaviour in a landlord–tenant context.

As already mentioned, a lease distributes property rights between landlord and tenant. The tenant acquires closely circumscribed rights to use the property, and the landlord acquires rights of control corresponding to the restrictions. In the tug-of-war of negotiation, the tenant may gain the relaxation of a prohibition, for example against transfer, in the form of an undertaking by the landlord that he will not unreasonably withhold his consent to an application by the tenant. In a case where refusal of consent would only slightly benefit the landlord while causing substantial deprivation to the tenant, the court has ruled that the refusal of consent may be held to be unreasonable where the benefit to the landlord of his refusal is unreasonably disproportionate to the detriment suffered by the tenant. So the court has stretched the intension of the concept of reasonableness to include an element of fairness.[31] The following case study rather points in the same direction.

CASE STUDY

The appeal court was called on to consider whether certain compensatory payments agreed by a city council to be payable to its employees were 'irrationally generous'.[32] These were lump sums in compensation for reduction of earnings consequent on the abandonment of established but uneconomic practices. The figure for compensation had been substantially reduced by a lower court.

The appeal court said:

> In fixing on the appropriate 'buy-out' figure the Council had to form a view, taking into account a number of factors which in summary were the long-term as well as the short-term savings in operating costs and the preservation of good industrial relations with its employees.

> In the opinion of the court, the Council had given anxious consideration to these factors and there was no basis on which its conduct could be found to be irrational.

Re-enter the reasonable man

The standard of rationality, according to the court, has regard both to long-term and short-term considerations. But doubt remains whether the familiar, legal measuring-rod of the reasonable man, acting reasonably and assumed to know the law, *necessarily* includes the expectation that he should at all go beyond the narrow performance of his legal obligations. It was assumed in the city council's case that the reasonable man *might* reasonably be sensitive to considerations of fairness, albeit on instrumental grounds for the sake of reputation or good future relationships. To satisfy the reasonable landlord criterion, however, the landlord must have regard to the tenant's interest as well as his own, and weigh that interest in arriving at a reasonable decision, regardless of instrumental considerations. In the provocation cases, the concept of the reasonable man was equated to the ordinary person who was measured for his degree of self-control in particularised circumstances. So it seems that the standard of reasonableness is a flexible one, varying with the category of social or economic relationship in which the reasonable man is placed. In other words, reasonableness, unlike fairness, is reconceptualised in legal language.

Opinion- and will-formation

In all of these situations the reasonable man is conceived to be a participant. The law looks to him for a yardstick for reasonableness in action. But Habermas speaks of both opinion- and will-formation: 'only legitimate law emerges from the discursive opinion-and will-formation of equally enfranchised citizens'. So his theory requires more from the reasonable man than his appearance in law as the reasonable actor. Concisely, as an ordinary person, say the figurative man in the Clapham bus, he must share with all other communicatively-engaged citizens an understanding of themselves, as a whole, as 'rational authors' of the law.[33] How is the gap that is now revealed to be filled?

Representation

In order to, at least, shrink the gap, I want now to propose a more exact description than 'meaning equivalence' for the relationship between the interpretation of the facts and the application conditions of the appropriate legal norm. That is, it will be remembered, the relationship that, according to Habermas, finally decides the issue. This comes down to what is for me the critical question, the relationship between legal language and ordinary language. I propose to adopt the concept of representation to denote the character of this relationship.

The notion of representation commonly appears *inter alia* in two areas that are fairly wide apart. One of these is occupied by the relationship between the sign and the signified. Semiotics studies language as one sign-system among other sign-systems. To say that a word *represents* its object carries a greater significance than the mere substitution referred to by the statement 'Let x represent the number of oranges' or the encipherment of a message in a code. In these cases, the signs are arbitrary and in themselves meaningless, and the relationship entirely factitious. To re-present in words is to present an object in a *significantly* different way. 'Presentation', in its common, contemporary usage as a synonym for style and in opposition to substance, refers to the art or technique of the seductive arrangement of words, images or objects. But, as it is understood here, *re*presentation introduces a second tier involving an additional layer of meaning.

The conception of representation is able to flesh out the criterion of 'meaning equivalence' referred to by Habermas. Thus we can say that the description of the application conditions of the appropriate norm expressed in legal language should *represent* the interpretation of the facts expressed in ordinary language. But this covers only part, the structural aspect, of what is involved in representation.

Fidelity

That aspect of representation which is important, other than the structural, is the normative. What is missing or goes wrong when what purports to be representation turns out instead to be misrepresentation? That the answer is fidelity shows up clearly if the focus is shifted from representation by words or images to the relationship between a commercial, legal or political representative and his principal, client or constituent. The lawyer in court, for example, defines his position thus: 'I represent X.' His duty, then, is to pursue X's real-world interests with fidelity within the horizon of the legal world. But does the conception of representation connote fidelity to the client's *instructions* or fidelity in the pursuit of the client's *interests*? The nature of the complex relationship of representation depends in turn on the fluid character of instructions and interests. Interests assert themselves in the determination of objectives while instructions draw guidelines for the means. Both are presupposed to be provisional. Both emerge from a dialogue and accommodation between the real world and the legal system with its distinctive ethics, culture and language.

In the sense that it takes place at the discursive level, this 'dialogue' is literally meant. Throughout this book the interplay between ordinary language and legal language has been on display on the judge's side in the case studies showing the absorption of 'fair, just and reasonable' and other flexible words into legal discourse and the assimilation of concepts of ordinary language by the process of reconceptualisation. In chapter 3, too, analysis revealed the readiness of judges in applying the law to supplant or at least supplement textualism by focusing on what might have been intended to be conveyed to the law's addressees. It is only against the background of representation in that sense that the judge can be portrayed as the citizen's representative and legal language be aimed at the achievement of 'meaning equivalence' between fact and norm. On the other side, as Habermas postulates, a process of opinion- and will-formation takes place through ordinary discourse based on *understanding* of the law. Thus, the presumption that everyone knows the law is justified.

Human rights

In this section I want to bring out the radical differences of rights-based law, especially its use of philosophical language from which the distinctive characteristics of legal language identified in the preceding section are missing. The Human Rights Act 1998 may or may not represent a watershed in British law. Its main impact so far has been in the sphere identified earlier as procedural justice. But whether or not the Act will exert a material influence in the direction of substantive justice remains unclear. The Act 'domesticates' the rights and freedoms of the European Convention on Human Rights by the incorporation of the convention into UK law. Rights, freedom of speech for example, were already part of British law under its 'unwritten' constitution. Also, the human rights catalogued in the Convention, which Britain was the first state to ratify, were already influential, although not decisive, in British law even before the Act's coming into force. Indeed, for the most part, the convention rights are still not decisive. Rights have not been given the power to strike down legislation. Short of that, 'so far as it is possible to do so,' legislation 'must be read and given effect in a way which is compatible with Convention rights' (s.3) although if the court is satisfied that a legislative provision is incompatible with a Convention right, 'it may make a declaration of that incompatibility'. (s.4)

The origin of the strong impact of rights on procedural justice can be traced to the conjunction of two competing tendencies. Ironically, the Labour Government initiated one and intensified the other. In its zeal for constitutional reform it introduced the Human Rights Act. On the other side, it (over)responded to public concerns about crime by plans to review evidential rules in criminal trials. These are designed to save money, speed up the forensic timetable and obtain more convictions. Inevitably, these aims are incompatible with the ideal conditions of procedural justice, already outlined. But a more down to earth consideration is that the measures impact on the newly incorporated Convention rights. For instance, there is the tension between the statutory measure eroding the accused's right to silence and his right to protection against self-incrimination. In general, many of the rights-based cases arise from claims that convicted persons have been denied the right to a fair trial (Article 6 of the Convention).

CASE STUDY

Expressing its sensitivity to public disquiet concerning the rarity of rape convictions compared with the number of reported complaints and, even more, the much higher number of unreported incidents (based on tip-of-the-iceberg speculation), the government passed legislation in 1999, whose objective was to gain more convictions. It provided that reference to a complainant's previous sexual history was inadmissible as a defence in a rape trial. Much more broadly, the measure, as well as responding to public concern, reflected the social acceptance of the moral and sexual autonomy of women in the aftermath of the 1960s.

The House of Lords had to decide whether reference to a prior consensual sexual relationship between a complainant and the accused might be admissible as evidence of consent in a rape trial.[34] Admissibility of such evidence would fall foul of the statute's blanket prohibition of prior sexual history. Yet, on the other side, where evidence of a previous relationship between complainant and defendant was relevant to the issue of consent, its exclusion would impinge on the right to a fair trial. Invoking the interpretative obligation in the Human Rights Act, the House of Lords held:

> [D]ue regard always being paid to the importance of seeking to protect the complainant from indignity and humiliating questions, the test of admissibility was whether the evidence, and questioning in relation to it, was nevertheless so relevant to the issue of consent that to exclude it would endanger the fairness of the trial.

The case is important from two angles. First, there is the court's interpretative obligation under the 1998 Act, as understood by the House of Lords. This was much more radical than the court's power, explored in chapter 3, to depart from the actual words to find an appropriate interpretation in tightly confined circumstances. The court now had a positive obligation to find an interpretation compatible with Convention rights if it was possible to do so. Not only might language have to be strained but words might have to be 'read down' and other words put in. The principle was that the legislature would not have wanted to infringe a Convention right if it had foreseen that that would have been the effect of the statutory wording.

The case also reveals an even more fundamental, jurisprudential issue. It did nothing to impugn the validity of the statutory objective to avoid the humiliation in court of women in matters regarding their control of their own sexuality. Yet this collides with the accused's right to a fair trial. So we meet again the problem of the inherent potentiality for rights to collide discussed in the context of Dworkin's theory in the last chapter. Collision issues are not resolved by the setting of limits to rights. Nor can rights be accommodated to one another. Nor, indeed, does such a collision strictly resolve itself into a question of, or be resolved by, *interpretation*, even though it is likely that the House of Lords correctly construed what Parliament intended when it enacted the interpretative obligation. What I suggest instead is that Parliament is *presumed* not to seek to infringe a Convention right unless it expressly counters that presumption in the terms of the legislation. In the latter event, the court would be obliged to resort to a declaration of incompatibility (s.4). This does not end the matter, for sometimes it is a Convention right that must yield. I will return to that point later in the chapter.

Collision of rights

Habermas's profound analysis provides a basis from which one can see why rights by their nature will collide. Modern law, he says, can be justified only by human rights and the principle of popular sovereignty. These underlie and roughly correspond to dichotomies, between self-determination on the one side and self-realisation on the other, and again, between liberalism and civic republicanism. The first perspective in each of these pairs is recognisably represented in the case just noted in the shape of the complainant's right to moral and sexual autonomy. This, it will be remembered from chapter 4, echoes the liberal principle mobilised by Dworkin to underpin the right to abortion. On the other side, the right to a fair trial, although designated as a human right, emanates from civic republicanism, our collective self-understanding as a political community.

CONCLUSIONS

Human rights and popular sovereignty, Habermas concludes 'do not so much mutually complement as compete with each other'. Neither can claim primacy.[35]

Above, I proposed that the adjudication process in cases turning on rights-based law did not involve textual interpretation. The same point was made in the discussion of Dworkin's idea of 'constructive interpretation'. A plausible inference from this might be that the language in which judgements are expressed in such cases does not exhibit the characteristics of legal language that have been identified. The hypothesis can be tested in the following case.

CASE STUDY

A tribunal had been set up to enquire into the events of 'Bloody Sunday', when members of the armed forces opened fire during an illegal march in Northern Ireland, as a result of which 13 civilians were shot dead and at least the same number injured. The soldiers who had opened fire applied to the tribunal to be granted anonymity when giving testimony to the tribunal in order to reduce the risk of reprisals by republican terrorist groups. Refusing the application, the tribunal adopted the stance that 'the risk to the applicants of disclosure could not be satisfactorily reconciled with and was overridden by the duty of the enquiry to carry out an open public investigation'. The soldiers appealed to the Divisional Court, which upheld their right to anonymity,[36] and the Court of Appeal rejected the tribunal's appeal against that decision.[37]

The substance of the case consisted of a competition between rights. On the one side was the public right to an open enquiry which ought to shape the procedures adopted by the tribunal in its search for the truth. This clashed with the security risk to the soldier witnesses and their families. The tribunal had conceded that, if anonymity were granted, its work would not be substantially impaired. That being so, the courts had no difficulty in holding that the safety of the soldiers and their families outweighed the right of the surviving victims and the victims' families to disclosure of the soldiers' identity. The point was made that 'the individual's right to life was the most fundamental of all human rights'.

This all seemed obvious enough, yet eminent jurists saw fit to argue the opposite point of view in the broadsheet press.[38]

The first comment to be made is on the timing of their intervention, which came after the first decision and prior to the appeal court hearing. This stirred a third Queen's Counsel into criticism of their action on the ground that their argument might produce a boomerang effect.[39] Not only might the thinking of judges be influenced at some level by what fellow-lawyers whom they respected intellectually had to say, but also the public might think that trial by newspaper would lead to bias. In the event, the Court of Appeal, by upholding the original judgement, demonstrated that it must have been either impervious to, or negatively influenced by, the interventions. Still, the point made concerning possible public reaction to media debate in advance of an appeal hearing was a shrewd hit at one of the QC's argument that the judges were interfering with the tribunal's duty to observe the principle of open justice in a democratic society. The tribunal's task was to uncover the truth, and fact-finding enquiries sometimes consider it necessary to protect their sources of information. To have exposed the soldiers to a substantial security risk in the face of their request for anonymity would have been to taint them with culpability without a trial.

Such a complete opposition between eminent lawyers, whose convictions were sufficiently passionate to make them resort to the press, and top judges, shows the difficulties of adjudication in cases where rights collide. The underlying presumption of legal certainty, that there is a single right answer, seems even more fictional in this area. But for the time being, the concern here is with the language in which the debate was conducted. Lacking its characteristic features, it may have been the language of morals, ethics or politics, but it was not the discourse of the law.

(Re)conceptualisation

Rights claim universality. When they compete, they do so in respect of appropriateness or applicability, not validity. When the courts decided that the soldiers' right to life should prevail, that did not imply that the victims' right to an enquiry in which their families and the survivors could have confidence was invalid or subject to any limitation which could be inscribed as a qualification of the right. Indeed, the claim underlying the right to openness, namely

CONCLUSIONS

that justice should be manifestly seen to be done, can be enlisted just as well on the soldiers' side. By allowing them to assist the tribunal to achieve its fact-finding goal without public disclosure, the tribunal gave them cause to believe in its impartiality.

The approach adopted by the analyses on both sides of the debate was the same: one right was weighed against the other. The right to life and the public right to open justice are both socially valued. They are not arranged hierarchically with predetermined weights. So both sides of the argument sought to convince by rhetoric. Thus, the court stressed the 'fundamental' nature of the right to life. In its turn, the other side referred to the 'fundamental' duty of the tribunal 'to observe the principle of open justice in a democratic society'. The fact that the invocations of fundamentalism on both sides of the argument cancelled each other out is unsurprising, since all rights can make a justified claim to be basic or fundamental.

Assuming that I am right in categorising the arguments as rhetorical, so setting them apart from arguments in legal language, can the recourse to rhetoric in this case be explained? The answer, I suggest, is that rights are not, and for the most part do not include, concepts. 'Openness' and 'life' have not been reconceptualised within the lexicon of legal language.

By contrast, when a decision turns on the appropriateness or applicability of a singular right, instead of a situation where competing rights both apply, matters are otherwise.

CASE STUDY

The European Court of Human Rights held that corporal punishment inflicted on a pupil in an English private boarding school did not constitute degrading punishment under Article 3 of the Convention.[40] This prohibits torture and inhuman or degrading treatment or punishment. The punishment had consisted of a slippering on the buttocks. Although the Court had misgivings about the automatic nature of the punishment and the wait before its imposition, it considered that the minimum level of severity to constitute degrading treatment had not been attained. Even then, the court divided, five votes to four.

The case is noteworthy because of the comparison made with one of its own earlier decisions. In that case, the victim had been sentenced in the local juvenile court to three strokes of the birch, administered three weeks later in a police station.

The court had held that to amount to degrading punishment. The comparison was based on a detailed but not necessarily exhaustive exploration by the court of the *concept* of degrading punishment. Such a legal conceptualisation makes possible movement in borderline cases in response to, or even ahead of, cultural shifts.

David Pannick has also noticed a loosening of the criteria in respect of the legal concept of torture as a result of the human rights jurisdiction of the Strasbourg court. This, he expects, will have a knock-on effect on the lesser concept of inhuman or degrading treatment or punishment.[41]

Grammar

For similar reasons, the grammatical features that were identified as typical of, and which largely contribute to the complexities of, the legal text are absent from rights-based law, the opposite being the case when qualifications, exceptions and rights of derogation are stated. See how the familiar tortuousness of legal grammar immediately reappears, for example, in the qualification attached to the right to freedom of expression (Article 10):

> The exercise of these freedoms, since it carries with it duties and responsibilities, may be subject to such formalities, conditions, restrictions or penalties as are prescribed by law and are necessary in a democratic society ...

Experience at conferences intended to promote human rights on a global scale shows that the reluctance of some states to enter into commitments expresses itself in the form of proposals to make rights subject to conditions and qualifications. The grammatical constructions embodied in such proposals, as in legal language in general, determine the illocutionary force of the provisions; in this case, by watering it down.

Reasonable or fair

In the analysis of its characteristics, the trio 'fair, just and reasonable' represented the flexible words which leavened the precision of legal language. Now, leaving out the middle term 'just', I want to consider the others in the context of the adjudication of issues arising from competing rights. In the Saville Tribunal case, the court judged that the tribunal's decision to refuse anonymity was unreasonable. Blom-Cooper, for his part, in attacking the court's decision, argued that a decision's 'unreasonableness' was insufficient to justify judicial review, the right standard being 'irrational', which he in turn rendered rhetorically as an affront to common sense. Against that I want to propose that, whereas reasonableness (or the reasonable man, acting reasonably) often operates as the fulcrum of legal decision-making, it is *fairness* that performs that function in the area of human rights law where rights compete.

Rights are observed as obligations. The fair value of a right, therefore, is measurable against the weight of the obligation or hardship it entails for another or others. From that viewpoint, the Saville Tribunal case can be seen as a judgement that the achievement by the victims of complete openness of the enquiry, by involving the soldiers' exposure to serious risk, would have been *unfair* to the soldiers. Again, in the case which concerned the admissibility of the sexual history of rape victims, the court canvassed the similar question of *proportionality*. A balance had to be struck between 'the important legislative goal of countering the twin myths' (that unchaste women were more likely to consent to intercourse and were less worthy of belief) and the accused's right to a fair trial. Fairness had to prevail.

The conclusion is that human rights cases may be shuffled into two categories: those where rights are limited or qualified, and those where rights collide or compete. In the latter category, contestation takes place and judgements are couched in language that does not partake of the key features that characterise legal language. Nor is the text amenable to interpretation in any special sense other than in the semantically extrinsic form of a presumption that the legislator, in saying what he did, would not have intended to infringe a human right.

It is fair to say that Habermas might find it difficult to agree to this conclusion. His thesis is that legitimate law requires both the protection of moral autonomy (through human rights) and popular sovereignty. Human rights must not be imposed by virtue of their moral justifiability alone but should be institutionalised by a process of self-legislation. Otherwise, 'the addressees of law would not be able to understand themselves as its authors'. The argument goes on:

> [they] are no longer free to choose the medium in which they can realise their autonomy. They participate in the production of law only as *legal subjects*; it is no longer in

their power to decide which language they will use in this endeavour. Consequently, the desired internal relation between 'human rights' and popular sovereignty consists in the fact that the requirement of legally institutionalising self-legislation can be fulfilled only with the help of a code that *simultaneously* implies the guarantee of actionable individual liberties.[42]

Can this requirement for a special language of the law, a *code* for the legal system be reconciled with my suggestion that, when rights collide, the discourse in which the debate is conducted and the decision formulated does not share the characteristics of legal language? I think that the answer is given by Habermas himself, to whom I am content to leave (almost) the last word:

> If there is an irreconcilable conflict of values instead of a conflict of compromisable interests, then the parties must jointly shift to the more abstract level of moral reasoning and agree upon rules for living together that are in the equal interest of all. That is just one of many examples of *interdiscursive* (my italics) relations. What matters here is that these relations are not *dictated* from the perspective of a superdiscourse. Rather, they emerge from the logic of questioning within a *given* discourse, with the result that the good is privileged over the expedient and the just over the good.[43]

This book enlists Habermas in its defence of lawyers' language.

NOTES

INTRODUCTION

1 Poll carried out by Sofres and reported in *Le Monde*, 18 November 1999. The poll's findings have been dramatically borne out in 2002 by the French Presidential elections. See also article 'Stay-at-home citizens', by Professor Whiteley in *The Guardian*, 1 May 2002, for details of the similar trend in the rest of the developed world (except Scandinavia).
2 Figures do not add up to 100 per cent because respondents reacted in more than one way.
3 Referendum conducted by Voteit, advised by ICM, reported in *The Guardian*, 31 May 2000.
4 Section 28 has now been repealed in Scotland.
5 The American thinker, Christopher Lasch, advocates a populist trend in his political philosophy.
6 In Marsha Clark and Theresa Carpenter, *Without a Doubt* (1997), New York: Viking.
7 Material taken from *Twelve Angry Persons* by Andrew Hacker in *New York Review of Books*, 21 September 1995.
8 *Ideology and Modern Culture* (1990), Cambridge: Polity Press, p. 246.
9 R. v. Taylors, TLR 25 June 1993.
10 Noelle Lenoir, reported in *Le Monde*, 21 March 2001.
11 In an article in *New York Review of Books*, 11 January 2001.
12 *New York Review of Books*, 22 February 2001.
13 Dworkin's approach to interpretation is discussed in chapter 4.
14 *Freedom's Law: the moral reading of the American constitution* (1996), Cambridge, MA: Harvard University Press.
15 Ibid. at p. 16.
16 *American Scripture: Making the Declaration of Independence* (1997), New York: Knopf.
17 The concept of judicial 'integrity' was developed by Dworkin in his *Law's Empire* (1986), Harvard University Press.
18 For a discussion of the debate between the 'moral reading' and 'original intent' theory, see chapter 4.
19 Ibid. pp. 265–305.
20 Ibid. pp. 321–2

21 Ibid. p. 342.
22 Ibid. pp. 342–3.
23 (1996), MIT Press.
24 Ibid. p. 33.
25 Dworkin, *Freedom's Law*, p. 343.
26 Habermas, op. cit. p. 354.
27 The proposal that even the sciences cannot escape relativism is generally attributed to Thomas Kuhn, in particular his notion of the 'paradigm'; 'Paradigms are never simply abandoned. Rather they accumulate anomalies until there is an eventual breaking-point.'
28 *De l'Interpretation* (1965), Paris: Seuil, p. 13.
29 See e.g. Goodrich, *Legal Discourse* (1987), Hong Kong: Macmillan Press.
30 How 'collision of rights' cases are resolved is the subject of discussion in chapter 5.
31 Title of one of Dworkin's earlier works.
32 *Sovereign Virtue: The Theory and Practice of Equality* (2000), Cambridge, MA: Harvard University Press.
33 *Freedom's Law*, p. 11.
34 *Habermas On Law and Democracy: Critical Exchanges*, eds Rosenfeld and Arato (1998) Berkeley, CA and London: University of California Press. p. 1.
35 Per Mr Justice Jonathan Parker in Schuldenfrei v. Hilton, TLR 12 August 1999.
36 M. Foucault, *Lectures 1970–1982 at the Collège de France* (1989), Paris: Julliard p. 67.
37 Cited in Klinck, *The Word of the Law* (1991), Ottowa: Carleton University Press, p. 219. The first quotation is from Mellinkoff, the second from O.C. Lewis.

1 BREAKING GROUND

1 DPP v. Noe, TLR 19 April 2000.
2 DPP v. Skinner (1990) RTR 254.
3 Phillips (1987) Glasgow: Ardmoray Publishing.
4 Ibid. p. 118.
5 Ahmadou Hampate-Ba (author and transcriber of oral traditions from Mali).
6 Goodrich op. cit.
7 See Phillips op. cit p. 118.
8 See Phillips op. cit p. 118.
9 In *The Guardian*, 7 April 2001.
10 The bill had no chance of becoming law due to lack of parliamentary time.
11 s.34.
12 The change in the wording of the caution has given rise to a rash of cases because of its apparent encroachment on the accused's right to silence implied by the presumption of innocence. The right to silence is fundamental to the idea of fair procedure guaranteed by Article 6 of the Convention of Human Rights, but the European Court has held

NOTES

that the right is not absolute (Condron v. UK, TLR 9 May 2000) The judge in the Jeffrey Archer trial famously directed the jury that it was open to them to draw adverse inferences from his declining to give evidence on his own behalf. (His conviction was reported in the media, *passim* on 20 July 2001.)
13 Research conducted by Shepherd, Mortimer and Mobasheri, and reported in the *Journal of Expert Evidence*.
14 Unfair terms in Consumer Contracts Regulations, 1994, S.1. 3159.
15 s.6.
16 Schedule 3, 1 (b).
17 *The Independent*, 11 December 1992.
18 Taken from article in *The Guardian*, 18 July 2001 by Ivor Gaber, pointing to the potential threat to the justice system of avoidance of jury service by the general public. Only one person attends out of every three people called, annually. Professional groups particularly, he says, boycott jury service. As a result, jurors are treated as 'verging on the simple'.
19 These cases were formerly reported and headlined daily in *The Times*.
20 Amin v. DPP, TLR 9 April 1993.
21 R. v. McDonald, TLR 27 March 1996.
22 Cowan v. Metropolitan Police Commissioner, TLR 31 August 1999.
23 Fellowes v. DPP, TLR 1 February 1993.
24 Greener v. DPP, TLR 15 February 1996.
25 Chief Adjudication Officer v. Faulds, TLR 16 May 2000.
26 Chaudhari v. British Airways, TLR, 7 May 1997.
27 R. v. Forest Heath D.C., TLR 16 May 1997.
28 R. v. Westminster City Council, TLR 18 April 2000.
29 Alex Lawrie Factors Ltd v. Morgan, TLR 18 August 1999.
30 Bate v. Chief Adjudications Officer, TLR 17 May 1996.

2 HOW CRITICAL LANGUAGE THEORY SEEKS AND THEN STRUGGLES AGAINST ITS OWN UNDOING

1 Textbooks by institutional writers have authority.
2 *L'Empire Rhetorique* (1977), Paris: Vrin.
3 See O. Reboul, *La Rhétorique* (1984), Paris: Presses Universitaires de France.
4 *Essay on the Human Understanding*, Bk III, chap. X, s. 34 (1979), Oxford: Clarendon Press.
5 *La Nouvelle Rhétorique et les Valeurs* (1976), Dalloz, p. 107, under the general title, *Logique Juridique*, Paris.
6 Ibid. at p. 116.
7 See *Logique Juridique*, passim.
8 Ibid. p. 116.
9 *L' Aventure Sémiologique* (1955), Paris: Seuil, p. 204.
10 Ibid. p. 135.
11 D.N. McCormick, 'The Motivation of Judgments in the Common Law', in *La Motivation des Décisions de Justice*, eds Perelman and Finers (1978), Brussels: Bruylant.
12 *Dennis Martinez and the Uses of Theory* (1987) Yale Law Journal, Vol. 96, p. 1,797.

NOTES

13 Ibid. p. 1,796.
14 *There's No Such Thing as Free Speech and It's a Good Thing Too* (1994), New York: Oxford University Press.
15 *Denis Martinez and the Uses of Theory*, p. 1,796.
16 English Version: *The Order of Things: An Archaeology of the Human Sciences* (1970), London: Tavistock.
17 *Madness and Civilisation: A History of Insanity in the Age of Reason* (1972), London: Tavistock.
18 Foucault's explanation on the book cover of the French edition.
19 (1967), London: Tavistock.
20 *Discipline and Punish: The Birth of the Prison* (1979), Harmondsworth: Penguin
21 *Lectures 1979–1982 at the Collège de France* (1989), Paris: Julliard, p. 67.
22 Ibid. p. 14.
23 *History of Sexuality*, Vol. 1 *Introduction* (1978), New York: Pantheon; Vol. 2 *The Use of Pleasure* (1986), Harmondsworth: Viking; Vol. 3 *The Care of Self* (1986), New York: Pantheon.
24 *Lectures*, op. cit. p. 147.
25 Reported by Didier Eribon in his biography, *Michel Foucault* (1989), Paris: Flammarion.
26 Extract from his lecture of 1982 entitled *The Hermeneutics of the Subject*, published in *Le Monde*, 23 March 2001.
27 Ibid.
28 Bennington and Derrida, *Jacques Derrida* (1991), Paris: Seuil p. 70.
29 Clark v. Associated Newspapers Ltd, TLR 28 January 1998.
30 Derrida, *Psyche* (1997), Paris: Galilée, p. 163 et seq.
31 Derrida, *Spectre of Marx* (1994), London and New York: Routledge.
32 Nagarajan v. London Regional Transport, TLR 19 July 1999.
33 *Ideology and Modern Culture* (1990), Cambridge: Polity Press, p. 33–41.
34 Speech was given at George Washington University in Washington, DC, and the text was published in *New York Review of Books*, 27 May 1993, p. 8.
35 (1969), New York: Pantheon.
36 Op. cit. pp. 235–6.
37 In *Lenin and Philosophy and Other Essays* (1971), New York: Monthly Review Press.
38 See Balibar in *Politique et Philosophie dans l'Oeuvre de Louis Althusser*, ed. Lazarus (1993), Paris: Presses Universitaires de France, p. 90.
39 See *For Marx* (1969), New York: Pantheon, p. 232.
40 See *Prison Notebooks* (1971), London: Lawrence and Wishart, p. 419.
41 Ibid. p. 419.

3 INTERPRETATION

1 *Les Limites de l'Interprétation* (1992), Paris: Grasset, p. 22.
2 Ricoeur, *De l' Interprétation* (1965), Paris: Seuil p. 19.
3 Ibid.
4 Lord Reid in Westminster Bank v. Zang 1966, AC 182, p. 222. This and some other examples in what follows are taken from article on

NOTES

General Principles of Interpretation in *Encyclopedia of the Laws of Scotland*.
5   Pepper v. Hart 1992, WLR p. 1032.
6   Ibid. p. 1043.
7   Ibid. p. 1042.
8   Ibid. p. 1042. Here the judge (Lord Oliver) directly contradicts Goodrich's contention that the law claims univocity for legal language.
9   Scottish Power v. Britoil, TLR 2 December 1997.
10 Pawley v. Wharldall 1966, 1 QB 373.
11 R. v. Gingell, TLR 21 May 1999.
12 Grey v. Pearson 1857, 6 HL Cas 61 p.106.
13 Caledonian Rly. Co. v. North British Rly. 1881, 8R (HL) 23 p. 31.
14 Smith v. Hughes 1960, 2 All ER 859.
15 DPP v. Bull 1994, 4 All ER 411.
16 Blythswood Investments v. Clydesdale 1995, SLT 150.
17 (1998), Princeton, NJ: Princeton University Press.
18 Henry M. Hart Jr and Albert M. Sacks in The Legal Process, cited by Robert Post in his review of Scalia's book in *New York Review of Books*, 11 June 1998.
19 Ibid.
20 Mock v. Pensions Ombudsman, TLR 7 April 2000.
21 Habermas, *Moral Consciousness and Communicative Action* (1990), Cambridge: Polity Press, pp. 29–30.
22 *Begriffsgeschichte als Philosophie, Gesammelte Werke*, 2, 77–91.

4 CONSTRUCTIVE INTERPRETATION

1   Title of one of Dworkin's works; see note 17 of Introduction.
2   *Freedom's Law*; see note 14 of Introduction.
3   Ibid. p. 31.
4   Ibid. p. 10.
5   Ibid. p. 76.
6   Ibid. p. 13.
7   Ibid. p. 11.
8   See *Law's Empire*; for fuller discussion, see p. 23.
9   See Ibid. p. 300.
10 Ibid. p. 205.
11 Ibid. p. 200.
12 As advocated in an article in *The Times*, 8 June 1999.
13 As he did through the mouth of one of his characters in *Henry IV, Part 2*.
14 Redmond-Bate v. DPP, TLR 28 July 1999.
15 See text published in *New York Review of Books*, 27 March 1997.
16 See *ante* for the distinction drawn between the negative obligation corresponding to another's right and the positive obligation arising from an entitlement.
17 R. v. Brown and others, TLR 12 March 1993.
18 In addition, a second independent doctor must see the patient and give a corroborative opinion.

NOTES

19 I based this judgment on my assessment of the way such a law would be applied according to British jurisprudence. But I have since been shown the report of a case which indicated that the Dutch courts may be prepared to recognise mental suffering alone as a reason for euthanasia. This seems to go much beyond what even Dworkin was advocating and, incidentally, shows the strength of the 'slippery slope' argument against euthanasia, cf. 'Ragged Edges of Euthanasia Laws'. M. Lensink and L. Pans in *Vrij Nederland*, 21 October 2000. The present law on euthanasia in the UK was upheld by a decision of the European Court of Human Rights rejecting the of a husband to assist in the suicide of his wife who was in the last stages of motor neurone disease. The case of Diane Pretty (now deceased from natural causes) was widely reported in the Press.
20 'A letter from Dr Kevorkian', Mike Wallace in *New York Review of Books*, 5 July 2001.
21 R. v. Sherwood, TLR 12 June 2001.
22 *Law's Empire*, p. 16.
23 *Between Facts and Norms*, p. 408.
24 Ibid. p. 33.
25 Ibid. pp. 223–4.
26 In *Moral Consciousness and Communicative Action*, p. 9.
27 *Between Facts and Norms*, p. 22.
28 Ibid. p. 270.
29 Ibid. p. 334.
30 Ibid. p. 38.
31 Ibid. p. 354.

5 CONCLUSIONS

1 X v. Criminal Injuries Compensation Board, TLR 5 July 1999.
2 Hackshaw v. Hackshaw, TLR 29 July 1999.
3 *Between Facts and Norms*, p. 33.
4 *Freedom's Law*, p. 31.
5 Ibid. p. 346.
6 Ibid. p. 304.
7 Cited in previous chapter.
8 *Between Facts and Norms*, pp. 317–8.
9 Re Stanley Casson, reported in *The Guardian*, 7 August 1999.
10 R. v. Marison, TLR 16 July 1996.
11 *Between Facts and Norms*, p. 218.
12 Op. cit.
13 Reported in *The Guardian*, 14 August 1999.
14 Homicide Act 1957, s.3.
15 R. v. Hobson, TLR 25 June 1997.
16 Luc v. The Queen, TLR 2 April 1996.
17 R. v. Morhall (Court of Appeal) TLR 17 August 1993; (House of Lords) [1995] 3 WLR 330.
18 R. v. Smith TLR 4 August 2000; (House of Lords) 1995 3WLR 330.
19 See Introduction for discussion of style.
20 White and another v. Jones and another, TLR 9 March 1993.

21 Dean v Allin & Watts, TLR 28 June 2001.
22 (1995) ,Paris: Editions Esprit.
23 *There's No Such Thing as Free Speech and It's a Good Thing Too*, p. viii (Preface).
24 Ibid p. 13.
25 Ibid. p. 4.
26 Ibid. p. 73.
27 R. v. Tagg, TLR 14 June 2001.
28 *Nicomachæan Ethics*, v. 15, cited by Ricoeur.
29 See *Between Facts and Norms*, p. 230.
30 Mc Philemy v. Times Newspapers Ltd. TLR 3 July 2001.
31 International Drilling Fluids v. Louisville Investments (Uxbridge), 1986. All E.R. 321.
32 Newbold v. Leicester C.C., TLR 20 August 1999.
33 Habermas's criterion for 'legitimate' law: see *ante*.
34 R. v. A., TLR 24 May 2001.
35 *Between Facts and Norms*, p. 99.
36 R. v. Lord Saville, TLR 22 June 1999.
37 R. v. Lord Saville, TLR 29 July 1999.
38 David Pannick, Q.C. in *The Times*, 29 June 1999: Sir Louis Blom-Cooper, Q.C. in *The Guardian*, 30 June 1999.
39 Richard Gordon, Q.C. in *The Guardian*, 6 July 1999.
40 Costello-Roberts v. UK TLR 26 March 1993.
41 *The Times*, 24 August 1999.
42 *Between Facts and Norms* p. 455.
43 *Habermas On Law and Democracy: Critical Exchanges*, eds Rosenfeld and Arato (1998), Berkeley, CA and London: University of California Press.

INDEX

abortion 118–19, 124
'accident' (case study) 47–8
adhesion 59
admitted opinions 60–1, 64
agreement (definition) 25
Alexy, Robert 164–5
Althusser, Louis 21, 82, 83, 84, 85, 86; *For Marx* 84
ambiguity 43, 66, 100
America *see* United States
anti-foundationalism 67, 68
apathy, political 2–3
application 106–8, 114, 149–53
appropriateness, and relevance 152
argumentation, theory of 59, 62, 63, 65–6; 'convincing argument' 113
Aristotle 53, 58, 65, 164
assertives and commissives 74
audiences: expert/specialist 62, 65, 66, 67; and rhetoric 57, 59–60, 65–6, 90; television 7–8; 'understanding' the law 148, *see also* reader
author, *intentio auctoris* (authorial intention) 92, 94–5
authority, and hegemony 87–8

Balibar, Etienne 86
Barthes, Roland: ideology 87; rhetoric 53, 55, 64–5; style 27, 49, 159; writer and text 69
'basic values' 136
beef, French ban on 10
Bentham, Jeremy 69
Berlin, Isaiah 130

'best conception' 117, 119, 121
binary distinctions: deconstruction 76–7; power–knowledge binary 26, 70, 83; text–context binary 76, 94–5
Blom-Cooper, Louis 177
'Bloody Sunday' (case study) 173–4
Bonham Carter, Lord 125, 126, 129
bottom-up approach 14, 18–19
breathalysis (case study) 29
Britain: abortion 119; elections 2, 130; freedom of speech 121, 125; human rights 25; law 1, 130, 160, 166, 170–2; law-making 125, 126; unwritten constitution 18, 121, 122–3, 170, *see also* Scotland
Bush, George W. 13

California v. *Simpson* ('O.J. case') 6–9
capital punishment 4, 14, 23, 119–20
case studies: application of the law 151; classical rhetoric 54–5; collision of rights 172–4; constructive interpretation 127–8, 133–4, 136–7; fair 163; fair, just and reasonable 159–60; freedom of speech 127–8; grammar 158–9; human rights 171–2, 173–4; ignorance of the law 29; interpretation 98–9, 100–1, 101–2, 103–4; invalid decisions 147–8; 'O.J.

186

INDEX

case' 6–9; ordinary language 45–9; parody or pastiche 74–5; reasonableness 167; reconceptualisation 154–7, 175–6; substantive justice 165–6; unknowability 33–5
catachresis 91
censorship 6
Clarity 42–3
Clark, Alan 74–5
Clark, Marsha 8
class relations 83–5, 87–8
classical rhetoric 54–9, *see also* rhetoric
closure 142–4
codes, linguistic 26, 142–3, 144
commissives and assertives 74
common and uncommon language 36
common knowledge, law as 105, 140
commonsense 86–7
communicative action 19, *see also* discourse
concept 91, 110–12, 153–7, 174–6
concept of justice 77, 86
connaissance de soi 71–2, 86
consensus-formation 87, 88
consent 133
conservatism 13–14, 17, 118
Constitutional Council (France) 11–12
constitutional and legislative intention 105–6
constitutional law, interpretation of 16, 23, 104–6, 116–17, 138
constitutional principle 135
constitutionalism, and fundamentalism 118–21
constitutions: American 15–17, 105–6, 116–21, 123–4, 125–6; written and unwritten 18, 121, 122–3, 170
constructive interpretation: consent 133; constitutionalism and fundamentalism 118–21; Dworkin 114–38; euthanasia 131–3, 134–5, 136; freedom of speech 121–8, 137, 138; Habermas 138–44;

individualism 130–1; integrity 116–18, 139; political correctness 129–30; political law 135–8; systems closure 142–4; systems integration 141–2
consumer contracts 41–2
contemporanea expositio 110
context 75–6, 96–8, 97
conviction (beyond belief) 59
Corax, *Rhetorical Techniques* 54
'core principle' 101
corporal punishment (case study) 175
'co-text' 75
Crime and Disorder Act 1998 125
crime, and public opinion 14
Criminal Injuries Compensation Board (case study) 147
Criminal Justice and Public Order Act 1994 38–9
criminal trials 170–2
critical element 109–10
critical linguistics 19–27; authority 87–8; deconstruction 52, 72–81; Foucault 68–72; Freudianism 78–81; Gramsci and authority 87–8; liberation 71–2; Marx and the science of history 81–7; Marxism 78–81; poststructuralism 68–9; power-knowledge binary 26, 70; rhetoric 53–67
cultural conflict 129

Dangerous Dogs Act 1991 46
dangerous driving (case study) 151
Death, Dr (Dr Kevorkian) 135
death penalty 4, 14, 23, 119–20
death of the subject 69, 81
decision-making 11–14, 62–3
decisions, Supreme Court 23
deconstruction: binary distinctions 76–7; concept of justice 77, 86; critical linguistics 52, 72–81; inexhaustibility of context 75–6; iterability 73–4
deeds (legal) 32
democracy 1–4, 18; 'illegitimate' law 146; juridical decision-

INDEX

making 66; majoritarian premise 15–16, 18; majority domination 138–9; people as originator of law 23; sovereignty of people 19
demonstration 59
Derrida, Jacques 21, 52, 72–81, 86, 96; *After Marx* 84
différance 72–3
diminished responsibility 155–6, 157
discourse: concepts and ideas 110–11; critical linguistics 69, 70; Foucault 26, 82, 86, 129; Habermas 25, 26, 27, 140, 149, 178; legal language 25–6, 27, 140, 149; rational discourse 164–5; social integration 141, 143
doctor's role in assisted suicide 131–2, 133, 134, 135
dogs, dangerous (case study) 46
donation, legal concept of 76–7
'*droit*' 51, 62
drunkenness (case study) 163
'due process' 136
duty of care (case study) 159–60
Dworkin, Ronald: constructive interpretation 114–38, 173; *Freedom's Law* 15, 16; and Habermas 18–19, 138–40; interpretation 22–3, 105–6; moral reading 14, 25, 91, 116, 137, 149–50; political ideology 13–14, 17, *see also* constructive interpretation

Eco, Umberto 90, 91–2, 92–3, 99; *The Limits of Interpretation* 94
Eighth Amendment, 'cruel and unusual punishments' 119
elaboration 114–15
elections 2, 19, 130
elitism 4, 35–6
England *see* Britain
English, Plain English Campaign 37–8, 40, 43
enthymemes 61–2, 64
epistemes (discursive practices) 68, 82

'equal protection' clause 115, 116
'equivalence' 24, *see also* representation
ethical code, journalistic 9
Europe, constructive interpretation 130, 132
European Convention on Human Rights 11, 25, 134, 170; case studies 171–2, 175–6
euthanasia 131–3, 134–5, 136, *see also* medically assisted suicide
existential issues 10
expert/specialist audiences 62, 65, 66, 67
expressibility 92

facts 64, 151–2
fair 160–3; case studies 159–60, 163; meritocracy 161–3; reasonable or fair 176–8
fair, just and reasonable 159–68
fairness, meaning of 161–2
fidelity 169–70
'fighting talk' 123, 128, 137
First Amendment, freedom of speech 121, 124
Fish, Stanley 67–8, 71, 122, 129, 160–2; *There's No Such Thing As Free Speech* ... 122
flexibility 44
Foucault, Michel: *Archaeology of Knowledge* 68; critical linguistics 21, 68–72; discourse and ideology 26, 82, 86, 149; political correctness 129; *Words and Things* 68
Fourteenth Amendment, deprivation of life, liberty or property 130
France: critical linguistics 20; language 60–1, 63, 65, 70, 72, 91, 92; law 1, 130, 160; legal language 51, 62, 116, 164; *Loi Barnier* 10
freedom and equality 22–3
freedom of expression 138, 176
freedom of speech 121–8, 137, 138
Freud, Sigmund 81, 86, 154
Freudianism 78–81
'frivolous' (case study) 48–9

fundamentalism: and constitutionalism 118–21, 137, *see also* originalism

Gadamer, Hans-Georg 21, 93, 110–13, 153
gay rights *see* homosexuality
Genette, Gerard 94
German language 116
Gesetz 116
golden rule (interpretation) 100–1
Goodrich, Peter 26–7, 36, 89
Gorgias 56
grammar 24, 158–9, 176
Gramsci, Antonio 21, 82, 86, 87–8, 130
Guigou reforms 12–13
guns, US law 4
Gunther, Thomas 24

Habermas, Jürgen; application 149, 150, 152–3; *Between Facts and Norms* 1, 18–19, 24, 93, 138; collision of rights 172, 173; constructive interpretation 115, 138–44; discourse 25, 26, 27, 140, 149, 178; and Dworkin 18–19, 138–40; interpretation 93, 109–10; justification theory 23–4, 165; legal language 145, 148; opinion- and will-formation 168, 170; reasonable or fair 177, 178; representation 168–9
Hague, William 130
Hand, Judge Learned 17, 18–19
'hate speech' 123–4, 125, 126, 129, 137
Havel, Vaclav 84
hegemony 86–8, 130
Hercules, Judge 23, 117, 139
hermeneutics 93–6, 99, 110–12, 120, 150, 153–4
historical materialism 86
history: American legal 116–17, 121; concepts and interpretation 110–11, 136; science of 81–7
Holland, euthanasia 133, 134–5

homosexuality 3, 14–15
How to Succeed in Business Without Really Trying (film) 161
human rights 170–8; case studies 171–2, 173–4, *see also* rights
Human Rights Act 1998 11, 12, 104, 170, 171, 172
Human Rights, European Convention on 11, 25, 134, 170, 171–2, 175–6; case studies 171–2, 175–6
Husserl, Edmund 19

identity issues 10
Ideological State Apparatuses (ISAs) 85
ideology: class relations 83–5; commonsense 86–7; deconstruction 86; hegemony 86–7; latent 83–4; polemical concept of 82–3; post-ideological politics 82; rhetoric 82–4, 85–6; society 83–5, 87–8; spin 82
'ignorance of the law' 28–9
'illegitimate' law 146–7
'import' and 'semantic intention' 105–6
incoherence 100
indemnity costs (case study) 165–6
independent observer 81
individual and poststructuralism 69
individualism 130–1, *see also* self
inexhaustibility of context 75–6
innocence/knowledge, presumption of 29–30, 32–3, 50
integrity 116–18, 139
intelligibility 41–4, 50
intentio auctoris (authorial intention) 92, 94, 94–5
intentio lectoris (what the text conveys to the reader) 92, 94, 103
intentio operis (what the text says) 92, 97
intention, constitutional and legislative 105–6
intentionalist theories 21, 105, 107
interdiscursiveness 78–9
interpretation 21–2; ambiguity and incoherence 100; American

INDEX

Constitution 17–18, 105–6; application 106–8; concept 91, 110–12; constitutional and legislative intention 105–6; context 96–8; critical element 109–10; the golden rule 100–1; hermeneutics 93–6, 110–12, 150; *intentio auctoris* (authorial intention) 92, 94–5; judgement 112–13; judicial discretion 107–9; judicial interpretation 52, 89, 95–6; legal hermeneutics 95–6, 99; legal language 89–90, 104–9; meaning of meaning 91–2; 'natural language' 99; purposive interpretation 101–2, 105, 108; the reader 92–3, 94; reading 90–1; reception 89–91; repugnance 100, 102–5, 106, 108; rhetoric 89–90, 93–4
'interpretive turn' 71
'intersubjective' 139
ISAs (Ideological State Apparatuses) 85
iterability 73–4

Jefferson, Thomas 36
journalism, ethics of 9
judgement 112–13
judges: appointment of 12; decision-making 62–3; instructions to jury 43–4; interpretation 21, 95–6, 104–9; as interpreters of constitutional law 16, 23, 104–6, 116–17, 138; judicial decisions and public opinion 63, 65; judicial discretion 107–9; judicial function 52, 139; judicial interpretation 52, 89, 95–6; political law 135–6
juries: judge's instructions to 43–4; 'O.J. case' 7, 8–9
just 164–6, *see also* fair; justice; reasonable
le juste 164
justice: concept of 77, 86; deconstruction 77, 86; open justice 28; procedural justice 164–5; substantive justice 165–6
'justice should be seen to be done' 28

'keep open' (case study) 45
Kelsen, Hans 146
Kevorkian, Dr (Dr Death) 135
knowledge: law as common knowledge 105, 140; presumption of innocence/knowledge 29–30, 32–3, 50
knowledge–power binary 26, 70, 83

landlord/tenant 166, 167; case studies 103, 158–9
language codes 26, 142–3, 144, *see also* discourse; legal language; ordinary language; plain language; political correctness
Lasch, Christopher 4
latent ideology 83–4
law *see* legal language; legal system
Law Society of Scotland 144
lawyer, consultative role 31–3
'lawyer's letter' 38
legal hermeneutics 95–6, 99
legal language: application 149–50, 152; constructive interpretation (case study) 133–4; critical theory 20–7; deficiency of 31; discourse 25–6, 27, 140, 149; flexibility 44; freedom of speech (case study) 127–8; grammar 24, 158–9, 176; Habermas 145; human rights debate 174; interpretation 89–90, 104–9; iterability 73–4; law as text 51–3, 103, 107; New Rhetoric 66–7; ordinary language and representation 168–9; philosophical discourse 22; reasonableness 24–5; reconceptualisation 24, 153–4; remoteness 35–7; style 27, 49, 159; systems theory 79, 144;

190

INDEX

theory and praxis 20–1; understanding 148, see also ordinary language; plain language
legal profession, as audience 62, 65, 66
legal system: authority and hegemony 87–8; Habermas and constructive interpretation 141–4; ideology 85; political pressures 11–14; and society 18, 23–4
legislation, intention and interpretation 105–6
liberalisation, and legal system 10
liberalism 13–14, 118–19
liberation 71–2
liberty 130, see also freedom
'liberty interest' 131, 132, 133, 135
'lifeworld' 140, 141, 144
limitations, on context 97
limits, freedom of speech 121–2
linguistic theory see critical linguistics
literal meaning 99
Local Government Act 1988 3
Locke, John 58
'loi' 51, 116
Loi Barnier 10
'lois' 51, 62
Lord Chancellor 12

Maier, Pauline, American Scripture 16
majoritarian premise 15–16, 18
majority domination 138–9
Marx, Karl 81–7
Marxism: critical linguistics 78–81; Gramsci 87–8; interdiscursiveness 78–9; negative justification 79–81; science of history 81–7
meaning: of fairness 161–2; meaning of meaning 91–2; plain language and intelligibility 41–4; reconceptualisation 153; relevance 76, see also interpretation
media 5–6, 6–9, 173–4

medically assisted suicide 131–2, 133, 134, see also euthanasia
meritocracy and fairness 161–3
Mill, J.S. 122
minority groups 123–4
moral philosophy, language of 25
'moral reading': application 149–50; constitutional principles 14; constructive interpretation 116; fundamentalism 119, 137; as interpretation 91; law and individual morality 126; rights-based law 25
moral responsibility 124–5

'natural justice' 148
'natural language' 48, 99
'natural meaning' 96
'natural ways' 84
Nazi regime 146
negative justification 79–81
negligence law 130
Netherlands, euthanasia 133, 134–5
New Rhetoric 21, 53–4, 59–67, see also rhetoric
newspapers 173–4
Nietzsche, Friedrich 73
normativity 35

'O.J. case' (California v. Simpson) 6–9
open justice 28
opinion- and will-formation 168, 170
oratory 56–7
ordinary language 37–8, 44–50; application 152; case studies 45–9; interpretation 91; representation 168–9; systems theory 79, 144, see also legal language; plain language
originalism 17, 22, 105–6, 115, 118, see also fundamentalism

paedophilia 80
Pannick, David 176
Parliament: interpretation 94, 95–6, 101, 102, 107–9, 172;

INDEX

law-making compared with US 125–6, 135–6; public opinion 5–6; sovereignty of 11, 96
parody or pastiche (case study) 74–5
passing off 75
patient, and assisted suicide 131–2, 133, 134, 135, 136
Perelman, Chaim 21, 53–4, 59–67
'person', concept of 119, 120
persuasion 55–6, 57, 59
Phillips, Alfred, *The Lawyer and Society* 30
Plain English Campaign 37–8, 40, 43
plain language 31, 37–44, 50, see also legal language; ordinary language
plane passenger (case study) 48
Plutarch 71
polemical concept of ideology 82–3
police caution 38–40, 43
political correctness 3–4, 68, 129–30
political ideology 12–14, 82
political law 135–8
political morality 114–15, see also 'moral reading'
political parties 12–14
political philosophy 57–9
political system 2–4, 11–14
pornography 123
positive discrimination 118
positivism 146
Post, Robert 108–9
postideological politics 82
poststructuralism 68–9
post-traumatic stress disorder (case study) 47
power–knowledge binary 26, 70, 83
power relationships 129
precaution, principle of 10
precision 44, 50
prejudice, risk of (case study) 136–7
'premises' 60–1; case study 45

presumption of innocence/ knowledge 29–30, 32–3, 50
principle 115; constitutional principle 135; 'core principle' 101; juridical interpretation 138; precaution 10; rules and principles 150–2
probability 56, 58, 60–1, 63–5, 66
procedural justice 164–5
propaganda 5, see also spin
proportionality 104
'proportionateness' 10
provocation (case study) 154–7
psychoanalytic theory 79–81, 86, 91
public opinion 14–15, 63, 65
'public place' (case study) 46
punishment: capital 4, 14, 23, 119–20; corporal (case study) 175
purposive interpretation 101–2, 105, 108

quasi-logic 61–2

Race Relations Act 1976 79, 125
racism 124, 125, 126
rape trial (case study) 171–2, 177
rational discourse 164–5
reader: *intentio lectoris* 92–3, 94, 103, see also audiences
reading and interpretation 90–1
reality, social 52–3
'reasonable doubt' 43
reasonable or fair 176–8
'reasonable' law 147–8
'reasonable man' 24–5, 156, 167–8
reasonableness 24–5, 166–8; case study 167, see also fair; fair, just and reasonable; just
reception 89–91
Recht 116
reconceptualisation 24, 153–7, 174–6; case studies 154–7, 175–6
reference to prior sexual relationshop (case study) 173
referendum on homosexuality 3
relevance 76, 152

INDEX

religious fundamentalism 16, 118, 137
remoteness 35–7
representation 4, 5, 7, 168–9; equivalence 24; political 2, 5
Repressive State Apparatuses (RSAs) 85
repugnance 100, 102–5, 106, 108
rhetoric 53–67; ambiguity 43; audiences 57, 59–60, 65–6, 90; basic premises 60–1; classical rhetoric 54–9; critical linguistics 53–67; defined 53; ideology 82–4, 85–6; interpretation 89–90, 93–4; juridical logic 62–3; New Rhetoric 21, 53–4, 59–67; as oratory 56–7; persuasion 55–6, 57, 59; political philosophy 57–9; probability 63–5; quasi-logic 61–2; rights and reconceptualisation 175
Ricoeur, Paul 19, 79, 91, 160–1
rights: collision of rights 172–4; constitutional rights, American 15–17; freedom of speech 123, 129; human rights 170–8; individual 16, 130–1; reconceptualisation 174–6; rights-based law 22–3, 25, 114, 131, 134; universality of 60, 96; women's rights (case study) 154–5, *see also* freedom of expression; freedom of speech
risk management 10
RSAs (Repressive State Apparatuses) 85
rules and principles 150–2

sadomasochistic practices (case study) 133–4, 135
Saville Tribunal case 177
Scalia, Antonin 22; *A Matter of Interpretation; Federal Courts and the Law* 105
Schleiermacher, Friedrich 94, 110
science of history 81–7
Scotland: landlord/tenant relationship (case study) 103–4; law 1, 166; Law Society of Scotland 144; written pleadings 152
self-control 156–7
self-defence 155
self, direct knowledge of (*connaissance de soi*) 71–2, 86, *see also* individual
'semantic intention' and 'import' 105–6
semblance (*'vraisemblable'*) 60–1, 63, 65
semiotics 72, 168
'seriousness of damage' 10
Shakespeare, William 57
sharia 16
sign-system (semiotics) 72, 168
Smith, Adam 142
social integration 141, 143
society: ideology 83–5, 87–8; legal system 18, 23–4
Socrates 58, 61, 62
sophists 57–8
sovereignty: of Parliament 11, 96; of the people 19, 177–8
speech-acts 74, 81, 123, 141
spin 5–6, 82
spoken word 32
statutory language 36, 41
Stein, Gertrude 154
Street Offences Act 1959 (case study) 100, 101
style, linguistic 27, 49, 159
subconscious 79
substantive justice (case study) 165–6
Supreme Court: abortion debate 118–19; Constitution 15–16 decisions 23; euthanasia 131–2; judges 13; political composition of 17; powers of 11
Swift, Jonathan, *On Poetry* 112
syllogism 61–2
systems closure 142–4
systems integration 141–2
systems theory 79, 141–4

tax avoidance 146–7
television, 'O.J. case' 6–9
terminology, and concept 111, 154

text: death of the subject 69, 81; deconstruction 73–4; *intentio lectoris* 92, 96, 103; interpretation 111–12, 114–15; law as 51–3, 103, 107; written and unwritten constitutions 18, 121, 122–3
text–context binary 76, 94–5
textualism 21, 22, 105–6, 107, 122–3
Thompson, John B. 8, 82–4
Tisias (case study) 54–5
top-down approach 14–18
Touraine, Alain, *Can We Live Together: Equality and Difference* 10
traffic control paradigm 108–9
trials: Clinton impeachment trial 23; criminal 170–2, 177; probability 56, 64
trickle-down theory 78, 78–9
Trollope, Anthony, *An Autobiography* 110

'understanding' the law 148
United Kingdom *see* Britain; Scotland
United States: capital punishment 4, 23, 119–20; Constitution 15–17, 105–6, 116–21, 123–4, 125–6; law 1, 4; legal milestones 22–3; power–knowledge binary 70; UK Parliamentary law-making compared with US 125–6
universal audience 60
unknowability 32–5

Valéry, Paul 56, 94
validity 26, 30, 112, 143; invalid decisions 147–8
'velvet' censorship 6
victimisation 79
'*vraisemblable*' 60–1, 63, 65

Walzer, Michael, *A Company of Critics* 78
Wittgenstein, Ludwig 19, 20
women's rights (case study) 154–5
World Organisation against Torture 155
Wright, Tony 36
writer *see* author
written and unwritten constitutions 18, 121, 122–3, 170

zeitgeist theories 78

For Product Safety Concerns and Information please contact our EU representative GPSR@taylorandfrancis.com
Taylor & Francis Verlag GmbH, Kaufingerstraße 24, 80331 München, Germany

www.ingramcontent.com/pod-product-compliance
Lightning Source LLC
Chambersburg PA
CBHW051644230426
43669CB00013B/2435